The Fir

Louder Than Words

3 True Stories of Ordinary Girls with Extraordinary Lives

Marni by Marni Bates

Emily by Emily Smucker

Chelsey by Chelsey Shannon

Edited by Deborah Reber

HCI TEENS

Health Communications, Inc.
Deerfield Beach, Florida

www.hcibooks.com

Library of Congress Cataloging-in-Publication Data

Shannon, Chelsey.
    Louder than words : the first collection three true stories of ordinary girls
with extraordinary lives / Chelsey Shannon, Emily Smucker, Marni Bates.
      p. cm.
    ISBN-13: 978-0-7573-1546-6
    ISBN-10: 0-7573-1546-1
    1. Shannon, Chelsey.   2. Smucker, Emily.   3. Bates, Marni.   4. Girls—
United States—Biography.   I. Smucker, Emily.   II. Bates, Marni.   III. Title.
HQ777.S438 2010
920.72—dc22
                                 2010015903

Publisher: Health Communications, Inc.
            3201 S.W. 15th Street
            Deerfield Beach, FL 33442–8190

Cover design by Larissa Hise Henoch
Interior design and formatting by Lawna Patterson Oldfield

Contents

Introduction
for Louder Than Words: The First Collection
by Deborah Reber

WHEN I FIRST PUT OUT THE CALL for teens interested in writing a book about their life, I had no idea what to expect. HCI Books had approached me a few months earlier about spearheading their next venture into teen publishing—creating the first-ever series of teen-authored memoirs—and I had jumped at the chance. Teenagers penning full-length books about their real, complex existences? What could be better?

But as I began searching for authors, I quietly panicked. Sure, the concept was great, but its success all came down to finding the right writers—talented teens with a unique, distinct voice, a captivating story, and the wherewithal to write a 30,000 word book in a matter of months while dealing with school, family obligations, part-time jobs, and a social life. What if I couldn't find the right girls to pull it off?

Still, I was passionate about the idea and was determined to make it work. So I took the "Field of Dreams" approach and embraced the quote made popular by the movie of the same name: "If you build it, they will come." I set about dreaming up what I wanted for the series and trusted the right young women would come along.

In a matter of weeks I found Marni Bates, a college freshman with a knack for narrative story structure and a willingness to write with candor and humor about her painful struggle with the stress disorder trichotillomania (a compulsion to pull out one's hair).

Soon after, I heard from Emily Smucker, a Mennonite blogger whose quirky perspective and unique outlook on the world brought her story of coping with perpetual sickness, a weak immune system, and the West Nile virus to life.

When an email from Chelsey Shannon landed in my inbox, I was blown away by the maturity and insight with which she wrote about losing her dad to murder when she was only thirteen, having already lost her mom to cancer as a young girl.

And so I had found the first Louder Than Words authors—three incredible young women who've experienced their own brand of pain, heartache, anxiety, and embarrassment, and lived to write about it.

As they got down to writing, Marni, Emily, and Chelsey showed up with a level of honesty and a self-awareness I wasn't fully prepared for. They were more than willing to put it all out there—the good, the bad, and the ugly. I loved watching each girl figure out a crucial piece of her personal story and find the words to share it so readers could connect with it, too. Even though I was their mentor through this whole process, I'm pretty sure I learned more from Marni, Emily, and Chelsey than they did from me.

If you're a teenager, you know all too well that life isn't all sunshine and rainbows. It's complicated, confusing, and messy. And even if you're not personally dealing with pulling, sickness, or the loss of a parent, no doubt you've got your own challenges, your own "why me?" moments. My hope is that in reading the stories in *Louder Than Words: The First Collection* you'll be able to remember that your life is more than the sum of your experiences. That though your "why me?" moments might shape who you are, they don't have to define your life. That the reality is, like the girls in this book, your life is Louder Than Words.

Chelsey

Part One

Last Minutes of Peace

i climbed the hill

          walking toward

home, where i don't know

          a disaster

is waiting, one that i

          won't

wake up from, won't

          disappear

The Beginning

I'LL BEGIN AT THE BEGINNING. I was born to family who were overjoyed at my arrival. Deeply in love, my parents were a biracial couple—my father, Blair, was black, and my mother, Amy, white. My parents dated for eight years before they were married, and by that time, my mother's large, Catholic family had accepted my father as a surrogate brother and son. My parents worked well together, both as lovers and as business partners. In the years before I was born, my parents ran a comedy club in downtown Cincinnati called Aunt Maudie's.

I was conceived shortly after the tragic death of my Aunt Kim in a car accident; a joy to balance a sorrow. My father filmed my mother's cesarean section and my subsequent birth. As my tiny, slippery self emerged from my mother, all he could say, with the utmost reverence, was, "Oh, my God." The first time my mother held me, she wept quietly. In watching the tape today, I can almost feel what she must have felt at that moment: relief, exhaustion, joy, awe, gratitude, and overwhelming love.

After my birth, we moved to a growing suburb of Cincinnati, Ohio, called West Chester and built a red, brick house to live in. I remember exploring our budding home as it slowly emerged from the ground up, my parents planting a small garden in the front, selecting paint chips and carpet samples. Ours was one of the first homes in the area.

Though my mother initially continued her work as a secretary during my early childhood, she soon decided to stay home with me, as, back then, my father spent much of his time on the road, staying in various cities as he pursued his career in stand-up comedy and music. Though she missed having him at home, my mother supported my father's endeavors, recognizing his talent.

The first few years of my life went smoothly and safely. But things started to change by the time I reached kindergarten.

When I was five years old, my mother was diagnosed with an acute form of leukemia, a cancer of the blood. Before my young eyes, the life was drained from my once vivacious and lovely mother, her face becoming pale and gaunt, her ebony hair thinning before giving way to baldness. By the time I started first grade, my mother was hospital-bound. By October of 1998, she was gone. My father was out of town when she died but asked my relatives who were staying with me to wait to tell me so he could break the news. As soon as he arrived home, he led me outside to the front porch of our house, and we gazed up at the velvety night sky, which was studded with stars that shone like diamonds. Deep in my heart, I knew what was coming.

"See that big, bright star up there?" my father asked gently, kneeling so he was beside me. I nodded.

"That's Mommy."

My worry confirmed, I clung to my father, beginning to cry. Though, in some ways, I'd known that my mother wasn't going to make it, I was still devastated that one of the most important people in my small world was gone.

A few days later, as I sat among my first-grade classmates and listened to my teacher explain my family's tragedy in words and concepts we could understand, I began to feel my life would always be different from those of my classmates—not necessarily less happy or functional, but definitely unconventional.

The years that followed confirmed my suspicions. Despite being a fairly happy and conventional family following the dark period of grief after my mother's death, there were still subtle nuances that distinguished me and my father from others in our community. The chief difference lay in my father's occupation. My father had transcended the realm of dingy clubs and hotels and begun to perform on cruise ships. He deeply enjoyed what he did and was quite successful at it. His work, however, made it necessary for him to leave me, his only child, roughly two weeks out of every month so he could perform at sea. This fact certainly didn't fit the mold of a typical suburban childhood. Unlike my friends, I didn't always have a welcoming parent to walk home to, a supportive face in the audience of a concert or recital, or a ride home from the bus stop in the rain.

Even so, I had a fairly happy childhood and learned to adjust to my circumstances. While my father was away, I stayed with our neighbors, the Rouses, whose daughter, Holly, was only a year older than me. Because we were next-door neighbors, I was never far from my own home. By the end of my thirteenth year, I had established a reasonably simple rhythm to my life: dad gone, dad home, the Rouse's house, my own. But a week before my fourteenth birthday, my life was drastically uprooted.

In my relatively short time on earth, I have learned that life, among many other things, is fully capable of taking detours from the path we envision for ourselves. These detours can be pleasant or traumatic, minor or deeply altering—but we all experience them, and we all must learn to deal with them.

In my life, the detours took the form of the premature death of my parents. These circumstances have simultaneously been the most difficult and life-changing ones I've had to deal with. The early losses of my parents feverously spurred me on to a path of change, healing, and a deeper understanding of myself. Though the grief at my parents' deaths—my father's in particular—seemed insurmountable at times, it also initiated my quest of discovering who I truly am.

Finding Out

THE DAY MY LIFE was altered irrevocably was an unsuspecting cold and gray January day. At school, I coasted thoughtlessly through my biology, language arts, and pre-algebra classes, distracted by thoughts of the weekend and my father coming home from his latest trip—a trip on which he'd brought his girlfriend, Monique, along. My only cause for concern was my failure to reach my dad earlier that morning, since he had told me the previous night I would be able to call him before I headed to school.

However, by the end of the day, I was no longer worrying as I walked up the hill from my bus stop with the boy who lived down the street. We laughed, talking about nothing in particular. When we reached the top of the hill, he parted from me, and I said good-bye. As I turned toward my house, I registered the two cars in my driveway: my Aunt Chris's green one and my grandparents' gold one.

Confused, I headed down to the end of the cul-de-sac where my house sat. *Why are they here?* I wondered. I knew I was spending the weekend at my grandparents' house, but as far as I knew, they weren't supposed to pick me up until the following day. And even if they were picking me up early, why were *both* cars there?

Slight panic filled me. My mind automatically jumped to the worst conclusion: *Did someone die?* I frantically scanned the possibilities as I closed the distance between the house and me: maybe my grandma or grandpa died, or maybe a more distant relative.

Finally, I reached the house. My grandma opened the front door before I had a chance to reach for the knob. Her eyes were sad as I gazed into them. She said hello, her voice scarcely concealing melancholy.

Why is she looking at me that way . . . like she feels sorry for me? I wondered as she embraced me.

"Why are you guys here?" I asked politely as I could, walking down the hall into the kitchen. My grandpa was there, as well as my Aunt Chris, who was passionately sobbing.

God, no . . . what happened?

I opened my mouth to ask, but my aunt came to me instead, holding me by the shoulders. "Something terrible has happened," she kept repeating. It became her mantra, her prayer to protect us all from the truth.

Disarmed by the presence of both of my grandparents, I had little notion of what might have happened, and why my aunt, who scarcely ever cried, was so upset.

"*What?* What happened?" I asked, growing angrier and more anxious with each repetition.

"Now, you can scream or do whatever you want when I tell you this," she finally managed through her tears. I attempted to steel myself, but the truth was far beyond my naive notions of what the worst-case scenario could be.

"Your dad has been killed."

What?!

Instantly, I felt angry. I wanted desperately to strike my aunt for telling such a joke; it wasn't funny at all. I was filled with hate toward my relatives for coming to my house and disturbing my afternoon with such cruel mockery.

Dad's coming home tomorrow morning, I wanted to snap at them. I don't know what you all think you're talking about.

Even so, I felt the world around me begin to slip away, my vision swimming as lightness filled my head. I couldn't stand . . . I couldn't think. Part of me, somewhere, knew that it was true. Part of me knew there was no joke—that they were not lying.

I felt the color drain from my face, and my relatives led me to the couch. My aunt sat down beside me and began to tell me what little details she knew: "Attempted robbery . . . shot . . . last night . . ."

Her words scarcely pierced through my fog of defiance. I felt so *angry*, more so than I'd ever felt in my life. But something happened. As she listed the details of the horrible crime, some part of me realized she couldn't have just been making it all up on the spot. Why would she? I saw the tears in her eyes, and I knew she wasn't lying. Then I started to cry too.

Aftermath

THE EVENING THAT followed was the most hollow and bizarre of my life. My Aunt Chris, my grandparents, and I prepared to wait the evening out and were eventually joined by the Rouses and other neighbors. Though a kind gesture, the company didn't really help much, as no one knew what to say. Silence permeated the house as it never had before. Our spacious family room was full, but no one spoke. We all sat quietly, lost in our own thoughts, our own imaginings and dreads of the future.

A sense of somber anticipation had fallen over us all. Though no one would explicitly state it, I had the distinct feeling I wasn't the only one who thought that, maybe, this would still all be revealed as a joke. It was as if we were all hoping—some of us praying—that if we sat quietly enough, we would hear my father's car pull up and he would enter through the garage, laden with luggage and some crazy story explaining the horrible mix-up. We'd laugh and cry from relief, and everyone else would go home. It would just be me and him, and I'd be happier than I've ever been.

This didn't happen, of course. We ordered pizza that I couldn't eat. Meager attempts at conversation were made, but mostly, there was silence. Disbelief clouded my thoughts as grief threatened to take over my heart. I simply couldn't believe it to be true. Not yet, not all of me.

After all, everyone knew murder didn't happen in real life or to good people. Murder belonged in faraway countries where it couldn't bother us or safe within the confines of a movie or TV screen, where it could be ogled at from a safe-enough distance. Murder, I maintained, did not belong in my world. It was simply inappropriate, and it certainly had no place in ending my father's life.

So I wouldn't believe it. I humored my family and the people who visited, but inside I mocked them, called them fools, for surely this was just an elaborate joke being played on us all. And when a television crew from some heinous, new reality show jumped out from behind the corner, or my dad burst through the front door, full of apologies and humorous explanations, I would be the only one not caught off guard.

Convinced that the sooner I went to bed, the sooner I would wake up from the nightmare, I retired at around nine o'clock, Holly joining me soon after. It was a dreamless void of a sleep, precisely what I needed to forget all that had happened.

The next day, I woke up early, the rest of the house still steeped in slumber. I rose quietly, not wishing to wake Holly. In my head, hope gathered. I was certain the previous night was just a horrible mistake, and that if I followed the hallway from my room to his, I'd find him within, safe and sleeping in his bed. He'd have arrived in the middle of the night. He'd be tired but wouldn't mind that I'd woken him; he'd just be happy to see my face. He'd get up, and we'd eat pancakes together. It was Saturday, after all.

This was the scene I felt sure awaited me down the hall behind his closed bedroom door. With caution, careful not to step where the floor creaked, I followed the path of refuge as I'd done after numerous nightmares and on countless mornings. He'd be there, sound asleep, just like all the times before.

I turned the knob and opened the door. The bed wasn't just empty—it hadn't been touched. I could tell by the smoothness of the sheets, the position of the pillows. It just looked like my dad's bed on any other day when he was away. I don't think I've ever felt a disappointment so crushing.

My parents' bed was grand: king-size and comfortable. My father had slept on the left side, my mom on the right. After my mother died, my dad kept to the left side for years, as if saving the right for her, should she ever wish to reclaim it. Sometimes, when I missed her, I'd go and lie on the right side. After a few years, Dad had migrated to the center of the bed. Still, in my mind, my parents had their sides of the bed. I lay on the left side and sobbed. I buried my face in the pillow, anxious to absorb whatever essence of my dad lingered on the fabric.

It was only at this point that I truly allowed reality to burst through my protective web of denial and rage. As I lay on my father's bed, I wept, feeling the deepest sorrow I've ever felt, in sobs that are usually kept inside, sobs that are accompanied by wails and aching chests.

After a while, I tried to distract myself. Sobs still falling from my lips, I rose from the bed and quietly shut his door behind me. I went downstairs to attempt to eat something but failed again. My body simply rejected the food.

I then tried to watch *American Idol*, which my dad and I recorded each week and watched together. But I couldn't focus. I could barely hear the television. All I could think about were my own words to my father in an e-mail a few days earlier: "Don't worry. I won't watch *AI* without you." I turned off the television.

Still, there was nothing else I could do. The reality of the situation had literally taken over my mind. I thought I had known distraction before, but nothing compared to my total inability to consider anything else but my father and his death. All I wanted to do was talk to him. I dialed his cell phone number several times, hoping against hope that he would answer, but the calls just rolled straight to voice mail.

Rather blindly, I grabbed a notebook and returned to my father's room. I began to write him stream-of-consciousness letters, in which I reverted to being his clinging little girl, begging him to come home, to make the nightmare go away. Only when I wrote could I stop crying. I wrote for most of the day.

1/21/06

Dear Daddy,

This has to be a dream. Please, let it be a dream. I love you too much to lose you like this. How could anyone take you away from me, and everyone else who loved you? And so many people did, Daddy. Oh, God. How could I ever live without you?

You taught me so much. You were such a fascinating person. How could you leave like this, when no one was ready for you to?

I feel like I'll never be able to enjoy anything again, Daddy. I can't eat, I can't watch television, I can't talk to anyone. All I want to do is sleep, where I can feel nothing. When left alone with my thoughts, I am tormented, and I keep crying, Daddy.

Remember on the day of my concert, when I said, "I don't want you to die?" It was almost like a premonition, I suppose. I kept thinking of Les Misérables, *the part where Valjean is dying too soon, leaving Cosette behind.*

It is too soon, Daddy. I thought we had years and years together, and we would be the best of friends.

But I take some comfort in the fact that I got to talk to you beforehand and tell you that I love you. And I can only pray that you are watching me from heaven, with Mommy finally by your side, watching me and loving me together, as you never could before. Is heaven nice?

When Aunt Chris told me, I was so angry. I didn't believe her, and I thought I would faint.

Daddy, I'm so glad I have all your e-mails, and your notes and voice mails.

I feel so alone—so, so alone and so empty. If only you could send me a sign, telling me that you're okay and Mommy's okay too.

My eyes are swollen from crying.

I'm so glad we always said I love you, and that you signed the books you gave me. There is so much of you in everything I own, in the house. This way, I can never forget you. I never will, Daddy. I'm far too attached to you for that. I'll write more later. I love you with all my heart.

What Happened

THE REST OF THE weekend passed in bleakness. My friends came over, comforting words and homemade chocolates shaped like roses in tow. There was fierce, blunt Abby; kind, considerate Kelsey; altruistic, analytical Bridget; and empathetic, sensitive Holly. I felt almost sorry for them. This level of involvement far surpassed all expectations of friendship between young teenagers, even if they were my best friends. Nothing in their lives had equipped them to comfort a friend dealing with the murder of her father.

As we sat in my family room attempting to enjoy ourselves, I

wondered what they would do when they got home. Would they sit
down with their families? Eat dinner? Laugh together? It seemed so
achingly probable—so *normal*—that I felt jealous of them and their
ability to get up and leave my house when it became too much for
them. They could simply call their parents and ask to be taken
home. But this overwhelming reality was now my life.

Amid company, and me crying, writing, and rather listlessly
beginning a scrapbook, Monique, my father's girlfriend, returned
from St. Thomas, deeply and understandably rattled. Monique had
been with my father when he was killed and was able to share addi-
tional details of the tragedy, despite, I'm sure, a horrible sense of
grief and shock.

One of Monique's first stops when she'd returned to Cincinnati
had been my house. She immediately began crying when I answered
the door and she saw my face, embracing me and apologizing over
and over. Once she'd calmed down and settled in the family room,
she sadly went into the details of my father's death.

As I already knew, the two of them had planned to spend the
night at a hotel in St. Thomas after a weeklong cruise in the Bahamas.
The next morning, they were to board a plane to Cincinnati and be
home in time for the weekend. They'd had a pleasant enough day in
St. Thomas before settling in at their hotel. Monique had had a bad
feeling about the hotel and thought the one across the street gave
off a much better vibe. However, the hotel they ended up in was
cheaper, and they figured it wouldn't make much difference for just
one night.

Unfortunately, they were wrong. Slightly after eleven o'clock that
night—no more than an hour after I spoke to my father for the last
time—a man entered their room while my dad and Monique slept,
squeezing in through the sliding patio door they'd left slightly ajar

to air out the room. My father awoke to the noise and rose from the bed, waking Monique as well. My father assumed the man had intentions of robbing them and told him to take whatever he wanted, so long as he didn't hurt anyone. Monique, nervous, began urging the man to go away, to not commit such a grievous crime that he would only regret. The man became agitated by Dad and Monique's words; likely he'd entered into the act assuming anyone in the room would remain asleep and he wouldn't have to deal with the reality of what he was doing. As he backed away, he shot blindly into the darkened room. The bullet hit my father in the chest.

Monique, understandably, began to panic. Dad, on the other hand, with his characteristic collectedness, sat down on the bed and picked up the hotel phone to call the front desk.

"'Call an ambulance,'" Monique told me he'd said with an amazing calm. "'I've been shot.'"

The help didn't arrive fast enough. My father—the man who had protected me, loved me, provided for me, and who I thought would always be there—sunk to the floor as the life drained from his body. Monique had knelt beside him as he died, had heard his final breath escape his lips, had seen his warm brown eyes close for the last time.

Miles away, I lay in my bed at the Rouses, totally unaware of what had just happened to my dad, and what would happen to me and my family as a consequence. Even though I was not there when my dad was murdered, as Monique told me the story, I could practically see the terrible scene unfold before me, and I felt a horrible ache in my own chest like the one my father must have felt in his as he died.

Back to School

MY ALARM BLARED at 6:15 AM on Monday morning, just as it had so many weekdays previously. I rolled from bed, mind fogged. As I attempted to focus on getting ready for school, my aunt materialized in my doorway.

"What are you doing?" she asked anxiously, still sounding somewhat groggy.

"Going to school," I replied matter-of-factly.

"But you're not ready!" she pleaded. "I think you should just stay home."

"No," I said calmly, but firmly. "I have to turn in a paper for my group."

That was true. I had spent the previous night completing the essay on *Les Misérables* my language arts group had assigned me. It wouldn't be late because of me. Somehow, in the midst of all the insanity and anguish that had been unleashed on me and my family, school was one of the only things I could think about. *I have to finish typing those questions. Isn't there a vocab test today? I didn't finish up that math homework.* The mundanity of it somehow comforted me.

"Plus, I want to gather any work I'll need to do," I added when she hesitated, but this was an excuse. Really, I just wanted to get out of the godforsaken house and escape from reality for a moment, to be swept away in the nameless, thoughtless current of students going from one class to the next. I wanted to be in control again, to be in a place where I always did well. School was my element—this strange place that was supposed to be home no longer was.

My aunt gave in when I made it clear I wouldn't be staying home, that I couldn't handle it. I set out toward the bus stop, the early morning chill familiarly nipping at my cheek. In my mind, it was my father, not my aunt, standing on the deck, waving good-bye, calling out that he loved me and to have a great day. I could almost hear his voice caressing my ear.

At the bus stop, my friends were silent. They were boys, uncertain of what to say. They watched me, begging me to give them a clue. Finally, I cracked a wry but lame joke, breaking the silence. I knew they knew about my dad, either from the news or from one of the neighborhood mothers. They laughed uneasily, folding their arms across their chests. We didn't say anything else. The bus came. Another Monday morning.

The rest of the day wasn't quite so routine. My first destination, the band room, had never seemed so formidable. The thought of walking across the front of the room, in perfect view of dozens of classmates, made me quake.

My friends flanked me as we traveled the hall, anxious to offer any moral support they could, but their bodies might as well have been transparent for how exposed I felt. As we made our way down the hall, the usually flowing morning banter stilted and unnatural, I wanted to turn and run home, in spite of my earlier insistence on going to school. But this was my choice, and I knew I couldn't back out.

When we reached the band room, my friends dispersed to get their instruments and I walked alone to get my bassoon, attempting to look dignified and strong and collected. But I knew how pale my skin was, how limp my hair, how messy my outfit. I knew they would know as much as I did, the story having spread across newspapers and local news channels. My family's tragedy had been circulated and regurgitated throughout the community and beyond, before we'd even had a chance to digest it ourselves. My loss wasn't even mine to tell.

I felt my classmates' eyes appraise me with a mixture of pity and discomfort. Always a shy and awkward person, being the focus of such attention would have made me uneasy even before I'd become an orphan.

Identity

ALL MY LIFE, I'd been a fairly reserved person. Since my mother's death especially, I'd been a pensive, quiet child who required much prodding before I'd genuinely participate in a conversation. I tended to shy away from meeting new people and sometimes even from conversing with friends and family members I already knew.

Some of my shyness had dissipated by the time I reached junior high, and I had a tight circle of interesting friends as well as a broader spectrum of acquaintances. In spite of this progression, by seventh grade, my self-confidence was at an all-time low. Though I generally liked who I was as a person, issues with my appearance caused my opinion of myself to plummet. I saw myself as overweight and ugly. And as these beliefs festered, they bred new ones: *You're incapable. You're so fat. No one will ever ask you out.* Eventually, even though I'd always considered myself to be a bright, intelligent person, I began to believe I had nothing of consequence to say, and that no one really cared, anyway. I consistently preferred fading into the background. Presentations and other such occasions where attention was focused on me were a nightmare.

These insecurities, in addition to continuing to deal with the aftermath of my mother's death, my father's occupational situation, and some difficulties in my friendship with Holly, made for a difficult eighth-grade year even before my father's death. I felt I was a nuisance to everyone who had to take care of me aside from my father—the Rouses, my Aunt Chris, my grandparents. I was generally dissatisfied with life and felt blue most of the time. Eventually, such statements as *Things would be easier if you weren't around* began to appear in my litany of negative thoughts. As a result, my father started taking me to see a counselor.

On top of this dissatisfaction, I was also finding it difficult growing up as a biracial young woman in a predominantly white area. Race, as a notable component of identity and personal history, was always slightly confusing to me. The majority of my friends, neighbors, and teachers were white. My father and his family were African-American. Though at the time I was much closer to my mother's family than my father's, racial stereotypes confused me, and I was never quite sure who I did—or "should"—identify with. Though I fit within my community for the most part, there were times when the differences seemed to far outweigh any similarities, when the color of my skin seemed to differentiate me from everyone else.

If it hadn't been for my close relationship with my father, things would have been that much more difficult for me. In the weeks that followed my dad's death, I sometimes wondered whether his murder was meant to punish me for feeling so depressed about my life, when really, it hadn't been all that bad. Like some higher entity watched my petty misery and thought, *You think things are bad now? Well, let's see what you think of this.* But I knew that wasn't really true. I knew my circumstances were just a horrible misfortune.

Following his death, I found it hard to explain our relationship to others who were not familiar with it. How could you really describe afternoons wasted together playing video games and eating sandwiches, laughing and talking as if there was no one else we'd rather be with? Or bedtime stories and sweet goodnights that were my favorite part of the day? Or the day when my father asked me to gaze up into the navy October sky and told me my mother had died?

I can't express how happy I was when my father allowed me to keep two cats as pets, in spite of our allergies, or how proud I felt when he'd praise my latest accomplishment in school or music, or how safe I'd feel when he pulled me into a hug. There was no awkwardness between us, a teenage girl and her father, as is always portrayed in popular media: we hadn't grown apart. We had remained close even as I got older because, at one dark point, we'd been all each other had.

So when I attempt to describe my relationship with my dad, I simply say that he was my best friend. I could talk to him about anything. We got along very well as people, and enjoyed having intellectual and cultural conversations. We would introduce each other to new hobbies and interests and make each other see things in a different way. I always knew our relationship was special, despite the setbacks of my dad being a single parent and being away much of the time.

My father's partial absence put a strain on our relationship, of course. But in some ways, this propelled us to be even closer and forced us to maintain a basic connection, even when he was away. We'd frequently e-mail and call during the weeks when he was gone, and in this respect, I probably talked to my dad more than many kids my age talked to theirs, even if their fathers were home.

Of course, there was the constant concern that my dad would miss something important in my life: band concerts, academic honors, and other such occasions. Though he tried his best to make it to everything, it simply wasn't always possible. The one day he refused to miss, however, was my birthday. Dad always made this day extremely special, giving me probably too many gifts. When I turned six, he even allowed me to have all my friends from school over for a sleepover. I relished celebrating my birthday because it reminded me of how special I was to my dad and how happy my parents had been to have me. Despite tradition, however, on my fourteenth birthday, a week after my dad had been killed, celebrating was the last thing I wanted to do.

Happy Birthday

IN THE WEEKS preceding my dad's death, we'd been making loose plans for my birthday. What I was most looking forward to was having dinner with my dad at the Macaroni Grill, my favorite restaurant at the time. So my family decided to hold my impromptu birthday celebration there. It was probably the largest birthday party I've ever had. We rented out the party room, and I was allowed to invite as many friends as I wanted. My whole family was in attendance, as well. As I laughed with my friends, opened their gifts, and enjoyed the food, it was almost carefree and pleasant enough to forget that my father's funeral was the next day.

Monique arrived toward the end of the party, concern etched in her expression, deepening the wrinkles of worry that had begun to line her face in the week since my dad's death. She pulled me aside.

"Me and your dad's family are on the way to the funeral home," she said. "Did you want to see him before they close the casket?"

This was obviously not a question I wished to encounter on my birthday—or at all. But it was there, and I was obligated to consider it.

I turned back toward my family and friends, some of whom were glancing back at me in slight worry, others not noticing me and carrying on with their conversations, light as they could be under these circumstances, and enjoying their food and wine. I saw my friends engage in silly banter, talking about him or her and what to do next. I saw Mike and Peri, Holly's parents, chatting with my own family. I saw my Aunt Trish and Aunt Erin, in from California, a rare sight for me. And I saw their smiles, much like my mother's, however wan. I saw my father's family: his sister, Carolyn, his brothers, Lester and Myron, his niece, Shaunda. I saw my Aunt Chris beside her boyfriend, Roger, laughing as she'd cried earlier that day, and her sons, my cousins, Nick and Andrew. I saw my grandparents, now having lost two daughters, a son, and a son-in-law, still breathing, still smiling, softly, as they were surrounded by their remaining progeny.

Around me, I saw life, however broken and saddened and fragile. And in my reverie, I became keenly aware of the life within us all—of the laughing, dancing, and joyful life that had once burned within my father. I knew it was gone now, extinguished far too soon. But I also knew it was that part of my dad I wanted to remember forever—not him lying motionless and mirthlessly in a casket, a mere shadow of who he really was.

I turned back to Monique.

"I don't think I want to. You guys can go ahead."

Monique voiced her support of my decision, gave me a hug, and left to say good-bye to my father in her own way. I returned to my friends and enjoyed the rest of my party. The funeral would be the next day.

Toward the End of the Party

i'm told
that i either can
or cannot go to see

his body.

it is a hard decision:

to see his body for the last time,
cold and lifeless,
dark brown eyes once warm, blank

or

remember him as he was,
full of life
and love.

well.

i guess it's not such a hard decision
after all.

Getting Ready

THE NEXT MORNING, I was awakened earlier than usual, not
due to my alarm clock or natural course, but by my Aunt Trish and
Aunt Chris. They spoke to me in hushed tones, under the impression that the gentle volume would lull me from my slumber more
effectively. Conversely, it annoyed me, only compelling me to roll
onto my side and go back to sleep. Unfortunately, this would not

stand. They managed to rouse me from my bed. I dressed quickly, my outfit entirely black, my face unusually pale and drawn, my curls artlessly pulled back.

Surprisingly, I had a healthy appetite, in spite of the unpalatable circumstances of the rest of the day. I ate a cheese omelet, a buttered piece of toast, and a small cup of orange juice. Shortly after I'd finished breakfast, our ride arrived.

As the others piled into the truck, I made my way to my father's study. While my fingers tried fruitlessly to fit the buttons of my black dress coat through their holes, my eyes searched the myriad shelves surrounding either side of my father's computer desk, all filled with expensive-looking hardback books, mostly biographies, with a few diet cookbooks and contemporary classic novels added for good measure.

It was a handsome collection. If a stranger had set eyes on the bookshelves, they would surmise, incorrectly, that my father had been an avid reader. Although my father was an intelligent man with a thirst for learning, he was more streetwise, with a minor in trivia. He could always answer any obscure popular-culture question, and he knew how to get this or that done. Dad was always willing to help out.

I knew for a fact that he hardly ever read novels, and while he enjoyed biographies, he didn't read them very often. He once told me he had trouble concentrating on the text itself and preferred audio books. I wondered why any of that mattered now that he was dead.

As my hands finally managed to push one coat button through its hole, my eyes fell on a copy of *Roots* by Alex Haley. I remembered my father's words about the classic: *Never let that book go, Chels. It's a first edition—worth a lot of money. It was mine in high school.*

I temporarily abandoned the buttoning operation to gingerly pull the novel off the shelf. Flipping open the front cover, I found my father's name written in clean cursive with blue ink. I smiled as I thought of how drastically his handwriting had changed; back then, it was legible.

I set the book back in its place. My eyes filled with tears. There was so much of him in the house, in everything I now owned.

I thought of myself in a new light: a girl, newly fourteen, standing in her dead father's study, all in black, a single tear streaming down her cheek. A girl who couldn't button her coat. I was alone. My family told me again and again I was not, but without him, I was. I was no longer anyone's child; such a terrible change of status wasn't supposed to happen so early in life.

I closed my eyes, and quietly sang a song my dad had sung to me years earlier when I'd joined him for Father's Day on a cruise. I wept more at the sound of my voice—broken, weak, and small—as I sang a song that celebrated fathers and daughters, something I felt I could no longer be a part of.

Premonitions

THOUGH MY FATHER'S death took me so off guard as to propel me into a state of temporary disbelief, I can't say I was totally without premonition. The week preceding Dad and Monique's cruise, I found myself feeling unusually melancholy about my dad's impending departure. Though such emotions were familiar when I was younger, I had since overcome my separation anxiety and learned to deal with him being gone.

He'll be back in a week, I'd tell myself. *It's not that long.*

So I was slightly confused as to why, as he began to pack his bags once more, I felt the inexplicable impulse to beg him not to go, to do anything to keep him from leaving on his trip. I spent as much time with him that week as possible, feeling oddly nostalgic, even as I sat peacefully with him in the family room.

Why do I feel so sad? I wondered. *Nothing is wrong.*

The day before my dad left, I had a band concert that I was very excited about. It was the second year in a row that I'd participated in Honor Band, a region-wide ensemble that included only the finest players from all the schools in our Ohio district. The rehearsals were few but intensive, consisting of only one Friday evening and a full Saturday to prepare for the Sunday concert. Needless to say, I was proud of my contributions and efforts, and couldn't wait for my family to see me play clarinet with the band, especially because we were playing a medley from *West Side Story*, one of my dad's favorite musicals.

I had a large group of friends and family come to my concert, including my dad, Monique, Aunt Chris, my grandparents, Holly, and Holly's mother, Peri. After the concert, we went out to dinner at O'Charley's in celebration of my achievement as well as my impending birthday. Over the restaurant's signature sweet rolls and potato soup, I enjoyed a pleasant evening meal with my family and friends. We even told our waitress it was my birthday and were awarded with a small, chocolate birthday cake. Across the table from me, my father told stories that charmed everyone, and the rest of my family were being their usual, quirky selves. Yet, even then, I felt a sense of sorrow and unease as I looked into my father's smiling, brown face.

Once everyone had finished eating and my father had fallen silent as people broke off into smaller conversations, I rose from my seat at the table, walked to him, and sat down on his lap, a ritual I hadn't indulged in since I was a young child. He looked at me in confusion but didn't shoo me away, as he used to when I was younger.

Unable to quell the sadness within me, I wrapped my arms around him and lay my head on his shoulder.

"Daddy, I don't want you to die," I said quietly, pitifully.

Understandably, he was puzzled and slightly perturbed.

"Sweetheart, I don't want to die either." I straightened up and looked into his eyes. "Why would you say something like that?" he asked.

I hesitated. What was I supposed to say? That I had some sort of ominous inkling my dad would be taken from us? That the peace we were enjoying at the table would soon be shattered? What good would saying such a thing do?

I shrugged my shoulders.

Always aware of politeness in mixed company but not without concern, he said, "We'll talk about it later."

With a nod, I rose from his lap and returned to my seat. We never did talk about it later, but what good would it have done? He would have felt concerned, I would have felt worried, and he would have told me it was all in my head.

The Funeral

ON THE CAR RIDE TO Christ Emmanuel Christian Fellowship, a nondenominational parish in Cincinnati at which my Uncle Charles was a minister, I didn't speak. I played Pokémon on my Game Boy to distract myself from what was about to occur. We arrived at the church early, and my aunts and I filed into the first pew. I felt lost.

In all the other funerals I'd attended—my mother's, my uncle's, and my Grandma Shannon's—my dad had always been right beside me, holding my hand and letting me cry into his shirt. Now, he was the one being buried, and I was all alone.

As the service drew nearer, the mourners began to arrive. I was struck by the immense crowd of people. An article in the *Cincinnati Enquirer* would later report that over two hundred people showed up. And all of them had formed a line in front of my pew to pay their respects to me and my family—many of them, even strangers, weeping as they pulled me into an embrace and told me how sorry they were.

There was my father's choral instructor from elementary school and his childhood friends. There were all my friends from West Chester, several of whom, in spite of a much anticipated band trip to Cleveland, had chosen to stay behind to support me. My friend, Amy, whom I'd known since first grade, and her mother, Lily, had flown in from Connecticut. My language arts teachers from both seventh and eighth grade, as well as my school counselor were there, and of course, the Rouses, my grandparents, Monique, my cousins from both sides of the family, my aunts from California, my Aunt Chris, my Uncle Lester and Uncle Myron, and my Aunt Carolyn, whose husband, Charles, was to officiate the service. Though my Aunt Pam and Aunt Kerry were unable to make it from California for the funeral, I knew they were with me in spirit. I felt almost overwhelmed by support and love, even in my sense of extreme isolation.

Once everyone's condolences had been offered and they took their seats, the service began. I found a surprising amount of comfort in my uncle's words, the soulful music and song, and the presence of those around me.

After the readings and a short sermon, people who had known my father well stood up in front of the crowd to give short testimonials, among them a man whom my father had known in his childhood and another longtime friend whom he'd known since high school. I was extremely touched to hear how my father had positively affected other people's lives.

When the testimonials were finished, it was my turn.

"And now we'll hear from Blair's daughter, Chelsey Shannon," my uncle announced to the congregation. My Aunt Chris immediately began weeping at the sound of my name, and I slowly rose from my seat to take my place at the podium, a letter I'd written to my father the previous day clasped in my hand. I took a moment to peruse the crowd before I began. It was easily the largest group of people I'd ever read to before, yet I didn't feel nervous.

"Hi, everyone," I said in an unpretentious, friendly voice. I cleared my throat as I struggled not to look down at the podium, hiding my face. With a small laugh at my behavior, I said, "My father was always telling me, hold your head up, you have nothing to be ashamed of." A chorus of affirmatives rang throughout the crowd. "So, I'm trying to work on that."

It was the oddest thing. In front of a two-hundred-person crowd, all eyes on me, eager to hear anything I had to say, I wasn't the slightest bit fearful or awkward or self-conscious. I felt full of a grace and ease that was entirely unfamiliar to me, especially under the circumstances, when I'd half-expected to break down and be unable to read my piece. But as I gazed into the crowd of people who had gathered to say good-bye to my father, I felt only peace and a willingness to communicate what I had to say:

My dear father,

You were stolen from me, from all of us, in the most unfair of ways, and much too soon. We should have spent years and years more together.

Our house still stands, the world still turns, but my life will be forever altered and forever incomplete without your gentle, unwavering love. You taught me and everyone around you so much, and you could brighten one's day with only a few words.

I keep thinking to myself, Who would ever steal away a man that I, and so many others, held so close and dear? *The tears I've shed are countless. You were the strength in my life, the comfort, the warmth, the love; you were the guidance, the support, and I always did my best to make you proud, and I still will. For you made me proud every day, and you still do.*

You were the most gentle and thoughtful of men. Why you? Why us? What will I ever do without you, Daddy? It is so hard for me to accept that from this trip, you'll never return, that you'll never again hold me in your arms, never again laugh with me, never again tell me you love me.

As we lay you to rest, we remember all the countless precious memories we all shared with you, or else we remember what a hilarious, cheering, kind man you were. I promise you that you'll never be forgotten by anyone who knew you.

As for me, I'll remember you as the best father I ever could have asked for. My eternal wish is that we could have had more time on earth together, but at the same time, I look forward to someday coming home to your embrace once more.

I love you, I love you, I love you, and I know you will help me, and all of those who you loved, pull through this.

The church erupted into applause, and the congregation rose to its feet. I felt something within me change as I smiled softly back at the crowd. Maybe I *wasn't* so worthless. Maybe people *did* want to hear what I had to say. Maybe I wasn't incapable, or ugly, or stupid, as I'd begun to believe. As I descended from the podium to return to my seat, I carried myself with a certain pride and hope, feeling as though my father's spirit was traveling beside me. As untimely as it seemed, I somehow knew this was the beginning of many changes for me that would ultimately be for the better.

The rest of the funeral consisted of a slide show put together by my cousin Shaunda. The pictures were set to my father singing from his CD, *Live at Sea*, which he'd released only a few weeks earlier. Images from my father's life drifted across the screen to the sound of his rich, baritone voice: my father singing his first solo at his childhood church at age five; my parents at their wedding; my dad holding a toddler version of me in front of autumn trees; and, most recently, photos of me, my father, and Monique at a production of *The Phantom of the Opera*, which we'd seen shortly after Christmas when it was touring in Cincinnati. Around me, my aunts had dissolved into tears as they gazed at a face they would never truly see again, the sense of loss magnified by the occasional appearance of my mother's image. I remained stoic, refusing to let myself cry, even as tears swam in my eyes and I had to bite my lip to prevent them from falling.

Looking back on it, I'm not exactly sure why I refused to let myself cry. I'd never believed that weeping indicated weakness and had been generally open about my feelings with the appropriate people. Most likely, I think the reason I remained emotionless was I believed if I cried, it would have meant he was really was gone. It would confirm everyone's horrific belief that these photographs and the tracks on the CD were the closest any of us would ever be to my father again. So I refrained from tears until we reached the cemetery.

It was remarkably warm and clear for a mid–January Cincinnati day. I was acutely reminded of something my father had said to Holly, Monique, and me on a recent day trip to the mountains of Kentucky. For some reason, we had been discussing funerals and how they always seemed to take place on rainy days. "It's not going to be raining at my funeral," my father had said with confidence. Of course, at the time, I had no way of knowing that his assertions would be so quickly proven true.

The large funeral crowd had shrunken by the time we reached the cemetery and gathered around a rectangular hole in the ground, the dirt freshly dug up beside it, the bright green cloth that's usually used for interment framing the hole. The coffin was beside the pit. I stared at it intently as a few final words were said and roses distributed to the immediate family, including me. Could this foreign, ever-oppressive wooden box, the kind that always struck me with the deepest sense of despair, really house my father's body? I half-believed it was empty or that they had the wrong man, that this was all just wrong.

My uncle stepped aside as the time came for us to approach the coffin and say a final good-bye if we wished. I was encouraged to go first. I merely stepped up to the coffin—the closest I would ever be to my dad again—and didn't say or do anything. But I did break into tears, for the first time that day. I began to weep, hopelessly, in agony, as a voice gently but firmly whispered in my head, *He is gone.*

Tender arms pulled me away from the casket and held me as I watched my other family members say good bye through stormy tears. The image is rather blurred now, but what sticks out most clearly in my memory is my cousin Andrew, kneeling by my dad's casket, head slightly bowed, hand on the varnished wood as he said good bye to the uncle who wasn't his uncle by blood, but who he'd loved, like the rest of my family, just the same.

I wept as the casket was lowered into the ground, and then it was finished. The guests bid my family good-bye and uttered one more "I'm so sorry" before dispersing into their respective vehicles and heading home. My dad's side of the family had rented out a hall for a reception, and many people joined us, but I had no appetite. I drifted through the rest of the day on autopilot, taking a bath in my parents' queen-size bathtub and reading condolence cards later in the evening before going out to eat with my friends Lily, Amy, Holly, and Jessica. I don't actually remember getting ready for bed that evening, but that's likely only because the oblivion that greeted me was so complete and welcomed.

Coping

THE DAYS FOLLOWING my dad's funeral were comprised of grieving his loss, dealing with the details of his murder, and attempting to rebuild my perception of "normal." Amid the isolation and despair, I had to go through the comparatively simple, yet emotionally taxing process of adjusting to my Aunt Chris's assumption of guardianship over me. I spent most of my time at home alone, unable to deal with the fact that, though I was still in the same house, my dad no longer lived in it with me and never would again.

Even so, had I not been allowed to remain in my house, I likely would have crumbled. Though it was merely a compilation of rooms filled with furniture and things, I took enormous comfort from remaining in the environment I'd inhabited for most of my life. In my mind, it seemed almost as though the house was the sole remainder of my immediate family. I knew it intimately: where the floor creaked when pressure was applied, the history of the color of its walls, which remote controls served which functions, where certain kitchen utensils lived.

My aunt's sons, Nick and Andrew, moved into the house with me temporarily so others would be there on the occasions when my aunt was unable or too tired to make the thirty-to-forty-minute commute from her job to my house. Though I cruised through those bleak days with a relative detachment and lack of involvement, my aunt understandably struggled to be present in West Chester as well as keep up her own condo in Colerain, where my grandparents also resided. Between acting as my caregiver, keeping her job, taking care of her house, and dealing with her own feelings of loss, my aunt likely had the most stressful time of us all.

The days were relatively quiet and full of melancholy. I attended school every day, though there were times when I was overwhelmed by the comparative triviality of eighth grade. Sometimes, I'd opt to visit my school counselor over being frustrated in pre-algebra or literature circles in language arts. I began to eat lunch in my English teacher's, Mrs. Falato's, room. Sometimes, I'd only attend half a day, having my cousin Nick pick me up and take me home to rest.

By February, I had sunk into a quiet state of depression, attempting to deal with the crushing reality that my dad wouldn't be coming back. One night, I had a dream that brought me incredible solace. I was in my dad's room, and it was spring outside. I looked out to see a green van pull into my driveway. Though I didn't recognize the car, I was filled with elation at the sight of it. I saw my dad, wearing sunglasses, step out, along with a woman who also seemed familiar. I ran to the front door of the house to let them in, throwing it open. Dad was standing there, with the woman and many others who had exited the car with him. When I jumped into his arms, I woke up.

As I sat up in my bed, I breathed heavily as if I had really been running. Though the dream had been extremely abbreviated, I felt joyous as I looked back on it. I hadn't dreamt of my father since his death, and I'd found immense comfort and joy in the dream, almost as if it were a message from him, telling me he was okay and he was here.

I rose from bed happier than I'd felt in weeks and went down-stairs into the kitchen, where my Aunt Chris was already eating. Grinning freely, I told her about the dream and how happy I'd felt. I was pleased when she shared my suspicion that it was more than just a simple nighttime reverie.

"Chels, remember after your mom died and I asked you if you had any dreams about her, and you said you did?"

I nodded. I remembered the dream well: my mother, as an angel, yet still bald from her chemotherapy, appearing to Holly and me. Only I could see her. My mother told me she was okay, that I didn't need to worry. I'd had a similar feeling of relief and gratitude back then.

"In my grief support group I went to after your mom died, they told us that the kids sometimes get messages, usually dreams, from whoever died, telling them everything is okay. That's why I was so excited to hear your mom had given you a dream. And now your dad has," she explained.

"Yeah. I'm really glad."

"And it's on the one-month anniversary too."

I hadn't realized it until she said it, but sure enough, when I looked at the calendar, it read Sunday, February 19th. My dad never failed to honor a special occasion

Nick, Andrew, and I tended to relax when we were home together, playing GameCube and watching television shows and movies. I felt bad doing so little when my aunt was constantly on the go, but I honestly didn't feel I could handle any more. In addition to consistently vegging out, I threw myself into art of all forms, spending hours singing while accompanying myself on the keyboard, practicing my violin and bassoon, writing poetry, and sketching. I even composed a short melody on the piano, a feat I had never attempted before.

Once the weather grew warmer, I took to going on long bike rides around the neighborhood. I'd ride aimlessly, aware only of the burn in my muscles as I pumped up a hill, the cool breeze against my face as I glided down another. My neighborhood was essentially a long, circuitous route. I could go as far as I wished and essentially wind up back in the same place.

In the early spring, Monique and I joined a community theater production of *The Music Man*, one of my father's favorite shows. Though I was merely cast as a townsperson, I took pride in the fact that I was trying something new and totally outside my comfort zone. Before my father's death, participating in a theatrical production, no matter how minimally, would have been out of the question for me, in spite of my love of musicals and interest in theater. I would have hated the idea of standing onstage for all to see, my awkwardness on display. But after the funeral and reading my eulogy for my dad, community theater seemed to be no large feat—it was even an enjoyable project to undertake.

In truth, I enjoyed being a part of the musical more than I'd thought I would. I made friends with a few of the other "townspeople" who were my age, and when we weren't onstage singing and dancing to cheerful songs, we'd laugh and chat in the back, applying over-the-top stage makeup and attempting to harmonize. After months of rehearsals, we put on our production in an outdoor amphitheater in the park, and to the tune of "Seventy-Six Trombones" and "Wells Fargo Wagon," I watched winter slowly melt into spring and the time following my father's death evolve from days into weeks.

Spending so much time producing art and riding my bike served as a much-needed escape for me. I didn't hide from my problems— to do so would have been impossible—but there were times when I required a break. When I did things like methodically teach myself to play the keyboard or spend hours sketching family photographs, I was able to focus on creating something, rather than on what had been taken away from me.

Writing became a major refuge, the outlet into which I poured all my emotions of fear, depression, and the occasional dash of anger. Although writing had ceased to be a primary pursuit of mine since grade school—when I was wont to begin a plethora of short stories but finish very few of them—I once again started writing journal entries, personal essays, and poetry. I was surprised to see writing resurface, especially in such an important capacity, but I was pleased. There was something very satisfying about seeing my thoughts and feelings crystallized onto paper. I wrote frequently, always attempting to refine my technique at conveying my emotions through words.

The Last Time

THE LAST TIME I saw my dad alive was in our kitchen, the night before he and Monique left for their cruise. I was in my pajamas and had gone downstairs to say goodnight before watching a movie with Holly, who was spending the night. My dad was on the phone, leaning his elbows against the counter as he often did. His itinerary for the forthcoming trip was on the kitchen island, as usual. Monique was also there, getting last-minute things together before retiring for the night.

I folded my arms around my dad as he wrapped up his conversation, resting my head on his shoulder. Tears sprang to my eyes for reasons entirely unbeknownst to me. My feelings of anxiety and dread at the impending separation bubbled over, and I felt as though I would never hug my dad again. I cried quietly so he didn't notice.

Wordlessly, Monique extracted her disposable camera from her purse and snapped a shot of this final embrace. At the time, I found myself mildly quizzical but didn't object. Later, when she presented me with two copies of the picture, I felt a deep gratitude for her intuitiveness.

I wiped the tears from my eyes as my dad hung up the phone. He turned to me and issued his usual going-away spiel: feed the cats, clean out the litter box, straighten up the kitchen, return his e-mails. I nodded along, not really listening, the sense of imbalance lodged in my breast. *Do I bring up my fears again or go with the flow?* I opted for the latter, not wanting to disturb him, especially not in Monique's presence. Instead, I agreed to his instructions, pushing my unease far away as I hugged and kissed him good-bye. As I walked up the stairs toward my bedroom, I had the distinct impression of leaving something I loved for the last time.

Once my dad and Monique had gone, I mostly forgot my earlier feelings of dread and fear. The week passed by in a completely normal fashion: on Monday I was off school for Martin Luther King Day, and the rest of the week was the usual mixture of school, homework, and music.

The last time I talked to my father was Thursday evening, right before I went to bed. He was in St. Thomas, in the hotel room where, a few hours later, he would die. Our conversation was commonplace. He said he'd call in the morning and that he and Monique would be back on Saturday. Distracted by what I was doing on the computer, I only half-listened to him, having no idea this would be our last conversation, in spite of my earlier premonitions. I tuned in for the end of the conversation, however, as we exchanged I love yous and said good-bye. I hung up the phone, closing any mortal connection between my dad and me.

Flying

When I was younger I was never afraid to fly.
With Dad sitting beside me,
I was confident that we would arrive safely—
in fact, no other possibility ever crossed my mind
and if we hit a patch of turbulence,
I'd cling to his arm for a moment
and I would be safe
and it would be over
and we would be fine.

Now,
I act brave,
like flying doesn't bother me,

when in truth,
it does a bit.
Gazing out the window
so far from the security
of ground and of him
I feel unstable, baseless
and when we hit a patch of turbulence,
I have no arm to cling to,
just false bravado
and broken reassurances.

Religion

For many kids in my school, eighth grade meant confirmation into the Catholic faith. And I was one of the many about to begin the process of confirmation, despite my tumultuous relationship with the church.

My mother's side of the family was devoutly Catholic, and before my mother's death, my mom and I regularly attended church. I absorbed the Catholic doctrine eagerly in childish wonder, even without really understanding what it all meant. I found the idea of God comforting and the concept of Jesus wonderful and generous. I said my prayers every night and set about to be as holy as possible. Until my mother fell ill.

When she was sick and after she died, my dad and I stopped attending church. I stopped praying at night. This wasn't specifically because I felt any anger at any God or because I felt particularly hopeless; rather, my mind was just consumed with other things, and I simply forgot about what used to be a sacred ritual of mine. Sometimes, in the dark days following my mother's death, I blamed myself for what happened.

Maybe if I'd prayed for her, I had thought, *she would have made it.* But such self-accusations were halfhearted. Somewhere, I already felt that nothing I could have done would have made a difference. I was even anticipating, in a sad way, my mother's death. When she'd grown quite ill, I drew her a picture of clouds and pearly gates that read "Welcome to Heaven." I don't know how she felt about that— if she felt hurt that all her efforts to stay alive were going to waste in the face of my muted acceptance or relieved for my silent blessing telling her it was okay to let go.

When she died, I did believe she went to heaven. And after I had the dream in which she appeared to me as an angel, the strength of those beliefs doubled. My mother, I steadfastly maintained, was an angel in heaven, watching over me.

It wasn't until I was ten years old that I began to question the Catholic doctrine. After my dad pulled through his depression following my mother's death and had gotten into the swing of being a single parent, we'd resumed attending mass. Not a Catholic himself, my father wanted to respect my mother's wishes of raising me in the faith. But the older I grew, the more I began to wonder if this was the right faith for me. Though I didn't disagree with any specific Catholic doctrine, I found it to be a very conservative faith socially, and this didn't sit well with me. My lack of agreement with Catholic positions on birth control, abortion, and homosexuality led me to research the faith, and in turn, others. When my father died, I was at a precipice of some great shift in my spirituality, just beginning to really examine what I believed in and what I did not. Interestingly though, by this time, I'd also resumed my nightly prayers, especially when Dad was away. During each trip, I asked God to bring him safely home.

When my dad died, I clung to the religious beliefs I'd been taught since childhood, praying even more regularly, thinking to myself that God was keeping him safe now, that God was watching over my family and me. I don't know if I truly believed this or if I just needed something bigger to believe in at a time when I felt so small and helpless. Either way, I'm glad I had it at the time.

But though I took comfort in the idea of God, I still wasn't feeling very warm toward the Catholic faith. Dad had started me on the path to confirmation before he died, and my Aunt Chris, a devout Catholic and my confirmation sponsor, wasn't about to let the matter fall by the wayside. So, following the initial shock of the tragedy, I resumed attending the bimonthly Sunday night confirmation meetings. The meetings felt like a social event, much diluted by the presence of chaperones and discussions about God. So many people from my grade were going through the confirmation process that I would have felt odd *not* attending.

My aunt asked me if I wanted to postpone confirmation until the following year, when I might be in a better place to consider my spiritual allegiance. The way I saw it, though, it was simply now or later, and better to do it now, in the presence of those whose company I enjoyed. My friends Bridget, Abby, and Kelsey, as well as a few other acquaintances from school, were never far from my side in all matters confirmation-related. And though I'm not proud of it now, I coasted through what was supposed to be a devotional, intentional process with apathy, along with a small seed of resentment.

Despite of my lack of commitment, I did receive an extremely precious gift through confirmation that I never would have otherwise. It was definitely the only occurrence in my life that I'll ever consider a miracle.

In April, the month before our confirmation ceremony, it was announced we would all be receiving letters of encouragement from our respective parents and sponsors. I thought it was a nice idea, but I didn't feel particularly excited, assuming I would only be receiving a note from my aunt. But when two envelopes were delivered to my hands, I knew from my father's trademark messy script on the front of one of them that I was mistaken. My pulse elevated as I fought to suppress the joy that filled my heart, knowing that if I expressed all the happiness I was feeling, I would burst into tears. I sat in the pew alone, ripping the envelope open with simultaneous eagerness and extreme care.

The card depicted a beautiful black woman on the front reading, "Never forget how awesome you are." The inside of the card read, *"Dear Chelsey, as you travel this journey never forget: Believe in yourself and have faith that the power within you can make your life whatever you want it to be. All my love, Daddy."*

Also enclosed in the card was a loose sheet of paper filled with his near illegible, sacred script:

1/8/06

My dearest Peanut,

My love for you is unending, and you continue to amaze me with your musical talents and ability for expressive writing. Both are a direct reflection of your emotional maturity, and both are great. Your zeal for the things you love is worthy of envy. I know the parent is to set the example for the child, and I hope I do, but in many ways you teach me so much. For these reasons and many more I am proud of you, and I know your mother would be too.

I love you without bounds!
Daddy

I savored the miracle of each word of praise and encouragement, knowing these were the final words from my dad I would carry with me for the rest of my days, a father's last words of love to a daughter in lieu of the proper good-bye that had been stolen from us all.

I attempted to read slowly, but it was impossible not to let my eyes race onward, absorbing every word he'd said. By the time I reached the end of the letter, quiet tears had sprung from my eyes, running down my cheeks and gathering at my chin. My friends came to my side, and I showed them the letter.

"My dad wrote this!" I said in quiet amazement, not caring that everyone was seeing me cry. I couldn't believe the magnitude of this miracle, a final surprise and parting gift. I could never have imagined such a treasure could come from something I'd been so unwilling to do.

My issues with religion were temporarily dropped, and I went on to be confirmed with the rest of my friends in May. The ceremony didn't mean as much to me as perhaps it should have, but it made my aunt happy, as well as, I imagined, my parents.

Perspective

UNFORTUNATELY, RELIGION wasn't the only thing my Aunt Chris and I didn't see eye-to-eye on. Whereas my relationship with my father had been one of easy harmony and accord, my aunt and I occasionally butted heads. It wasn't that I disliked her—in fact, I loved her very much. She was one of the adults in my life who I found to be extremely responsible and unselfish. However, our communication styles differed, and we held distinctly separate interests. Whereas I was interested in art and literature, my aunt was into the outdoors and horses. It wasn't that we didn't make attempts to connect. It just didn't always work out when we did.

Chiefly, though, after my aunt became my legal guardian, I began pushing her away simply because she was not my father. Conversation wasn't as easy between my aunt and me. She didn't pack my lunches the same way. She didn't give the same hugs or laugh at the same things. And though I knew perfectly well that none of this was her fault, I couldn't help but disengage, even becoming short with her, despite how much I knew it hurt her.

I've always seen my Aunt Chris as a very dutiful person. She essentially took charge of the situation after my dad died, making tough decisions and stepping up to the plate at times when others couldn't. Even in the midst of grieving her brother-in-law, she was able to take care of me. Maybe I pushed her away because I knew she would always be there.

Aunt Chris continued to take me to see Donna, the counselor I'd been seeing since before my dad's death. In the last fifteen minutes of each session, Donna would invite my aunt into the room, and the three of us would have a check-in. These were often uncomfortable conversations for me. My aunt would allude to dissatisfaction with my behavior or her own emotional turmoil, and I would squirm in my seat. I didn't like facing the fact that Aunt Chris, who had always been so strong, was having troubles, too, and that they were partially my doing.

One counseling session in particular stands out in my mind. For some reason, my aunt asked her son, Nick, to drive us to the therapist. As usual, Aunt Chris came in during the last portion of the session, while Nick remained in the waiting room. We assumed our usual dialogue, and my aunt began to talk about the stress of maintaining both my house and her condo while still going to work and making sure I was taken care of, all on top of dealing with the loss of my father.

The therapist, Donna, said simply, "This is very hard for you."

My aunt nodded curtly, her voice adopting the matter-of-fact hardness it did when she was attempting to remain unemotional. "Yes. Yes, it is." Then she started crying. Then she started sobbing. It was as if Donna's simple words had opened the floodgates to the pain within my aunt—someone was finally noticing that she, too, was suffering, even if only in silence. Though she rarely cried in front of the rest of us, it didn't mean she never cried.

My aunt continued to sob through the rest of the session and the car ride home. Nick was stoic in the driver's seat, and I was lying prostrate in the back, facing away from the front. Neither of us said anything or tried to comfort her. We both realized this was something that needed to happen.

After this incident, I attempted to cultivate a stronger sense of empathy for my aunt, reminding myself when I felt the urge to snap at her or push her away, that she had feelings remarkably similar to mine.

Leaving Home

IN THE LATE SPRING, my Aunt Trish flew in for an extended visit from California. Though I loved all of my aunts dearly, I was probably the closest to my Aunt Trish. We'd enjoyed a special emotional connection since my childhood, and I was very pleased for her to visit. It was actually a test run of sorts, as she was considering moving back to Ohio to live with me. For a month, she lived in my house, temporarily relieving Aunt Chris of some of her stress.

At that point, Aunt Trish's nurturing disposition was just what I needed.

But Aunt Trish was also keen on stripping down the house, removing memories from it that were becoming too painful. With the question of moving increasingly in the air, she began the process of taking down pictures and packing away miscellaneous bric-a-brac. Rather than feeling angry, I felt gently saddened, the increasing lack of discernable warmth and character in the house matching my growing feelings toward it. I loved my house, but without my father, it just wasn't the same. It had become a stranger's home even before my aunt removed the pictures. By late spring, it became clear that I would be moving out of the house I'd lived in for most of my life. My father hadn't been faithful with paying off the mortgage, and my aunt's income was not ample enough to make up for his mistakes and support the two of us. Though I knew moving was a practical and, in some ways, healthy choice, the idea of leaving my home was very hard to bear.

One of the most difficult things, however, was unpacking my father's suitcase. The last suitcase he ever packed had been shipped to the house long ago, placed beside his bed, and shut away. His room had remained my refuge in the months following his death, and when I lay in his bed or holed myself up in his spacious closet to get away from it all, I would sometimes consider going through the suitcase. But the prospect was too painful, even though I knew it would have to be done eventually.

One Saturday morning, my Aunt Trish and I sat in the hallway outside his bedroom door and unzipped the black bag I'd been avoiding for so long. When she opened the lid, my father's gentle scent permeated the air, and tears sprang to my eyes. As I unfolded the T-shirts and unpacked his toiletries, I wondered what my father had been thinking as he'd packed his things for the final time: *Was he anxious to come home? Weary after a day of sightseeing? Excited to see me again?* I would never know.

With my Aunt Trish's gentle guidance, much of the house was packed away without incident. The most difficult part came when, one day, Nick was helping me pack up my room. As I sat motionless on my bed, Nick would hold up this object or that—an article of clothing, a knickknack, a book—and ask me "Pack or leave?" With one-word responses or a curt nod of the head, I watched my belongings—this small cell of my life—be pared down so they could fit into a few cardboard boxes and be carted across town to my aunt's condo until concrete plans could be made.

After a while, I asked Nick if we could take a break. He nodded. "This is hard," he said simply.

I nodded back, trying my hardest not to cry, but I scampered from the room as tears began to roll down my cheeks. It *was* hard. Though moving was certainly a part of everyone's life at some point, this moving was different. I wasn't one hundred percent sure where I was going, who I was going to live with, or even what school I'd be attending. With this moving, there wasn't even a semblance of certainty.

Toward the end of her visit, my Aunt Trish told me something I'd already realized: she wouldn't be moving back to Ohio. This disappointed me deeply, but I acted callous to protect myself. Even so, she invited me to stay with her in California during the summer, and perhaps consider moving out west with her. I agreed to visit, not making any promises about moving.

The rest of the school year was shaped around preparing for my visit to California. During my looming sojourn out west, I knew my family would finish packing up the house and move all my belongings to my aunt's house across town. When I came back—if I chose to come back—it was clear that I would be returning to the condo, not my house in West Chester.

Needless to say, melancholy permeated the final days before my trip, in spite of the sultry promise of summer. I became acutely aware of how I spent my final days in my house, not wanting to squander a second spent within the red brick walls. I'd stay up very late at night, anxious to absorb whatever bit of the house I could. One night, after a productive day of packing up my room, my bed was strewn with an assortment of belongings, and I ended up sleeping with a blanket on the floor.

On the last night at my house, I grabbed a pen and a flashlight and sat inside my now-empty closet, the secluded cell of my room I'd disappeared into when I'd needed a quick escape from reality. On the sidewall of the closet, near the bottom, I wrote the following inscription:

This is Chelsey's room, now and always.

Then, I turned off my light and went to bed, ready as I'd ever be to venture out into the world, away from my house, my dad, and the life I'd known so well.

Part Two

Sojourning

I FELT UNUSUALLY LIGHT and free on the plane to California. I'd only packed clothes that would carry me through a few weeks' stay, along with a few recreational essentials. Everything else had been left in the house to be boxed up and moved by my family, either to a storage space or to my aunt's condo. I looked forward to seeing my Aunt Trish again, as well as my Aunt Kerry and Aunt Erin, who I hadn't seen since the winter.

Aunt Chris and her boyfriend, Roger, were accompanying me on the flight, but after a few days at my Aunt Trish's, they would be assuming their own path to a more northern part of California to visit Roger's sister. For my part, I had mixed feelings about this vacation, which had the possibility of becoming a long-term move. Part of me was deeply grateful for the chance to escape Ohio and focus on my own healing rather than stewing in the maelstrom of depression. I believed the dry California heat and salty, forgiving ocean could help me become attuned to emotions other than grief once again, could breathe new life into a life turned stale by tragedy. Another part of me, however, was reluctant. I knew that when—

if—I returned to Ohio, everything would be difficult. My house would no longer be mine, and I would be living with my Aunt Chris. I wouldn't attend my old school anymore. The Ohio I'd known for the first fourteen years of my life would be entirely changed. As I gazed out the window of the plane, I wondered how I could miss home since I didn't even know where home was.

We flew into the Santa Barbara Municipal Airport as the sun sank below the horizon and the western sky was being painted a dusky palate of purples and grays. My Aunt Trish and her husband Michael greeted us at the airport. We all piled into their car, exhausted yet talkative, and drove off into the mountains as the moon rose overhead. I had never been to this part of California before. To me, California was a rather pedestrian state, atypical only in its pronounced commercialism and abundance of beaches. But this was a California I was unfamiliar with: mountains higher than I could imagine, coated with sparse, reedy trees and separated by seemingly depthless valleys. We drove on thin, serpentine roads that hugged the mountainside for dear life.

Along the road, my aunt explained the part of town she was living in, a community known as Santa Ynez in the town of Los Olivos. She and her husband Michael were acting as tenants for a wealthy woman's property while she was away, tending to her horses and dogs, as well as working on renovating the house. The house itself was part of a gated development set in a largely undisturbed California mountainside. The area was secluded, peaceful, and calm.

When we finally passed through the gates of the neighborhood and pulled up to the house, I felt a uniqueness around me. The air was so clean as to almost seem liquid, perfumed slightly by the scent of desert. The moon was brilliantly white, as if bleached clean by the clarity of the air framing it. The stars twinkled with a dazzling effect I'd never before experienced. The vegetation sur-rounding the area, however sparse, truly seemed to be salient, breathing with the earth, emitting clear oxygen to be absorbed by our lungs.

The next morning, I found a similar sense of comfort and solace in my surroundings, though they themselves had done a veritable about-face: The sun was shining, the air dry and warm, the sky gen-tly littered with cirrus clouds. Birds sang cheerfully as a gentle breeze stirred the sparse foliage.

I could stay here for a while, I thought to myself noncommittally as I joined my family for breakfast. And I did. After my Aunt Chris and Roger continued on their trip up north, I stayed with Aunt Trish and Michael, slowing getting to know Santa Ynez and its neighbor, Los Olivos. I found ample time to rest, write, read, and sleep, which had been my Aunt Trish's intention. The house behind the gate, set discretely in the woods, was a retreat, a hidden oasis of peace that I bathed in without hesitation. The only Internet there was dial-up, and I rarely bothered with it; there was no cell phone signal from the house. It was a change for me, who, up until that time, frequented MySpace and was usually texting someone or another. But in California, I was forced to be still and quiet with my own thoughts.

Healing

MY TRANQUIL SURROUNDINGS didn't always mean peace for me, though. There were times when I felt consumed by depres-sion or uncertainty for my future, and I'd retreat to my bedroom to write or cry. I had plenty of time for reflection; I ended up writing a collection of twenty-five poems that told the story of my father's death, as well as several other individual poems and personal essays.

My Aunt Trish gave me space when I needed it and an empathic ear when I felt like talking. We'd always had a special relationship, but this trip solidified our bond. We'd spend time together talking, cooking, and running errands. For the first time in a long time, I was unconcerned with such trivial matters as homework assignments and cleaning my room, and was able to focus on more substantial things.

One of the most special things I did during my stay in California was visit a certain beach. I'd been to the ocean plenty of times in the past, having often accompanied my father on cruises, as well as visiting California before. I was always intrigued by how unique each beach was—how the mood, temperature of the water, and texture of the sand differed. One morning, my aunt told me we'd be going to a special beach that few people knew about. We packed snacks, sandwiches, and drinks for the day and set off on the two-hour drive. Unlike most of the beaches I'd visited, this one wasn't advertised and didn't attract large numbers of families. The path to this beach was flanked by mountains and seemed to go on and on. We didn't speak much in the car. My aunt focused on driving, and I gazed out the window in silent reverie.

When we finally arrived, I was anxious to see what all the fuss was about. The beach was unlike any I'd ever been to before. There were only about ten other beachgoers to be found. Oddly, though it was warm, the sun was blocked out by clouds, and a cool wind was blowing. We set up camp, pinning a large beach towel down at the corners with our picnic basket and shoes, before I approached the water's edge and tested it.

As I slowly waded into the freezing water, I couldn't help but laugh at myself. No matter how unpleasant, it was nearly impossible for me to visit a beach without going into the water. I suppose oceans had some personal significance for me and always would. My father had worked on the ocean, often sending me gorgeous photos of the different beaches he visited or the sun setting on a horizon made entirely of waves. When I went with him on cruises, I'd take walks around the ship and lean against the railing of the deck, breathing in the moist, salty sea air. While the rocking of the ship at night made some people nervous or nauseous, I found it relaxing, like a mother gently rocking her child to sleep, and even after I returned to stable land. I would imagine the ground moving for a few days.

The sea fascinated me with its mysterious depth and power. It was one of the few places humanity hadn't entirely explored—one couldn't rattle off a complete list of facts about it without hesitation. This impressed me. Any place that had resisted the inquisitiveness—and arrogance—of humans deserved respect in my book. I loved stories about the ocean, from real tragedies like the sinking of the RMS *Titanic*, to strange phenomena like the Bermuda Triangle.

Visiting the sea had always felt like a homecoming to me. I'd often spend time finding a small relic of it that I could take home: a shell, stone, or sample of sand. Occasions where I could swim in the ocean were very special, almost sacred, particularly because I lived in a landlocked state. I was blessed in this respect by having family in seaside California and a father who'd worked so closely with the sea.

As I waded into the freezing water, goose bumps exploding on my skin, I turned around and waved to my Aunt Trish, who was reclining on the beach towel. Turning and attempting to gather courage to get my head in the water, I remembered the first time I'd visited a beach with my Aunt Trish.

Not long after my mother died, my father sent me to California to visit with my various aunts; I was about six years old. Aunt Trish took me to the Santa Monica Pier one day, and I was eager to take a quick dip, even though, at the time, the vastness of the ocean scared me, as it does most kids. I went in nonetheless and was having fun until a huge wave arose from the depths of the sea without warning. Panicked, I scrambled to the shore toward my aunt, only to lie in that unfortunate area where the wave hits sand, where its impact and pull are the strongest. Fearing I'd be sucked into the ocean and drown, I screamed, but my aunt moved forward, grabbing my little forearms with her hands.

"I've got you," she said calmly, as the ocean continued to urge rather insistently that I join it. I felt myself slipping out of my aunt's grasp—but then, suddenly, the pull subsided, and I was safe. I could see by the wideness of my aunt's eyes that I hadn't been a baby for feeling scared.

But she'd said she had me, and she had. For the years that followed, my Aunt Trish had always had me, whether by sending me unique care packages or acting as an empathic and nonjudgmental ear.

That day at the Santa Monica Pier was fresh in my mind as I reluctantly removed myself from the freezing water, returning to the towel with my Aunt Trish. I spent the rest of the afternoon collecting interesting stones to take back to my loved ones as souvenirs— the beach was oddly littered with pebbles of every shape, texture, and color—and relaxing on the blanket, eating and drinking.

By the time we piled back into the car and headed for Santa Ynez, I felt a balance between exhaustion and peacefulness. The ocean had somehow restored something in me, and I was happy to take relics of my visit home with me, wherever home was.

Kindness of the Wind

I pretend the wind pushing the tree branches outside
is waves crashing against the sand of a beach—
no injury meant to the wind,
but I covet the sea
and the depth of her mysteries,
her capacity for nurturing,
free, fierce power of will,
and
destruction.
I wish
we were closer,
that we met more
than once a year.

Our meetings are magic.
She cradles me.
I hear her wisdom,
etch it into my heart,
but she washes it away
with one solid wave
replacing it with New.
Her sageness is ancient
but ever-changing
as quicksilver.
In the crest of her wave, I listen
as she threads seaweed in my hair,
wrinkles my skin.

Sometimes the wind meets us there,
drying me along with the sun
as I lie on the beach,
exhausted.
The wind listens to the ocean,
tries to remember the sound
of her waters flowing, never still,
and the wind imitates her for me
on nights at home
when I'm feeling unsure.
How sweet the wind is, how thoughtful,
but it is not the same
as the sea.

New Beginnings

EVEN AMID THE TRANQUILITY of California, my life back
in Cincinnati was still on my mind. My Aunt Chris, who returned
to Ohio two weeks into my visit, didn't give me frame-by-frame
updates of what was going on with the house, but she had told me
that all the possessions had been cleared out and no one was living
in it any longer. My cats, Honey and Pickle, were with her in
Colerain, and whatever stuff I hadn't designated as wanting to take
with me was either sold, donated, or put into storage. In some ways,
I was beyond grateful for not having to actually move things out of
my home and see it slowly empty of all personality. In others,
though, I felt detached and ignorant as to what was going on.

The question of schooling was also weighing on my mind.
Basically, I had three options: attend an all-girls Catholic school as

my aunt and grandparents preferred; attend the district school, Colerain; or apply to a new school that had only recently come to my attention: the School for Creative & Performing Arts (SCPA) in downtown Cincinnati. Though I'd never heard of it before, I was intrigued by SCPA. Given my rocky history with Catholicism and my quiet disdain for the orthodox, SCPA seemed like the optimal choice. Plus, I was eager to refine my newfound interest in writing, as well as continue with my musical education. I slowly began gathering information about SCPA, coming to learn that it was a fourth through twelfth grade school that specialized in seven areas of the arts: technical theater, drama, instrumental music, vocal music, visual arts, creative writing, and dance, as well as, of course, basic academics. The school was located in an area of Cincinnati called Over-the-Rhine, widely regarded as one of the most crime-ridden parts of town, but I didn't initially pay much attention to this fact. I was seduced by the uniqueness of the school: I could barely imagine a place where the arts, not sports, were the most valued pastime— where my habit of writing could potentially pay off. I put together a portfolio of writing samples and shipped it off to the school while I was still in California. Though I was entirely uncertain as to whether or not I would get in, I found the summer reading list on the English department's web page and eagerly began reading and writing the papers.

My efforts, of course, didn't go unnoticed by my Aunt Trish, who took this as a sign I wouldn't be staying on with her in California. Being both a lover of diplomacy and a hater of confrontation, I never directly told her I wouldn't be staying and she never asked. Though she was probably disappointed, she supported my endeavors, which ranged from getting my junior high to fax my transcripts, to getting Aunt Chris to set up an interview, to me completing the prerequisite material for the major for which I'd be auditioning: creative writing. I scrambled to get everything together as the final audition date for the upcoming school year drew nearer.

In the end, it was my interview at SCPA that brought me back to Cincinnati, causing me to finally put a return date on what had been an open-ended plane ticket. After a month's stay in California and a great deal of resting, thinking, healing, and learning, I was ready to pursue what I envisioned to be the best path for me at the time. With tears in my eyes, I said good-bye to my Aunt Trish and thanked her for all she'd done for me, feeling sorry our plans hadn't worked out the way we'd hoped but confident I was doing what was right.

Adjustment

IN SPITE OF MY excitement for the SCPA interview, returning to Ohio wasn't easy. On the drive home from the airport with my grandparents and aunt, I expounded upon all the things I'd learned and the experiences I'd had with great zeal, unwilling to show the anxiety and sadness I was feeling at the prospect of going to Aunt Chris's condo instead of my house. When we pulled up to the condo complex I knew so well, my grandparents having lived there since my birth, I took a deep breath and lugged my suitcase upstairs, trying my best to be optimistic.

The room that had once been a spare bedroom and a place for my cousin Andrew to stay on occasion was now my bedroom, housing all my things. My cats had moved in and were anxious to see me. I slowly began unpacking my suitcase, trying to shake the sensation that I wasn't home yet, that this was just a layover and I shouldn't get too comfortable.

I tried not to dwell on my living situation as I prepared for my audition. On the big day, I dressed professionally in black dress pants, a white camisole, and a black blazer. I wore one of my mother's gold necklaces around my neck and carried one of my father's rings in my pocket. To me, this was more than just an attempt to get into a high school. Though I had backup plans, I didn't accept any of them. "If you don't get in here, you're going to go to McAuley," my aunt had said. I had nothing personal against McAuley High School, the all-girl alma mater of my mother and a few of my aunts, but in my heart, I didn't feel it was the right place for me.

So for me, this interview was the only option. I didn't know what I'd do if I didn't get in. Though I hadn't started writing seriously since earlier that year, I wanted SCPA with an intensity I was familiar with, and I wouldn't let myself fail.

My grandfather drove me downtown, all the necessary materials in my hands and butterflies in my stomach. Though it was simple enough to gather some writing samples and send them to a woman I didn't know—the creative writing teacher, Joy Fowler—it was quite another to sit with her face-to-face and explain why I felt I deserved to attend SCPA.

I checked in and waited for my turn to arrive. When it did, I acted with a cool professionalism that I hoped masked my true anxiety. But contrary to my notions, Dr. Joy wasn't a mean woman who was bent on ripping me apart. She was a middle-aged, soft- but clear-spoken woman with pleasant hands and long, wavy hair the color of iron. She wore gold, half-moon glasses, a long, old-fashioned dress, and socks and Birkenstocks. Her eyes were hazel, contrasting against her olive skin and sleet-colored hair: they were sharp and quick, but simultaneously warm and empathetic. So I didn't feel awkward explaining my recent change in circumstances to her after she'd given me feedback on my portfolio and asked me a few general questions.

"I'm so sorry for your loss," she said sincerely, letting her words take up the space they deserved. "But I'm very glad to have you with us."

Not letting my hopes climb too high—I wouldn't find out whether or not I was accepted until a few days later—I thanked Dr. Joy for her time and met up with my grandfather.

My good feeling turned out to be correct. I'd been accepted into SCPA, and I'd never felt happier—for the first time in a while, I felt like I had at least some control over my future. I would be pursuing a unique high school career and spending my days in a creative environment.

It was only after I was accepted that the logistics of attending SCPA settled in; namely, how I would get to school. Since my aunt worked relatively close to our home and my new school was far out of the way, being driven was not an option. Taking the city metro bus was my only choice. Though I wasn't averse to this for any snobbish reasons, the prospect did make me, a timid suburban girl, slightly nervous. The idea of passing unaccompanied through some of the most urban parts of town frightened me, much as I'm embarrassed to admit that now. Wisely, my aunt rode the bus with me to school once so I'd get a feel for the process, then had me ride it by myself a few days before school. I felt like a baby, being escorted and eased into such a simple concept, but I knew it was necessary. I was vaguely aware that it was going to be a different world, though just how different, I didn't know . . . yet.

When on the Bus

I.

There is a woman on the bus
who does not let go of her cigarette.
It rests patiently between her fingers,
unlit, whole, and full of potential,
just waiting to be inserted
between her thin, chapped lips.
She wears sweatpants and a T-shirt
and holds her cigarette
even as she kisses her child
on his yellow head,
smiling down upon him
with lips yearning for her cigarette.
As soon as they get off the bus
she lights it.
With a drag and a grin,
she is satisfied.

II.

There is a man on the bus
with two pieces of luggage.
He is quiet and stressed
and looks about the bus frequently,
features taut.
He leans on his knees into the aisle
and an older man asks him to lean back
so he can see out the window
for his stop.

The luggage man tells him
to shut the hell up.
This unbidden hostility disturbs me
and amuses others.
I later learn that he'd been seeking a flight
since morning
and had failed to make it out.
"Do I get off here?"
he asks the driver.
I wonder if he's going home.

New School, New World

MY FIRST DAY AT SCPA proved to be strange, to say the least. I woke up early, jittery and anxious, and dressed in the outfit I'd put together the day before. I rode the bus without incident, though I was paranoid the entire time, especially when a man with apparent mental deficiencies told me he liked my purse. But I survived. I even survived the two-block walk from the bus stop to school, during which I pictured myself getting hopelessly lost.

Though I made it to school, I didn't quite make it to class, instead spending most of the morning in the main theater, which had been turned into a holding ground for displaced students. Apparently something was wrong with my schedule, and the school had no printout for me to follow. I sat quietly, reading, until someone handed me a temporary schedule, which I proceeded to read incorrectly, consequently going to lunch twice and missing my biology class. In any case, I had missed what I'd most been looking forward to—creative writing. So the rest of the day passed in relative quiet as I suffered through gym, English, and world history. I rode the bus home and collapsed.

The next day was better. My schedule ironed out, I now knew I was to go to Dr. Joy's class at the sound of the first bell. Slipping in quietly without looking at anyone, I took a seat at a table where only one other girl was sitting. I busied myself with putting my bag under the table and getting paper out when the girl's words cut into my consciousness:

"You just had to ruin it, didn't you?"

I looked up, wide-eyed in confusion.

"I was sitting here alone, the table all to myself," she continued, "and you had to ruin it for me." She said it with a smile on her face, but I had no idea if she was kidding or not.

"I'm sorry," I said in a small voice.

She laughed. "Oh, it's okay, I guess," she said and began talking to someone else.

This girl, I later found out, was named Gillis, and she was just one of the many characters in my writing class. True to my wall-flower mentality, rather than talking to these people, I'd sit back, watch them, and classify them: Ashley and Avery were the smart ones. They would usually sit together and answer Dr. Joy's questions when no one else would. Heather and KJ were new, like me, but both juniors; Heather was a slight blond girl who was also a visual art major, and KJ was a tall black boy with dreadlocks who wrote captivating spoken word. There was Alexa, a part Puerto Rican, part African-American, part German girl with curly hair and an uncanny interest in Hitler; and Brianna, a black girl with a kind round face who had equal parts spunk and sweetness. There was Keegan, a tough-looking Irish kid who was, interestingly, one of the few people I talked to regularly, and Caprice, a soulful African-American girl

who was always friendly to me. There were also several other classmates who didn't speak up as much.

Dr. Joy decided to have a theme for each week. The first week's
theme, at the suggestion of a girl named Megan, was self-introduc-
tion. Through our written assignments, which we shared at the end
of the week, I learned fragments of information about everyone and
enjoyed listening. But when the time came to read mine, I was nervous. Not sharing wasn't an option though, so I approached the
podium, trying my best not to scan the crowd.

I clutched my piece in my hands. I had grappled over what to
write about. *What part of me do I want these people to see first?* I'd
wondered. Having not even spoken to most of them, I knew what I
wrote about would be of critical importance in their first impressions of me, and even drafted a few different versions. In the end,
though, I decided to read the one I'd written about my racial identity, about being "mixed," as people were apt to term it.

Without preamble, I launched in. "People call me 'mixed,' as if I
were paint or some other inanimate substance to be blended and
manipulated." To my relief, my opening line drew a few laughs, and
by the piece's end, I was greeted with warm applause. KJ smiled at
me as I took my seat, and I felt slightly more at ease regarding my
place in the class.

But even if I felt I belonged there as a writer, I never thought I'd
quite be one of "them." Instead of talking to the people around me,
I spent idle moments writing in a notebook I shared with Abby and
Kelsey back in West Chester. Whenever we saw each other, we'd
switch notebooks, thus keeping up on each other's thoughts. Clinging
to the notebook helped me feel connected to my old friends and not
completely alone at my new school.

One day, when Dr. Joy was sick, my creative-writing classmates sat together around a table, laughing and playing cards. I watched but didn't join in. And it wasn't for lack of opportunity. No one was outright mean to me, and a few people, like Heather, Keegan, KJ, Alexa, and Caprice, even made efforts to talk to me. But I just wasn't into it. Making sure I said the right thing and coming off as clever seemed like way too much work when I was still dealing with the loss of my father, moving into a new house, and attending a totally different school. Though most everyone seemed genuinely interesting and I would have liked to know them better, it was just easier for me, the wallflower, to sit off to the side. In a way, I was pleased with myself for creating what I hoped would come off as a mysterious yet intelligent persona. In other ways—in deeper ways— I was upset with myself for not actively seeking acceptance and building new friendships.

My academic classes were even worse, socially speaking. I barely talked to anyone in biology, history, or English. And then there was algebra. My teacher, I was convinced, was "a Cajun monster from hell," as I once described him in a diary entry. Mr. Samis was a loud man who seemed to feel the appropriate volume level for speaking was what most others would consider shouting. He didn't let us use calculators in class, had an extremely specific format in which we were to complete homework, and was deeply dissatisfied if we spent his class time doing anything other than algebra, as I soon found out. Shortly after I was placed in his class, I opened my book to read after completing the homework he'd assigned. Retribution was swift.

"Put it away!" came a hideous bellow from above me. I looked up in panic.

"Do some work, Ms. Shannon," he said in disgust. "*Math* work." And he stalked away.

Shaken, I did the only thing I supposed I could do as a girl who had barely been yelled at her whole life and certainly not for simply reading: I cried. I don't know if Mr. Samis or anyone else noticed. I partially hoped my teacher would, so he would apologize. But if Mr. Samis realized I was crying, he didn't say anything.

So I hated him for a while, and, as a result, doubled my efforts in his subject, eager to do my math not only correctly, but also without error in his punctilious format. Each day that he checked my work over and had no criticism to offer was a triumph. Ironically, the hard work that was intended to spite Mr. Samis led him to a sort of respect for me. I'd become one of the "good kids," the quiet ones who always did their homework. Even so, I was wary, until one day when I realized that first impressions—or impressions in general—are not always correct.

On the year's anniversary of my father's death, a local news channel had apparently shown a short tribute to him on the nightly newscast. The next day before the bell rang for algebra, Mr. Samis called me up to his desk. Supposing he was going to yell at me for something, I prepared for the worst and was thus extremely surprised when he went on to say, "I saw the news story about your father on the news last night. I'm very sorry."

I was so shocked, I could barely formulate a response. Not only had this man who had described himself as "mean, nasty, and ugly" on the first day of school seen the story about my dad, he'd cared enough to mention it to me the next day. After that, anytime someone would insult Mr. Samis or talk about how much they hated his class, I would defend him.

Lost in the Shuffle

IN SPITE OF MY NEWFOUND chumminess with my algebra teacher, I was making no strides with my peers by the second semester of school. I expounded upon the situation in a LiveJournal entry:

So, so, so, so bored.

Pretty much, my social life at SCPA . . . sucks. Time for some soul cleansing and such.

Begin emo rant.

So, I haven't really been talking to anyone. I haven't been trying to make friends. So people just think I'm weird, or emo, or quiet, or all three. Or they just talk to me because I'm smart and can help them with whatever. And I don't exactly appreciate that; but hey, it's understandable.

So yeah. While everyone's making friends and talking—new kids included—I just sit on the sidelines like a jackass. I mean, I've been shy all my life, but I still had plenty of friends. It never was a problem. But now, where I'm going into a situation where I have no one, it is a big problem.

It's like I have so much to say, but I just can't say it. Something holds me back. I'm afraid they won't listen, or they'll think I'm stupid. It's just like everyone feels bad for me even though they don't even know about my situation.

And I hate it so much. The whole thing sucks, because I like the school, and I know I'd be having a good time if I had my friends there. But they aren't, and they never will be. So it just sucks. I drag my ass down there every day, try to write, fail to speak to anyone, and come back here, only to repeat the whole thing again.

To be fair: I do appreciate the writing part of it. It's not all I'd hoped it to be, but I am growing as a writer. And that's always good.

But I miss my friends in West Chester. I miss doing things with them and going places, being with people my age and not worrying about what they'll think of me—just being Chelsey and having a great time. And sometimes I wish I were going to the freshmen building with them. It would be the typical high school experience, cliques included, but at least I wouldn't be so damn lonely.

And then, to top it all off, it's pretty much all my fault. I've barely exerted any effort.

deep breath

End emo rant.

In addition to this social maladjustment, I was continuing to deal with the culture shock of going from living in a suburban, middle class, predominantly white area to attending a school located in a very rough part of town with a great deal of cultural diversity. The diversity didn't bother me, but it did open my eyes as to how much I had missed out on when it came to half of my heritage. Around me, I heard people—white *and* black—speaking in Ebonics and using slang I was neither familiar with nor understood. Cultural references went miles over my head, and as I struggled to keep up, I underwent a minor crisis of racial identity, which had always loomed at the back of my mind as a biracial girl.

By societal standards, I acted like a white girl. I didn't listen to hip-hop or rap, or watch BET. Frankly, I didn't know what a weave was and never fully understood why my father was so adamant about me applying lotion to my elbows and knees until I started attending SCPA. But even as I learned about the part of my cultural background that had somehow been excluded from my experience, I still felt separated from other black kids, not only because of the lightness of my skin, but by my culturally homogenous background.

The Anniversary

IN MY FORMER naïve perception, cities weren't places to spend a lot of time in. They were considered dangerous in comparison to our sheltered suburbs. In spite of my father's upbringing in Cincinnati, my own exposure to the area was limited to the occasional trip to the downtown Macy's for Christmas shopping or the Museum of Natural History and Science. Walking down city streets made me nervous, even as I slowly conquered my fear of the bus.

I had never quite been aware of the relative affluence of my former home until I began attending SCPA. Occasionally, kids would make jeers about West Chester and how rich and spoiled people who lived there were. The first time I heard such a comment, I was too surprised to feel remotely offended. And when I considered it, the people of West Chester did lead fairly charmed lives. Most of my friends and neighbors had lived in large houses, as my dad and I had, complete with kitchens stocked with food and fancy appliances and family rooms hooked up with cable, a widescreen television, and the latest gaming systems. Large wardrobes and expensive handbags were the norm. Of course, I knew every family in West Chester didn't live in such comfort, nor am I suggesting that those who did were selfish or decadent. But I did come to realize that not *everyone* lived so comfortably.

Attending class with kids from a spectrum of backgrounds helped me gain perspective on my own life and place in the world. I was also exposed to kids with piercings in odd places and hair dyed odd colors, as well as many kids who were openly homosexual or bisexual, neither of which were the norm in West Chester. I embraced these aspects of SCPA, considering them positive by-products of an environment where creativity was honored. Though SCPA was far from perfect, it was supportive of kids of all different ideologies, backgrounds, colors, and personal styles. I felt myself settle into a wonderfully chromatic and vivacious student body, even if I did so quietly and without drawing much attention to myself.

It was while I was finally starting to adjust to my new life that the one-year anniversary of my father's death arrived. That day, my dad's side of the family picked me up from school to head over to the cemetery and then to a small gathering at my Aunt Carolyn's house. Since my dad's death, I'd been spending more and more time with his siblings and their children, building distinct relationships with them that I had, for some reason, missed out on while my dad was alive. I rode quietly in the backseat as we made our way to Walnut Hills Cemetery, reflecting on a year gone by.

In some ways, everything felt so different, like my life in West Chester with Dad was eons ago, instead of just a year. Simultaneously, the pain and disbelief I still felt at his death was so fresh, it sometimes felt as though he had been killed only days earlier. I was almost shocked when I considered the adjustments I'd made to my daily life, and, even more profound, that I had endured one of the worst losses I could imagine. In the beginning, I'd thought the grief would kill me—that it would be just too much to bear. And yet, here I was. True, I was secluded and hadn't made many friends. I usually went straight home after school, crawled into bed, and watched television until it was time to go to sleep. And sometimes, when it did become too much, I'd simply weep. But somewhere within me, I knew that all my despair and pain was temporary. I knew that although this was enormously difficult, I would one day overcome it and be the happy girl I'd once been, however alien that girl seemed at the same time.

When we reached the cemetery, I joined the small semicircle of my family members peering down at my father's grave, where I could so well remember laying him to rest. By then, there was a headstone, reading simply "Blair E. Shannon. June 1, 1959–January 19, 2006. Son, Father, Brother, Husband." The sight was relatively new to me. I didn't come to the cemetery frequently, maintaining that it was only a body, that my father's essence was around us, within us. But it felt appropriate to pay respect to his spirit in this way.

Once everyone had arrived, I read a piece my family had asked me to prepare for the occasion.

1/19/07

Dear Daddy,

A year has gone by since you died. I reflect on the past year without you, and wonder to myself, have I become a better person? Are you proud of who I am now? Have any of us changed?

A year ago today, you were still living. You were vivacious, full of life and light. A year ago tonight, you were gone, with such caustic abruptness that took us all by the most unpleasant surprise.

You were not there to stand with us when we bore the horrible news—for once, you were not there for me to cling to or lean on. I'd endured deaths before, but you'd been there for me. This time, you were the one who was gone. My pillar of strength had been demolished, and I was totally lost.

The next few months were a blur for me, as I'm sure they were for many of us. I felt like I was in a daze, some sort of prolonged, demented nightmare that would not let up, no matter how much I wished it away. I simply could not believe that my dad, Blair Shannon, was dead—killed, no less. Though you were human and mortal, it somehow seemed illogical in my mind that you could really be gone.

Moving out of the house was really hard for me. I knew it had to be done, but you and I had many memories there. Whenever we go back to get something from there now, I am filled with pain and reminded of you. There is no home for me without you.

I think everybody has been having a hard time, even people who don't say much about it. It's hard for me, because you were always there for me to talk to, and now you're gone. I guess people think I'm doing okay. I'm not a lot of the time—the year has been extremely trying for me, as could be expected—but I will be okay, eventually. I'm not rushing anything.

A lot of people—Americans, especially—seem to think that once a year of grieving has passed, the worst part is over, and we should all move on. It's not like that at all. Anyone who's ever lost someone they loved knows there is no formula or set amount of time that will ease the pain. I feel I haven't even started yet; I've been too preoccupied with moving and starting at a different high school.

What hurts the most is that you were killed, and no one has been caught so far. I hope every day that something will be done—that some sort of justice will be served. It would certainly make me feel better, but I know that wouldn't bring you back. That wouldn't erase the pain we've all felt over this past year. Although I honestly hope your killer will be caught, I doubt he ever will be. But if any kind of karma exists, I'm certain he'll get what's coming to him.

Your being gone now makes me appreciate all the special little things you did for me. Like the way you packed my lunches, or the notes you'd leave me in the morning, or how you'd call me every day you could while you were gone. Since you were such a good dad to me, I feel very deprived now, but I would rather   have   had   a   great   dad   for   a short time than a bad dad for my whole life any day.

I hope you're proud of me, going to a totally different school and all. I think you'd be surprised at some of the things I do every day. I've been trying to be brave for you and try new things.

I think everyone should take some time today to think of how things have changed: who they've grown closer to, who they've drifted apart from, how perceptions of our own selves have changed, what is important to us now, and, of course, special memories of you.

I think of you every day, and I'm pretty sure most of the people here today do as well. I don't know what happens in the afterlife, but I hope very much that I will see you again. Even though I can't hug you anymore or hear you tell me you love me, I carry you in my heart every day. You're a part of me always.

Love,

Chelsey Kimberly Shannon, Your Peanut

My family thanked me for my words, and after a few prayers were said and tears were shed, we ate a light dinner at my Aunt Carolyn's and watched a copy of the slide show that had played at my dad's funeral. In some ways, since the pain and absence were no longer a shock, I was able to feel their effects more fully. This time, I cried with abandon.

In spite of my sadness over the circumstances, I felt happy that I felt comfortable enough with my dad's side of the family to share such an occasion with them. I hadn't grown up feeling especially close to my father's brothers, Myron and Lester, or his sister, Carolyn, but we seemed to have bonded during our family tragedy, as is bound to happen. I found myself beginning to spend time with my uncles and aunt outside of family holiday gatherings, as well as my dad's niece—my cousin Shaunda—and her family. I was grateful to finally build relationships with people who had known my dad with a similar intimacy as I had.

Still Adjusting

SINCE I'D MOVED INTO my aunt's condo months earlier, I was finally beginning to feel more comfortable. I'd painted my room (albeit a pale green that I later regretted) and rearranged the furniture to my liking. Things with my Aunt Chris were still rocky, however. It wasn't so much that our relationship was flawed. The more I dwelled on it, the more I realized that there was one main source of our problems: my Aunt Chris was not my dad. This was, obviously, neither of our faults. The move was a big adjustment for us both. Having already raised her own kids, my aunt probably never imagined she'd have to take on another teenager. Even if only in my own mind, I felt the need to walk on eggshells, to never mess up.

You're not hers, I reasoned. *She's under no obligation to keep you here.* And, sometimes, if I was feeling particularly sad, I'd think, *She doesn't really want you here.*

Going from my laid-back, permissive dad, to my structured, type A Aunt Chris was also a major shift. While my dad had no qualms about spending lazy days at home doing nothing but watching movies, my aunt saw free days as perfect opportunities to clean the house, or, if the house was already clean, to "get organized," one of her favorite euphemistic phrases. We also experienced the basic clashes that naturally arise when you share a living space with a new person.

The worst memory I have of my early days of living with my aunt was during a time that occurred in late autumn. I had just been visiting a bookstore and called my aunt to ask her to pick me up on her way home from work. In retrospect, I fully acknowledge my tone was rather bossy and impolite. But at the time, I had no such notion and thus was surprised when, after being picked up and heading down to my grandparents' condo to say hello, I walked in the room to hear my aunt complaining to them about my behavior.

"I am not her maid," she said fiercely.

It was one of those awkward situations where you walk in at just the wrong moment. Objectively, I knew what she said was true. She *wasn't* my maid, and I should have asked her for a ride more nicely. But in my fragile emotional state, any expression of discontent concerning me—especially one not addressed to me directly—was only indicative of the fact that I was a nuisance, that Aunt Chris didn't really want me around. I began to cry in spite of myself as I made my presence known. My grandma rose to comfort me.

"I just asked for a ride," I said through my tears. "Jesus Christ," I added before I could stop myself. Big mistake. Any derivative of God's name used in vain should never be uttered in the presence of strident Catholics or there would be hell to pay. Their response was swift and full of outrage. My aunt rose from her chair to chastise me, both she and my grandma barraging me: "You must *never* say that."

This reaction upset me further. They seemed far more shaken by my use of language than how upset I was. I dashed into my grandma's bathroom and locked the door, settling onto the floor, light still off. My grandma came and knocked softly on the door after a few moments, but I didn't respond. After a while my family left me alone, and my tears intensified, becoming shuttering sobs that escalated into hyperventilation at intervals. I attempted to calm myself down, but whenever I thought of my aunt's words or my grandmother's disappointment, it became harder and harder to breathe.

The bigger picture hurt too. *I don't belong here,* I thought miserably. *What the fuck am I doing here? I'll never be happy. I might as well die.*

A half hour went by in this manner, me lying on the floor, attempting not to pass out from hyperventilation. Partially, I didn't leave for so long because I was truly upset; partially, I didn't leave because I didn't want to face my aunt, who was apparently so dissatisfied with me.

As I splashed cool water on my face after finally calming down, I heard someone come into the adjacent bedroom. Preparing myself for a continuation of the conflict, I was surprised to find my grandpa standing there when I opened the door. He opened his arms to me, and I laid my head on his shoulder, beginning to cry again. He gently rubbed my back and didn't ask for an apology or say anything, understanding that sometimes words are simply unnecessary. He led me back into the kitchen, where my aunt and grandma were sitting at the table. I slunk down into my seat, unable to look either of them in the eye. Though I wasn't ashamed of my language, I did regret upsetting them, and I knew they likely didn't understand why I was so upset, probably finding my reaction babyish and histrionic. I didn't feel like explaining I wasn't just upset because Aunt Chris was annoyed with me. It would have raised too many questions—and drawn too many words of placation—to explain that I was upset because I felt like a bother.

Instead, I apologized to my aunt for acting like a brat and using God's name in vain. She apologized for upsetting me. I ate a bowl of cottage cheese, and my aunt and grandma joked lightly for the rest of the meal. Soon, the incident was forgotten, but I couldn't let go of all the huge feelings Aunt Chris's simple words had brought up for me—that at the end of the day, I was an imposition.

My daily life living with Aunt Chris took some getting used to. My life with my dad had been unique, especially because he was gone for roughly two weeks out of the month. But when he was home, he was very much *home*. He ran errands during the day, leaving afternoons and evenings free to be spent with me. This was probably how we developed such a strong relationship in spite of his absences. When we were at home together, we would spend a lot of time talking, watching movies, and eating leisurely meals. We were aware of each other's quirks, likes, and annoyances, and were comfortable in each other's company.

With my Aunt Chris, there wasn't as much free time. She worked regular hours as a nurse, and after getting off, she was often required to spend an hour or two at the barn to take care of her horses. By the time she came home, exhausted, she didn't feel much like talking, and frankly, after a long day of school, riding the bus, chores, and homework, neither did I. So rather than spending evenings together as my dad and I probably would have, my aunt passed the hours before bed in the family room while I sequestered myself in my room. I just didn't have the energy to try to build a relationship like the one I'd had with my dad, especially when I'd been forced to realize even the strongest relationships can end suddenly and traumatically.

The sad part of it was, before I'd moved in with her, my aunt and I had enjoyed each other's company as aunt and niece. We would do fun things together and not worry about rules or stepping on eggshells. Though we were (and are) very different people, we'd try to do things the other person liked, compromising and trying out new activities. My aunt even expressed her sadness at losing this fun, lighter aspect of our relationship following her assumption of guardianship over me. Maybe she felt the only way for her to be my guardian was through an outlined set of rules and a stern stance. In some ways, she was right. My childhood hadn't had much structure, having been shaken up by the death of my mother and my dad's unusual career. Though I enjoyed the lack of ordinariness, part of me had always craved structure. I would make chore charts, budgets, and to-do lists for fun. I made an hour-by-hour schedule of how to spend my summer days and stuck to it. Now, instead of me being responsible for adding organization to my life, someone else was doing it for me. Though I enjoyed structure to an extent, this didn't always mean I enjoyed the idea of someone else imposing it on me. I would sometimes fight with my aunt over stupid things like doing the dishes, or give her attitude when she asked me to clean my room. Even in my own ears, I sounded like a brat. But I didn't care.

These setbacks were comparatively minor, however. What most bothered me about my relationship with my aunt was how lukewarm it was—how the condo still didn't feel like home to me after six months of living there. I wondered if it ever would.

Home

You could say the house was sacred,
and i dream of it often,
floors tread upon all my years,
grooves and creaks old friends,
walls painted beige then fuchsia then pumpkin,
and i was there for it all.
The red leather sectional was my refuge,
the little-used green-pink living room
the temple of my thoughts,
my energy scattered and shared,
encased by the red brick exterior.
I thought it was the place that made the peace,
the safe,
the warmth—

or at least,
i thought it had some power of its own.
But when you left,
home died.
When you left,
home became a house.
Now, in my dreams,
it doesn't even feel like home
when you're there too.

Remembering

AS I CONTINUED TO settle into SCPA and the condo in
Colerain, I was still very much adjusting to the reality that my father
was gone. I was also becoming deeply aware of the effect of having
lost in my life a loved one who was murdered as opposed to dying
of illness or old age. With my father's death, there was more
anger—though not necessarily at the person who had actually killed
him. I was angry at the situation more than anything. That my
father had been taken away by a person, not a disease or time, made
his death seem all the more unfair. Though I tried not to think of it
much, the idea of Dad dying in such agony and fear pained me on
a fundamental level. It wasn't the same with my mother, who had
slowly winded down, and who had likely known she was dying,
however terrible that was in its own right. With my dad, minutes
before he died, he'd been bright and vivacious as ever—then suddenly, he was simply gone.

My Aunt Erin in California initiated a lawsuit for negligence
against the hotel my dad and Monique had stayed in that night. As

Monique had described it, the entire establishment had been shady, and though they had balconies that were accessible from the street, they hadn't had any security cameras.

Though I didn't think a lawsuit would hurt matters, I didn't devote myself to the idea, nor to the idea of my dad's murderer being caught. The way I saw it, he was a faceless, nameless criminal, and for all we knew, he could be dead now, or moved away, or have changed his mind about the way his life was going. Maybe he had never committed a crime before. Or maybe he had a long history of such incidents. We'd never know. I tried not to concern myself with the details and legal aspects of my dad's death. Though such a familiar, pragmatic approach probably comforted some of my family members—the most natural thing to do when someone you love is harmed is to seek justice—I preferred to deal with the emotional side of things.

At the same time, however, I couldn't imagine what Monique must have been going through each day, having seen my father die and having been in the room in his last moments. I couldn't imagine the blame she must have laid on herself, the tortured wonderings of *What if,* always *What if.* Though we hadn't been very close during my father's lifetime, Monique and I began spending more time together following his death, partially because, in some ways, she was the closest person I had to my dad, since they were together during so many of his final days on earth, and partially because I knew I was the closest person *she* had to my dad.

One day, while driving home from an outing together, we started talking about my father as we often did. Monique began to describe my dad's final day with an attention to detail I'd never heard before. Her voice broke when she began to describe my dad jumping up from the bed when he heard someone slide the balcony door open, and she paused.

"I'm sorry," she said. "You probably don't want to hear this."

"No," I replied gently, but honestly, "I do." I had an almost morbid curiosity about that short window of time when my father had gone from living to dead.

She described to me how they'd passed the day and evening, how they'd been sleeping peacefully when my dad awoke to the sound of the balcony door opening, how alertly and quickly he sprang from the bed. She told me how she panicked, how she wouldn't be quiet, no matter how many times the intruder—a young man holding a gun—shushed her. She said he was agitated, standing in the balcony bathed in light, maybe because he was afraid someone would see his failed attempted robbery. She said my dad was calm, that even in such a moment of fear and chaos, he was sure and still as the earth, attempting to reason with the man, saying he could have anything he wanted as long as he harmed no one. But the man was too agitated and shot into the room before running off, gaining nothing, taking so much.

Monique told me how my dad sat calmly on the hotel bed and picked up the phone to call the front desk. "Call an ambulance; I've been shot." But it was too late. The bullet had hit him in the chest, the precious receptacle of human life. He sunk quietly to the ground with a grace, Monique said, you wouldn't expect of a man his size, but what more could you expect from my father—charming, genteel Blair? It was only fitting that he died quietly, with a dignity and serenity that I never could have mustered if I was laying on the floor, knowing my life was quietly draining out of me. Monique knelt beside him as his breathing stilled, comforting him as best she could. How could you comfort a dying man who had so much life and so much to live for? What could you do or say?

She told me how slowly the paramedics moved when they arrived, as if they knew it was already too late. She said they were inattentive and almost casual, an attitude that infuriated her. And then he was taken away in the ambulance to a hospital where he was pronounced dead.

There are things about her story I'll never understand. Why my father? Why my family? Why did the bullet have to hit his chest? Why couldn't the ambulance have been faster? Why hadn't they stayed in another hotel? And, more deeply, what did my father think of in those last, fading moments? Did he cling to the hope that this would be righted, that it would turn into a frightening but ultimately safe travel anecdote to tell to friends? Did he think he would see my face again, or did he blame himself for leaving me an orphan? Or were his last moments tranquil as his demeanor, quietly accepting, if gently regretful?

I'll never know. None of us will. But as Monique finished telling me the story, breaking into soft tears, I felt her pain, the pain of my father, and, acutely, my own loss. I sincerely hoped my dad's final thoughts hadn't been ones of anger or remorse or blame, but ones of acceptance, peace, and love for those he was leaving behind. Given the type of person he was, they probably were.

Awake

Back from my break,
I'm here,
ready to live again,
ready to feel my lungs
expand with air
again.
My hibernation—
self-induced isolation—

is gone now
(I hope forever),
and I am ready to live.
I am ready to be.
So I spread out my fragile wings
and fly.

Reevaluation

WITH THE SPRING, something began to change within me. As the earth slowly awakened, bursting into bloom, I began to disentangle myself from the web of sorrow and isolation that had ensnared me since my dad's death. I'm not sure why, exactly, because sadness and solitude were comfortable for me, if not enjoyable. Maybe it was because it had been over a year since my dad had died, and I knew he wouldn't want me to be so sorrowful on his account. Maybe it was because I refused to continue to feel dead inside as the world around me sprang into life, enjoying its youth. Renowned developmental psychologist Erik Erickson's theory of psychosocial development states that adolescence is a period devoted to developing one's identity. If anything, mine had been lost amid the grief, turmoil, and stress of moving to a new school. Though I had spent a lot of time with myself in reflection and healing, I still felt like I didn't really know who I was. What were my values? What did I believe in? What did I like? What did I want to do with my life? All previous conceptions of these notions were thrown to the wayside with the jarring death of my dad, and I felt the need to rebuild myself from the ground up.

I consciously decided to start with religion. Uncomfortable with the idea of not really having a name for what I believed in, I decided to research different religions. I quickly learned I was no longer a Catholic, and, even further, that I no longer believed in the divinity of Jesus Christ. This was a startling realization for me, in spite of the fact that this knowledge had long been lurking in my subconscious. It's easy when rejecting one's predetermined brand of Christianity to say, "Well, I still believe in Jesus." I had said the same thing for a while to reassure my aunts and other relatives. But it simply wasn't true for me anymore. The idea of a human being so divine—divinity itself—had long been foreign to me, and suddenly I was able to say with reasonably strong conviction that I didn't believe it.

This was thrilling. I no longer felt like a pseudo-Catholic, trying and failing to adhere to a doctrine that had never resonated with me. Almost immediately, I felt truer and more at peace with myself. I began to explore non-Christian religions specifically, because I still wanted to feel I was a part of some larger group, not wanting to be thrown off as some spiritual rogue. My interest in nature and the sacredness of the earth led me to the path of Neopaganism. The concept of a nurturing, natural divinity, characterized as female, appealed to me, as did the ability to connect with the divine without the necessity of "official" intercession and the absence of absolute punishment or reward or a hierarchy of holiness. Despite my happiness with my newfound faith, I knew my aunt likely wouldn't be so pleased, even though I'd found an underlying connection between Catholicism and Paganism. Still, I felt the need to tell her about my discovery. I wanted to be open and honest about who I was becoming.

It took awhile for me to gather the courage to speak up on the topic. I decided to do so when Roger was around, so it wouldn't turn into too intense of a conversation, or, even worse, an ugly one. One evening, as we dined at Red Lobster, I sat up straight, looked them both in the eyes, and said I had something to tell them.

"I don't believe in Jesus," I said simply.

Their reaction wasn't as extreme as I'd feared, but it wasn't warm, either.

"Why not?" my aunt asked. I didn't really have an answer. To me, the real question was, why would I? Why did she believe in Jesus, or God, or heaven? Faith isn't something anyone is born with. It has to be cultivated. The default, if you think about it, is to *not* believe. It's not as if we're born with an innate sense of loyalty to a certain religion or any religion at all. It's something that is learned and practiced as one grows older, if one chooses to do so. And, after much conscious thought, I realized a traditionally religious path wasn't right for me.

My aunt, on the other hand, was the opposite. Religion was one of the most valued aspects of her life. She always strove to be a good Catholic and cherished the notion of salvation and heaven when times were rough. And I admired her tenacity and devotion. I had once been the same way, I had to admit. But now, from an objective standpoint, I knew I didn't need unproven, albeit pleasant, assertions to comfort myself about my parents' deaths. Though it would be lovely to believe they were sharing a cloud in heaven watching over me, this wasn't necessarily the case, and I didn't have to comfort myself with something that may or may not be true. It was enough to me that my parents had loved me while they were alive. Though I did assert that some part of them—spirit, essence, *something*—was still around me, I didn't believe I would someday join them in heaven or see them again.

Rather than delve into the psychology and philosophy of my decision—things I wasn't entirely clear about myself yet—I told my aunt that I no longer believed, but that I respected her spiritual beliefs and hoped she would do likewise for me. The conversation veered after that, for which I was grateful, but I knew the matter wouldn't be permanently dropped. A few times, following a morning spent in church or on the car ride home from some function or another, my aunt would bring up the topic, again asking why I didn't believe or saying she thought my change of mind was a phase. I wanted to explain my thoughts to her. I wanted her to understand I hadn't stopped believing in Christ because I had lost both of my parents early, or that my lack of faith wasn't the product of some foolish spiritual rebellion but the result of an analytical questioning of my own values and beliefs. But I never went into these explanations with my aunt, fearing they would only lead to conflict. I kept my responses concise and sparing, and she would usually move on. Even though I wanted Aunt Chris to understand me, I knew it would be hard for her to see things my way after she'd spent her whole life believing in Christ and practicing Catholicism. And even if we disagreed, I wanted our relationship to be as peaceful as possible.

New Visions

ANOTHER PART OF my newly structured identity was my vegetarianism. It was a concept that had always been a part of my peripheral consciousness: I had often given up meat for Lent as a younger child and was always compassionate toward the plight of animals. In the spring of my freshman year, I met a boy named Robert who rode the same bus home as me and was a vegetarian. Partly wanting to impress him and partly genuinely curious, I went about the task of researching vegetarianism and people's motivations in adhering to such a lifestyle. Without much effort, I was exposed to a plethora of information about the animal agriculture industry, the cruelty farm animals endure, and the health benefits of a plant-based diet. After my research, the decision to become a vegetarian was snap and without hesitation.

With my shift to vegetarianism, I became more aware of my body, its needs, and nutrition. As most vegetarians do when they make the switch, I researched what nutrients were necessary—for any human, not just plant-eaters—and how to obtain them without eating meat. Becoming a vegetarian forced me to eat more mindfully. Suddenly, I couldn't eat whatever my grandmother cooked or my aunt brought home. So, I began to prepare my own meals, mostly out of necessity. I didn't know at the time that it was the beginning of a love for cooking.

My heightened attention to my body was generally unprecedented and led to a much greater comfort in my own skin. I felt synchronized with my person. For once, my body wasn't just a shell. It was a corporeal extension of me that I was in touch with and, yes, was even beginning to like.

It wasn't perfect, of course. I still maintained excess fat on my stomach, left over from my father's period of depression after my mother's death, during which I mostly ate Chef Boyardee, as Dad wasn't feeling up to cooking. And I still maintained typical adolescent insecurities. But for the first time, I didn't feel the need to hide my body when crossing in front of a room full of people. When someone would compliment me, I would actually believe them. I took better care of myself because I actually liked my appearance. I began to see my dark, curly hair as an asset instead of an uncontrollable liability. I learned to care for my specific hair instead of following general beauty regiments. I began to drink less milk, and my sinuses cleared. I felt I had more energy. A picky child, cutting out meat forced me to try new things, namely vegetables and beans. I grew to like most of them—actually, came to like most any food when adequately prepared.

Though I was devoted to my cause, I wasn't without temptation. One memory in particular comes to mind: my cousin's graduation party. The fried chicken smelled wonderful, and there I stood, not far from it, with my mostly empty and certainly insubstantial plate of raw vegetables and pasta salad. It would have been so easy to simply grab a piece of chicken from the steaming platter and partake, but, reflecting on the information I'd gathered about animal suffering, I knew I had no choice but to refrain. The act—and my adoption of vegetarianism in general—helped me cultivate a compassion and awareness for other beings that I had been without before, as well as the discipline to refrain from always indulging myself whenever I wanted something.

Community

IN THE EARLY SUMMER, I became involved in a wonderful organization called Women Writing for (a) Change (WWf[a]C). Imagine a quiet, calm, open room and a circle formed of large, comfortable pillows. There is a candle in the middle of the circle and girls perched on the pillows. The facilitator reads a poem to begin the class, then a stone is passed from hand to hand as each girl checks in with the group, summarizing her week up to this point and giving feedback to the poem. Then we write, responding to the poem or another prompt or whatever else comes to our minds, and we share. But absent from our sharing is any self-consciousness, or pretentiousness, or competition. We share from our hearts, and our words are received with open minds. There is no applause when a reader finishes—only a quiet, calm chime, an equal response to pieces short or long, happy or sad, lyrical or straightforward. Around you, even if the girls are strangers, you feel surrounded by love and caring.

Women Writing first entered my consciousness when I was still living in West Chester. An old friend of my father's had attended classes there and thought it would interest me when she learned I had a renewed interest in writing. However, at the time, we lived so far from the writing hall (far, interestingly enough, from everything that would play an important role in my later life) that I never pursued it. However, during freshman year, Avery, a girl from my writing class at school, would often talk about Women Writing and how much she enjoyed it. Reminded of the organization, I decided to sign up for the summer class and see what it was all about.

At first, I was self-conscious as usual, worrying my words would be judged, judging them myself. It felt strange to read something directly after I'd written it. I knew—or thought I knew—that for a piece to be exemplary, it would have to go through much editing and revision. However, within a few days of the summer class, I settled right in, comforted by the flickering of the candle, the quiet of the space, the lack of judgment from my listeners, the honest, clear voices of others.

One of my favorite aspects of Women Writing was small groups, which were exactly what they sound like. For fifty minutes, we would break from the large group into smaller, preassigned groups, in which each member received an equal amount of time to share whatever she wanted and receive whatever specific feedback she requested. I enjoyed both listening intently to others and having a concentrated period of time for my voice to be heard.

Initially, the idea of reading my work for seven or eight uninterrupted minutes felt daunting, but once I let my defenses down and stopped worrying about criticism and skill level, I found it surprisingly easy and deeply enjoyable. Small groups also helped me learn the value of specific feedback. Like most writers, I'm familiar with having someone read a piece of my work, only to have them smile, return it, and say simply, "It's good,"—not for lack of sincerity, but for lack of knowledge of what else to say. In small groups, I was encouraged to ask for the specific feedback I wanted from my group members—whether it be questions of craft, how well I conveyed my emotions within the piece, or the emotional reaction of my listeners to the piece. If we wanted, we could even request silence. At first, when my group asked me what kind of feedback I wanted, I was tempted to respond, "I don't really care. Tell me whatever you want," not wanting to feel demanding or fussy. But the truth was, I *did* care what they told me, so I consciously made an effort to ask for specific feedback. Like many aspects of Women Writing, this is a principle I've learned to apply to life in general: ask for what you need.

Another lovely aspect of Women Writing was the read-back lines. At the end of each class, there was a read-around, which is where we went around the circle, and each person chose to read from her own work or pass to the next person. The rest of the group listened and wrote down lines or phrases from the readers' pieces that caught their ear. When everyone had read or passed, each person read the lines she had jotted down—read-back lines—in random order, sometimes slightly overlapping each other. It was a reprise of the read-around, a symphony of words. I would feel honored whenever I heard a line from my piece read back, serendipitous and united when someone else read a line I too had written down. I'd make an effort to say a read-back line at least once, to have my voice heard.

Undoubtedly, Women Writing for (a) Change helped me find my voice and, moreover, find the courage to project it without fear.

Women Writing's tolerant, warm environment was the perfect place for self-discovery. I could write about virtually anything I wanted. No topic was too sad or seemingly insignificant for exploration, and my words were always met with genuine praise. Whereas I usually felt like I was wasting people's time when I shared in creative writing class at school, I felt worthy and respected at Women Writing, largely because I had learned to respect my own worth. I felt camaraderie with my fellow writers and nurtured by the facilitators. By the time the final, public read-around arrived, I felt a similar grace and ease in reading my piece as I'd felt when I read at my dad's funeral.

Aside from helping me find my voice, write from my heart, and, eventually, come to love myself, Women Writing also introduced me to the idea of feminism. Though it had always been on the peripherals of my consciousness, I didn't really know much about it and certainly not what it meant to me. Although I realized that many people rejected the term *feminist* as extremist, I came to accept the label with open arms. Feminism, I learned, wasn't a matter of putting down men or about female supremacy—conversely, it was about gender equality, finding worth in both genders, and realizing that each person has both masculinity and femininity within them. It was quite simple and logical to me, and as soon as I thought about it I knew I was, in fact, a feminist.

West Again

SHORTLY AFTER WOMEN Writing ended, I headed out to California. My Aunt Trish was no longer tending to the house in the gated community; she and Michael were now renting a house in the same town. My time with Aunt Trish was no less valuable or connected; we continued to have long, in-depth talks, cook together, and watch films. We also made jam and took trips into Santa Barbara.

That summer, we visited another secluded beach, this one in Santa Barbara. It took about a half-hour to walk from the parking lot down a treacherous cliff to the beach. Few bathers dotted the sand, some taking advantage of the clothing-optional policy. My aunt and I set up a towel in a secluded area of the beach. I stripped off my swimsuit and plunged into the water, the vulnerability I felt complimenting my experience that year. I'd been stripped to the core emotionally, pushed far out of my comfort zone by attending a new school, living in a new home, uncovering new parts of myself. But, along with the vulnerability, like swimming in the ocean without the protective layer of a swimsuit, there was also freedom. In my new, unbound life, I had been free to discover who I was, free to uncover any hidden potentials, build new expectations for myself. I swam a long time in the water that day, peaceful and calm, simply enjoying the sensation of being enveloped by the sea.

On that trip, I began to wonder once more if I should stay in California. Though SCPA had provided eye-opening changes, I wasn't entirely happy there. I hadn't made many friends and wondered if a girl of suburban heritage such as myself could ever fully adapt to a more urban lifestyle. Additionally, my life with my Aunt Chris was still rocky, even if it had calmed down somewhat. Simply put, I was safe, but I wasn't very happy.

As I began to talk options over with my aunts, gathering perspective and thoughts, I started wondering if I could really be happy anywhere. Of course, I was still grieving. Wasn't discontent to be expected? Wasn't it better, as I'd initially thought, to be living in a place that was at least somewhat familiar and near my old friends?

At the same time, the appeal of moving to California was alluring: I could start fresh, try to forget what had happened, enjoy life in a two-parent household, and form stronger bonds with my other relatives in California. Both options—staying or going—had their merits as well as their drawbacks, and it was very difficult to decide which would be best.

By the time I left California, I felt ninety percent certain I would be returning before the end of the summer, moving in with my Aunt Trish and enrolling in the local high school. I felt excited but still slightly torn. I didn't want my Aunt Chris to think I was ungrateful for her generosity, nor did I want to upset my grandparents. The night I returned to Ohio, I decided to talk with my Aunt Chris about my pending decision.

She was already in bed when I went to her, but she agreed to talk to me anyway.

"I'm thinking about moving to California," I said bluntly.

"I know."

"What do you think about that?"

"Well," she said objectively, "I know you and Trisha have a strong bond. I think she and Michael are good for you in ways I'm not. I feel like sometimes you're looking for nurturing from me, and I'm just not really good for that."

I nodded. That was all true.

"But I want you to realize that sometimes, when you visit a place, it seems nicer than it really would be if you were there all the time."

"Yeah," I agreed. The thought had occurred to me.

"And if you move out there, you're there for the rest of high school. There won't be any back and forth." It wasn't a decision to be taken lightly.

She expressed her understanding for my desire to move, but gave me another perspective to consider. "It's been good for you to be here, so you can see your friends and Grandma and Grandpa, I think," she continued. "So maybe you should stay here for a few months, go back to school, and see if it's any better. If it's not, maybe then think about going. You can't leave right away, anyway. If you move, you have to tie things up first."

I was quiet a minute, absorbing her logic and impartial analysis. "That sounds like a good idea," I said, referring to her plan of staying in Cincinnati for a few months. It seemed like a good compromise.

"And . . ." I hesitated. "I just want you to know that I appreciate you letting me stay with you." To my surprise, I started crying. "And you've just always—" I broke off in tears, unable to finish.

"Always been there?" she asked, and I nodded. "I always will be," she continued in her matter-of-fact manner. "Whether you decide to stay here or not."

A Family of Friends

I ENDED UP DECIDING to stay in Cincinnati. After going back to SCPA and realizing what a great opportunity and unique high school experience it was, it seemed like the right choice. Though I probably would have benefited from living with my Aunt Trish and Michael, I also realized moving away wouldn't solve all my problems or allow me to forget. I couldn't just escape the situation by changing where I was living. Instead, I stayed in Cincinnati, in some ways to finish what I had started.

In the end, this turned out to be a good choice for me. The more time elapsed since moving out of my old house, the more outgoing I became, slowly growing more comfortable with revealing the new-found parts of myself to others. I made more friends at school and no longer felt I was stuck in a depressive rut.

That year, instead of being with Dr. Joy for creative writing, I was taking playwriting with Ms. Lenning, a class comprised of the other sophomore writing majors, as well as KJ, Heather, and a few new additions. Alex was new to the school, a year older than me, and a can-do fashionista who added great sparkle to our class. Kelsie was a junior who had attended SCPA the year before I had started. A fierce, loving girl, we wrote our first play together and ultimately became good friends. Sandrina was a rebel with a heart of gold. I came to think of her as a punk with endearingly obscure tastes and a sweet heart. There was also Keloni, a senior who also majored in art and was amazingly talented, but always humble. I became close to these people, as well as the others who had been in my writing class the previous year. By the end of the year, I had established a deep, meaningful connection with almost everyone in my writing class. We formed a pseudo-family of sorts, sharing phrases and inside jokes. Suddenly, I was in the midst of a wonderful community of people, each one different and adding his or her own personal flare to the group. It amazed me that I was so close to everyone when the previous year I had felt sure I would never be a part of things.

I became particularly close with Avery, a girl I had met freshman year who shared most of my non-writing classes, and who was also in my Women Writing for (a) Change class in the fall. Though I was still close with my friends from West Chester, I needed a close friend who went to the same school as me. As she was a familiar face, I began opening up to Avery in the beginning of sophomore year, exploring my newfound, if embryonic, outgoing nature. I was slightly intimidated at first, as Avery was very intelligent and an excellent writer. But the more I talked to her, the more I saw she was also a funny, interesting person and we had a lot in common.

Our friendship was cemented about a month after school began. I had been planning a dinner party for my friends from West Chester, and Avery and I were talking about food and cooking in chemistry one day.

On an excited whim, I turned to her and said, "Hey, I'm having a dinner party on Saturday. Do you want to come?"

She seemed surprised but pleased at my spontaneous invitation. "Sure," she said, nodding.

It was a curious intersection of what I'd come to think of as my old life, West Chester, and my new life, SCPA. Despite my slight anxiety, the party went well. Abby and Bridget got along well with Avery, who was brave in the face of meeting new people. We enjoyed dinner together and played Scrabble before everyone headed home. Afterwards, Abby expressed her relief and happiness that I'd found a good friend at my new school.

From there, my friendship with Avery blossomed. We enjoyed the typical movie nights and sleepovers, as well as our more unusual brand of bonding: cooking. Our conversations about food turned into ideas about what to make. Early on, impressed by my cooking at the dinner party, Avery suggested I come over to her house to bake an apple pie one day. Though we actually never made the pie, it was a charming notion to me, and I knew then that Avery and I would be close. Over the months that followed, we made chocolate French toast sandwiches, black bean burgers, spaghetti, strawberry short-cakes, fried potatoes, homemade pasta, lasagna, artichokes, cheese-cake, blackberry scones, pancakes, macaroni and cheese, lemonade, and all manner of other things—all the while talking, laughing, and learning to work together.

Another signal that Avery was in my life to stay was the fact that she shared her birthday, June 1, with my dad. Unlike many people, Avery was neither uncomfortable nor overly sympathetic when I talked about my parents. In contrast to most of my friends, Avery had never met my dad, and she was always eager to hear about him.

Our friendship was further solidified by our participation in the Young Women's Feminist Leadership Academy (YWFLA), through Women Writing for (a) Change. YWFLA was a program designed to help young women cultivate general conscious leadership skills, as well as lead a writing group in the Women Writing for (a) Change style. Though I had only been participating in Women Writing for about six months, I knew it was an important place for me to be, and I was eager to participate in it in any way possible.

I never considered myself much of a leader, probably due to my lack of self-confidence. I also felt that way because I wasn't particularly bossy or assertive, qualities I thought were essential to good leadership. Through YWFLA, I learned I was wrong. YWFLA helped me gain confidence in my leadership abilities and myself in general. The program consisted of two retreats at a convent tucked away in Kentucky, as well as eight weeks of Sunday evening classes. Over this time, we learned about leadership, feminism, the sacredness of honoring our voices through writing, and how to lead consciously, not pedagogically. I became close to the other girls in my class—Jaime, Janela, Julia, Megan, Karen, Alicia, and Avery—as well as our facilitators, Jenn and Sami. I slowly became aware that there are many brands of leadership, and that the bossy, in-your-face kind isn't necessarily the best. As the time drew nearer to complete our practicum—a required project where we were to put the information and skills we had learned to practical use—I felt confident I would be able to lead a circle.

My practicum took the form of a weekly circle for seventh and eighth grade girls once a week after school. The circle lasted for seven weeks and was built around topics that had been important to me at the girls' age, like family, friends, and identity. Though I only had three girls in my group, along with the occasional attendance of my YWFLA mentor, Marissa, I felt important ideas were exchanged, and the girls seemed to find the circle a positive space for them to write and explore their thoughts and feelings. I was happy to give them a peace similar to what I'd found at Women Writing the previous summer. By the time our circle was over, I felt comfortable in my leadership abilities, and my self-confidence had grown.

At one of the YWFLA retreats, I wrote the following piece:

> After a childhood incident of attempting to light an Advent candle and getting burned in the process, I have been afraid of fire, lighting matches, and the potential for destruction that it has.
>
> Now that I have successfully lit my first match, I feel amazingly powerful. It was frightening at first, when the match finally took and ignited, but I didn't panic, only calmly lit the candle—my candle—and quietly basked in the glory of the light. I imagined doing the same in my own circle of girls: lighting the candle that would brighten the space where their voices were to be heard. They would stare into the flame I had provided and feel safe, worthy, held.
>
> Humbled yet amazed, I realized I had the power to ignite. I had a fire burning inside me, someplace, and I was now able to share it. I was brave. I was capable of doing, leading, learning—everything—for in spite of my affinity for the quiet, stable earth and my former fear of passionate, wild fire, I finally had lit a flame.

Celery

I cover my pale green walls with posters—
Phantom of the Opera
Sweeney Todd
The Joker
(and perhaps ironically)—
Peace—
because the color is not like me.
I am not faint.
I am not boring.
I am not weak.

Now I yearn to paint each wall a different shade,
represent the fragments of me:
Dark red, my passion,
Ocean blue, my dreams,
Chocolate brown, my comfort,
Pure purple, my soul.

But when I moved in,
I wanted it painted pale green.
Pale green for a pale girl,
distillation of her former self,
pale pitiful shade,
yearning to scream.

And I could scorn my former self,
embrace our alienation.
I could paint over the green
with fresher, newer hues,
colors that have no problem shouting out.

Or I could cover it with pieces
of who I am now,
of what I love now,
but still let that green peek out.
I don't want to forget it.
I don't want to forget her,
the girl I used to be.

And I know that green is the color
of growth.

Epiphany

BY THE TIME I graduated from YWFLA and completed my sophomore year of high school, it had been two years since my dad's death. I found myself deeply amazed at the growth I'd experienced and the pain and turmoil my family and I had overcome. I thought of myself two years earlier, a freshman just starting at SCPA. I was broken by my dad's death, frightened to be in an entirely new environment, and unkind to myself. Now, though I continued to miss my dad very much, I no longer felt a constant aching in my heart. I had found my place at SCPA, flourished in my art, and discovered a wonderful new set of friends, as well as maintained a connection with old ones. I had discovered new parts of my personality and learned to love myself. Like my father had told me to do so many times, I had finally learned to keep my head up.

By the time I headed out to California that summer, I felt eons away from the person I'd been the last time I'd touched down on the California terrain. Back then, I'd been an uncertain girl, caught in a flux of indecision, befuddled by the vicissitude of life. Now, I was a mostly happy girl, enjoying my ever-growing friendship with Avery and cherishing my place in our community of friends. When my Aunt Erin picked me up at the airport, she told me I seemed like an entirely different person.

I enjoyed a relaxing visit in California, spending time with my Aunt Erin, Aunt Kerry, and Aunt Trish. At one point, we all gathered at my Aunt Kerry's house for dinner, and my Aunt Chris and Roger, who were also vacationing at the time, were included. It was a rare occasion where my life and family at home intersected with my life and family in California. Amid my aunts, uncles, and cousins, and thinking of all my friends at home, I felt deeply aware of the abundance of my life for the first time in a while.

It was also during that trip that, one night while researching religion, I discovered I was an atheist. Atheism had always sounded like a cold, scary realm that I would never quite bring myself to: "Well, I'm not a Christian, but I do believe in God." But the more I considered it, I didn't think I did. I didn't think there was any greater being controlling human existence, caring about what we did or didn't do. I hadn't for a while. Yet a spiritless existence seemed empty to me, and I did believe that, somehow, my parents were still around, even if they weren't your archetypal angels in a cloudy, perfect heaven. It was a difficult paradox to explain, and one I still don't completely understand. I guess it's fair to say that I believe in some greater energy or unity that bonds all living things together—something greater, more powerful, and more significant than humans. Some people call that thing God, but I don't because the term implies a personal quality to the energy, a deity with thoughts and emotions, and this was an idea I rejected. Whatever it is, it is bigger than us, beyond understanding by our limited consciousnesses, and not something to be praised, in my opinion, but simply acknowl-edged and respected.

After a bit of research, I became aware of the notion of theism—that is, the belief in a deity that controls and/or cares about human goings-on. And since I didn't believe in such a thing, I was techni-cally an atheist. Bingo! It was like something finally clicked. Coming to atheism wasn't, as I'd previously envisioned, the result of long nights of thinking or a deeply tragic event. It was simple logic. And instead of feeling lost or pointless, I actually felt happy. From now on, I could do good things just for the sake of doing them. I didn't have to worry about being judged or being good enough. I felt miraculously free. And, contrary to general conceptions, I wasn't "angry" at God for "taking" my parents away so early. The way I saw it, no one controlled what had happened to me. It's just how things turned out, and there was certainly no one to blame.

However, because of my belief in some realm of mysticism, I began to refer to myself as a spiritual atheist: one who has a sense of spirituality, but rejects traditional theism. I suppose some people would call such an ideology a watered-down paradox, and in some ways, it is. But it worked for me, and I was happy to finally find a faith—or lack thereof—to call my own.

Instructions

Give up God. Stop thinking
that everything happens for a reason,
that you'll be rewarded for the good.
Stop wondering
if you'll be punished for the bad.
In fact,

give up good and bad,
mere objective perceptions.
Give up fairness, justice,
give up religion, the idea of holiness,

then give up guilt.
Be bad and don't apologize.
Be bad and be accountable,
but guiltless.
Be good and expect
no greater reward
than being, doing, feeling.
Give up living for a utopian, far-off future,
free of guarantee—

and take up living for living:
realize
there needn't be anything else.

Liberation

I MADE ANOTHER big discovery that summer. Though I'd had a lovely time visiting, I found myself wondering what was going on at home and missing everyone each day. That year, I didn't even consider staying in California. However unglamorous, I realized that, for now, Cincinnati was my home. I felt happy and excited to return.

On the last day of my visit, I was finally able to visit the ocean.

30 June 2008

Today was beautiful. Aunt Kerry drove me—just me and her—down to Los Angeles to Aunt Erin's house. We listened to Damien Rice and talked. The boys were supposed to come with us but ended up staying behind.

When we got to L.A., Aunt Erin had prepared a little birthday celebration for Aunt Kerry. It was belated but nice. Aunt Kerry was surprised and happy. We ate and talked.

That night I laid on the floor of the living room listening to my family have a passionate discussion about politics—so typical. Then we ate some chocolate cake for Aunt Kerry's birthday. Then we decided to walk down to the beach as the sun was setting.

I wanted to go because my other California objective was to, of course, swim in the ocean. During my visit, I'd been twice to a beach but hadn't swam either time, so I was a little frustrated. So we walked to the beach and took some pictures, and then Aunt Kerry and I walked down to the shore. On the way down, I had these fanciful little visions of me going into the water in spite of my clothes. But I didn't really think I would because the sun was setting and I thought the water would be cold.

But when we reached the shore, the sun was smiling before it disappeared behind the hills in the distance. There were a few people splashing in the water. The sand was bathed in the warm pinks and oranges of the sunset, and the light reflected off the water, and it looked warm. I left Aunt Kerry at the shore to see how warm the water was. It was perfect. And I knew I had to go in. I went back and wrapped Aunt Erin's shawl, which I'd had around my shoulders, around Aunt Kerry's and kicked off my flip-flops.

"I want to go in," I said.

"Do you think you can?"

"I think so."

Then I ran into the water. No hesitation. I just went in and when it was deep enough, I submerged my head, and my heart was singing. I was finally with it again, the water, the ocean, and it welcomed me. My dress billowed around me in the water. I didn't even bother to take my jewelry off. I raised my arms in the air because I was joyful. Waves washed over me, and I was joyful. I turned around and waved at Aunt Kerry, and I was laughing, swimming, and soaking in the smell, the sensation. And soon Aunt Erin and Uncle Javi joined Aunt Kerry at the shore, and my family stood there watching me swim in my dress, free and happy. Javi took pictures.

At some point, I got out of the water, dress plastered to my body, hair dripping. I felt high. I stumbled about and felt so happy and complete and in-touch and couldn't stop smiling.

Aunt Erin was admiring me because I was brave for just plunging in, and I felt brave and beautiful.

I walked home dripping wet, and we were happy, and Aunt Kerry was happy and laughing, and I love her so much. She was very close to my mom. She lived with my parents when when my mom was pregnant with me and I was a baby, and I love to be with her. We can talk for hours. And we did.

We came back to Aunt Erin's, and I took a warm shower, and my skin felt so soft, and I felt relaxed and warm and perfect. Then Aunt Erin made me a cup of chamomile tea, and I put honey in it. When it was time for Aunt Kerry to leave I wanted to cry because I love her. We hugged three times, and I hoped hard that she would come home for Christmas with her sons.

After Aunt Kerry left, Aunt Erin and I went upstairs and put on my dad's CD, and I drank my tea and another cup afterward, and we played Scrabble. We both played a good game. At one point, Aunt Erin's letters spelled "Cincy" and "me," and then, shortly after, mine spelled "Ohio." Cosmic much? Honest.

Aunt Erin cried a little when my dad sang "If I Can Dream," and I smiled when he talked about me on the CD, and I wondered what he would think if he saw me now. And while we played Scrabble, I talked about how I've changed, and she talked about how I've changed, and I said how happy and overwhelmingly ready I am. We talked about my dad and everything else. I told her I was an athe-

ist now, and she reacted openly and warmly and said, "You're discovering all different parts of yourself out here," and it's so true.

We did tarot cards, and then we went to bed. And here I am now in this cozy little room in a twin bed that I love. And I've been wanting to write this journal entry since I got into the ocean, but more importantly, I was participating. I was loving my family and laughing and appreciating what characters they are and feeling high from plunging into the ocean and just smiling and drinking tea, and it was just beautiful.

I can't wait to see the pictures Javi took of me while I was in the ocean. Because that's perhaps the happiest and most peaceful and held I've felt. I swear. The happiness just coursed through me, bubbling over, and I laughed and smiled and loved.

Aunt Erin gave me one of my mother's rings. And Aunt Trish gave me one of my mother's nightgowns. And Aunt Kerry wanted to give me one of my mother's jackets, but there was no room. She'll continue to hold it for me.

Does this mean something? Do they think I'm ready now? I think I am.

I'm just changed. I'm so ready for something to happen, something to change. I feel so bold, so beautiful, so prepared.

And each of these wonderful women, my aunts, understands this so acutely, what I'm feeling, where I'm going. They love me so much, and I love them. I'm so grateful for them.

Not bad for my first day as an atheist. I've found more beauty in this day, not believing in any god, than I have in many of my other days as a theist.

I never want this day to end. But it will. I go home tomorrow. I get in at seven, and I'll be close to all the other people I love again. I'm ready to go home. I'm ready to start these changes, this life, this love.

This trip has been so full of growth and learning, much of which is just coming to fruition now. I'm fully realizing it. As I told Aunt Trish, this is the first time in my life I've ever been really aware of my own growth.

I think that's all. It barely touches the surface, but I can't say everything. I loved this day. I love my family. I love this existence.

Not Quite the End

IT'S HARD to know where to stop my story because, in truth, it is continuing, and I'm still growing and changing. It's also difficult to tie everything up neatly and without leaving any dangling questions. So here's where I am now as I write this.

I'm still at SCPA, almost a senior. I love it more each day and am so grateful to be in an environment that is creative, diverse, and liberal. I've had a few recent successes in writing and continue to develop my skills in narrative and poetry, as well as playwriting.

I continue to be an atheist, feminist, and vegetarian. I still don't consider myself a strict atheist, however. I still believe there is something ethereal inside each one of us and some greater connection among every living thing.

My relationship with my Aunt Chris has improved; my relationships with my California aunts, friends from West Chester, Avery, Monique, my dad's side of the family, and my new friends from SCPA are still going strong. I've lost track of a few people along my way, but I still wish everyone who has been in my life the best.

I still think of my dad often, of course, and miss him, though not semi-constantly, as I once did. At some point recently, I learned to stop living in the past, in a state of constant regret, anguish, and what-ifs. I've learned to draw happiness and love from the people in my life now, though my dad will always be in my heart, as will my mother. My parents planted the seed of my potential seventeen years ago. It's my responsibility now to make sure that it flourishes, whether or not they are here to see it grow and blossom. I'm not sure if they are or not, if life after death is just a pleasant pipe dream or if it's reality. But in my heart, I have two angels following me, watching me as I go.

Postscript

Football Game

Sitting in the stands,
just watching football players
be walked down the field
by their parents.
How proud those parent seem
to parade their strong boys
in front of the crowd.
Some boys hold their mother's hand,
I notice,
pointing it out.
She is quiet for a moment.

Does that ever make you sad?—
her voice
so quiet
against the contrast
of the noisy high school fans.
What?
I ask, not sure what she means.
Does that ever make you sad?—
again, as if I hadn't heard her.
I follow her gaze
and understand
but before I can answer:

If you ever need a parent
to walk you down some aisle
   I'll do it.
I smile.
The players keep walking.
Thanks.

Home Videos

When I watch old home movies
I can see into a world
that is far, far away
and I was hardly even part of.

I hear the laughter of my mother
and the smiling face of my father.
And I see them happy together
and me in the middle of it all.

I see the faces of aunts and uncles
long passed away,
living happily in that captured moment
unaware of what will happen someday.

Me: I'm unaware as well.
The grinning, chubby baby
sitting on my parents' laps.
I don't know they'll both be gone within years.

Eventually the tape comes to an end.
The recorder must have thought,
"They won't care about seeing that,"
when it's the only thing really worth seeing.

The happiness becomes,
once more, a thing of the past.
There's but one thing to do:
rewind the tape and watch it again.

Book Club Discussion Questions for CHELSEY

1. *CHELSEY* includes some of the author's poetry and other writing she created in the aftermath of her father's murder. In what ways do you think writing helped Chelsey cope with her grief?
2. Have you ever suffered a loss like the death of a parent or loved one? In what ways was your experience of mourning and grief similar to Chelsey's? How was it different?
3. After her father's death, Chelsey's life is uprooted again, as she loses her childhood home and has to figure out where she wants to live and go to school. What other challenges do you think Chelsey faced in redefining her day-to-day reality?
4. The author includes a number of poems in her book. How does the poetry feel different from the rest of her writing? Does it convey her emotions or experiences differently? In what ways?

5. While the focus of *CHELSEY* is on loss and recovery, the author also tells a parallel story—that of her search for a religion or spiritual framework that feels like a fit. Why do you think this search for meaning is so important to Chelsey?

6. Do you think being brought up in a certain faith makes one more or less likely to want to explore other religions? Have you ever embarked on a personal quest to find spiritual meaning in your life? What did you discover about yourself?

7. Have you ever experienced something that seemed too overwhelming and horrific that, at the time, you questioned whether or not you would survive it? How did you get through that difficult time? What surprised you most about your recovery? Has it continued to affect you today? If so, how?

8. The author writes about her relationship with the ocean throughout the book. What do you think the ocean might symbolize for Chelsey in her personal journey?

9. What do you think was a pivotal moment in Chelsey's story where she realized she would survive her loss and would ultimately be okay?

About the Author

Chelsey Shannon attends the School for Creative and Performing Arts in Cincinnati, Ohio. When she's not writing, she enjoys cooking, reading, and studying astrology.

Emily

123

Three Wishes

IF YOU HAD THE CHANCE to have three wishes (no wishing for more wishes), what would they be and why?

Okay, I admit, it would be easy to think of three easy answers:

1. That I would never get sick again.
2. That I would never get homework in the coming school year.
3. A nicer video camera.

It's also quite easy to get whatever your heart desires in three wishes, despite the whole "no wishing for more wishes" deal. You could wish:

1. That there would be no more suffering.
2. That whatever we wanted would appear like magic at the snap of our fingers.
3. That everyone would live happily ever after.

See? You could get everything in three wishes.

Oh, whatever. So I think the question is dumb. Who ever listens to me anyway? Maybe I'd better go take my temperature to see if it's gone down a fraction of an inch yet, and go lie in bed where I belong.

A Feeling

I'VE BEEN HAVING ANNOYING stomachaches lately. Sunday evening I had another one. So I sat out the whole church service, sipping tea and reciting Isaiah 40 to myself. I always recite Isaiah 40 to myself when I have stomachaches. It is very comforting.

I felt better by the time the service was over. My siblings and I went to our cousins Justin and Stephy's house, where we played soccer, ate food, and then just sat around while the guys played a game. It was during that time I began to know I was probably getting sick, because there is a certain feeling you get when you are getting sick. It's not just headache and sore throat—it's a sort of woozy feeling.

When we finally got home, which took a long time due to my brother Matt's game playing, I took my temperature and had a sky-high fever.

Arg zarg. I don't want to be sick again. How will this affect my plans?

At least it's happening now, and not during school.

Plans

WE WERE HAVING A NORMAL youth function at my church—sitting around, talking, and having fun. We were mostly talking about what to do for a fundraiser. Should we do another slave auction, where kids from the youth group get auctioned off as slaves and have to do their owner's bidding for the day (within reason, of course)? That was the only idea anyone threw out, even though no one seemed to like it very much.

Then Phebe said, "I think Emily should write a play for us to perform."

A murmur of approval and a nodding of heads swept through the room. I glowed. A play! Could I actually write a play? I've written skits before. Actually, I usually just make them up and tell people what to do so I don't have to bother with scripts. But could I write a whole play?

"Okay, I'll do it," I said.

I'm gonna write a play! And the youth group is gonna perform it!

Wow, I have so many things planned for this year. I want to take college algebra at the community college, because I don't think I'm smart enough for advanced math, but I want to take *some* math this year. Plus, then I'll get some, you know, college experience.

I also want to get a job, because I can *finally* drive. And I'm going to be a senior, and at my school, that means I don't have to be in school full time. Oh yeah, and there is the little fact that I need money.

Somewhere, Mom found out about some community writing classes, and I think it would be so much fun to take one with her.

Oh, and now that I can drive, I can finally see if I can find some community theater or something to participate in. I'm tired of knowing nothing about drama other than what I make up.

This year I'm also probably going to be yearbook editor. I mean, Justin and I are the only ones who even know how to put pages together, and he was editor last year.

And now, this play! I'll probably have to direct it too, because who besides me can direct a play? Well, J. D. can, but I don't think he would really want to direct *my* play. I'll probably be put in charge of costumes too. I can't wait!

Wow. Yes, I know that is a lot. I'll probably have to drop something. Or several things. Still, I am looking forward to being *busy* for once.

Now I just need to get over this dumb sickness and *get started!*

Change

WELL, WELL, WELL. I am better I guess. Or at least, well enough to be doing things again, which pretty much translates into better.

And tomorrow is school. The summer is over. But what will the school year bring? It's my last year. Do you know what this means? Everything is changing, changing.

Sometimes it seems like things will always be the same, especially my family. My brother Matt will always talk about leaving the church, moving out, and getting a girlfriend, but never do any of them. He'll always be short on cash. And everyone will laugh when he says crazy stuff.

My sister Amy will keep going cool places and meeting cool people. She'll joke about getting a boyfriend but never actually get one. And she'll always come home.

Ben will always hate girls and love sports.

Steven will keep on doing silly stuff and make everybody laugh.

Jenny will be cute and get on my nerves.

Forever and ever.

But it's all changing. It really is. I can deal with all that, I think. All my siblings changing. But I don't know if I can deal with me.

For now, I have one more amazing senior year left.

Amy

MY BIG SISTER AMY is gone, far away teaching school in South Carolina. And every time someone over twenty-seven or so tries to have a conversation with me, the first thing they always ask is, "So, how is your sister doing?"

Here's the problem. I don't really know.

We don't talk on the phone. I don't especially like talking on the phone. We don't really e-mail, either. We did instant message each other for the first week or so, but then, well, she never got on anymore.

So these people keep asking, "How is your sister doing? Is she enjoying teaching?"

And I go, "Umm . . . I think she is. Uh, I think she's doing pretty good. Last I heard from her she was at least."

"Do you talk to her much?" they ask.

"Well, we instant messaged for a while," I say.

"What's instant messaged?" they ask if they don't know what it is.

And that's the way it goes. Over and over again.

So you can imagine my happiness when, the other day, I was online and realized that Amy was too. I sent her an overjoyed message. She returned one. That was when strange things began to happen.

I wrote her a message. She wrote back saying, "Emily? Are you there?"

I wrote her another message. She wrote back. "Emily? Are you still on?"

Extremely frustrated by now, I wrote a third message.

I heard the telltale "ding" telling me I had an instant message. It was some sort of ugly brown message telling me that my last message could not be sent.

I wrote another frustrated message, banging out something on the keyboard that looked like this: "sdkjfejkl fhkdhfdjhxdjk."

Pretty soon I heard that ding again. "sdkjfejkl fhkdhfdjhxdjk could not be sent."

That's when I gave up. I still don't know how my big sister is doing.

Braving It

I WOKE UP THIS MORNING and didn't feel so hot.

Mom is gone on a trip. Did I mention that?

I didn't feel too good. I didn't feel too horrible, either. But I felt like I was sick, and I knew I had better stay home from school.

I called Dad. He was very unsympathetic and made me cry, but I think that was partially because my emotions were very fragile, due to being sick.

So after that very annoying conversation, I was allowed to stay home. I slept. And slept and slept and slept. When I woke up and went downstairs to eat some fish leftover from last night, the phone rang.

It was my dad, who also happens to be my teacher. He wanted to know if I could come to school for the rest of the day. I agreed, partially because I was feeling a little better but mostly because I felt guilty for staying home. I don't exactly know why. But I felt really icky the whole time I was at school and didn't get much done.

It was so much worse when I got home. Being sick always brings me down. But this takes the cake, what with Dad sending me on guilt trips for the stuff I don't do, no one thinking I'm that sick because I force myself to do so much, and the house falling to pieces before my eyes. The floors are getting dirty, the fridge is starting to smell, and the laundry is piling up. It's horrible.

Ten Random Facts About Me

1. I don't actually mind the smell of skunks.
2. I like cleaning the little gray fuzzies out of hairbrushes. And cleaning the threads and hairs out of vacuum cleaner heads.
3. There are six kids in my family—two older than me, and three younger than me. I love having a big family. I would often just as soon hang out with my family as with friends.
4. One of my favorite foods is pie dough.
5. My favorite character in *The Lord of the Rings* (the movies at least) is Gollum.
6. I'm a Mennonite, which is a denomination of Christianity that shares a lot of principals with the Amish. (But we don't ride around in buggies and we're allowed to use electricity.)
7. I fall asleep more easily in the middle of the day on the living room couch when my siblings are running around than at night in my bed when everything is quiet.
8. I dream every night about pretty much everybody—people I've randomly stood in line with, people whose Xanga sites I've happened across. There's a good chance I've even dreamed about *you* before.
9. I go to a Mennonite school with only 31 other students.

Everyone there is really close-knit and friends with everyone else. My dad is even one of my teachers.

10. You know the screensaver that has those pipes that go all
over the place and then fade away? Well, sometimes instead
of a ball on the end of a pipe joint, there will be a teapot.
If a computer is set to the pipes screensaver, I will sit and
watch for teapots for hours.

Dreams

I'M THE KIND OF PERSON that if nobody wakes me up, I
won't wake up. That's just the long and short of it.

So when I'm sick and staying home from school, and both my
mom and big sister happen to be gone, I have to have some system
of waking myself up or else I'll sleep until 3:30 PM, when everyone
gets home from school.

I came up with a solution. I enlisted the help of my sister's clock
radio, which wakes you up with—you guessed it—the radio, instead
of annoying beeping that's hard on poor, sick little ears.

This seemed to work other mornings, but this morning, instead
of waking up, I started dreaming about *American Idol*.

The girl onstage was amazing. She had gone against all the fashion stylists and everyone who told her what to wear and what to
sing. She was wearing a pioneer era dress and was singing a song
about wanting to do things that would last for life, not just the here
and now. She also kept singing about God. I thought she was amazing. My hero.

But everyone was making fun of her. The next contestant got on
stage and sang her own song. The point of this contestant's song

was to make fun of the pioneer contestant's song. It was sad. Then Miss Pioneer contestant got back onstage and sang with the other contestant, and they argued about what is important in life while they were singing.

I wanted the pioneer contestant to win so badly. I was so proud of her. But then I realized the third contestant was none other than this awesome guy from my youth group, Brandon!

So while I was sitting there, earnestly trying to decide if I should be rooting for Brandon or this amazing girl who wasn't afraid to voice her beliefs about what is important in life, I woke up and realized that the radio was blaring. Well that explains it.

Blood Draw

I GOT A BLOOD TEST TODAY. Two weeks is a long time to be sick. My mom is beginning to think this isn't just another Emily flu but something else, like mono.

So we drove to the Harrisburg Medical Clinic and went through the whole rigmarole . . . the tight rubber band thing on my upper arm, the spongy ball to squeeze, my mom holding my hand, the doctor telling me I have a good vein, closing my eyes as the needle plunges into my arm.

Wow. Some blood draws don't really hurt. This one did. When it was over, the doctor asked me what I thought of my first blood draw, which was crazy because I've had my blood drawn countless times before. I'm the sick one, you know?

I wonder if I do have something besides Emily flu. I wonder when I'll get better. I'm tired of being sick. I'm falling behind, and I'm feeling useless.

But what can I say? God is with me.

Waiting

I'M STILL SICK.

Yes, it has been almost three weeks now. That is a long time, even for me. It's rather depressing. I got blood drawn a week ago, and Monday they told us they had—gasp!—overlooked my tubes of blood and not sent them in. So I had to get more blood drawn, only the second time it barely hurt at all, thank God. And perhaps sometime soon we shall see if I have some horrible disease or if it's just an extra long bout of Emily flu.

I am having a bit of trouble writing the play, in that it is too short and making it longer is turning out to be harder than expected.

Perhaps tomorrow we will know whether or not I have mono.

When You Are Well

I'M FEELING A LOT BETTER, thank you very much. I thought it would never happen, but look here, it has.

Lots of things have happened recently.

I went to church, and multitudes of people congratulated me on being better now. It was lovely.

In the afternoon, after lunch, I went to Stephy and Justin's house. It was just like old times.

We were messing around with their old video camera when Justin came in and flopped on the bed. I decided to interview him. I said he was a famous poet, since he's always writing poems like "I was walking in the woods, looking for some goods; my feet were bare, then I saw a bear." Stuff like that.

I wanted to name him something else, something besides Justin Smucker, so I scanned the room looking for ideas. My eyes fell on a packet of pictures from Wal-Mart that was sitting on the shelf in the closet.

I pushed the red button. "I am honored to be here, interviewing the renowned poet, Wall Mart," I said.

In a bored monotone Justin replied, "I like walls. Walls inspire me."

Wow, it was funny. I was glad I was behind the camera so it didn't film me laughing. I'm pretty good at laughing silently. But the camera was shaking.

We talked about his past romances with Kay Mart and Dairy Mart, and his current one with Bi Mart.

"Is *Bi* short for something?" I asked.

"There's two of them," said Justin, "you know, cause *bi* means two. Like a bicycle has two wheels."

"So . . . she has two heads?" I asked, not quite understanding.

"No," said Justin, with a perfectly straight face, "there's just two of them."

Stephy and I about died laughing.

Life is so amazing when you are well. The further I get on in my life the more I realize sickness could have the potential to ruin it.

Like with college algebra, for instance. As seniors, Justin and I were going to carpool to the community college and take it together this winter. It would be fun if our friend Bethany would too, but she'd just as soon do the least amount of work required to graduate.

But now, with my recent sickness, my parents aren't sure they want to pay for a college course if I'm gonna get sick in the middle of it and fail. Justin is pretty optimistic. He says I've used up all my sick days this year, so I can't get sick again. I don't think he wants to drive all the way to Albany several times a week by himself.

I think I'll most likely stay well for college algebra. But how can I convince my parents of that?

Communion

SOMETIMES IT FEELS like up is down and red is blue.

And sometimes it feels like I will be sick forever.

Sometimes it feels like I'll never be able to do anything in life, to go anywhere in life, because I'm sick all the time.

And other times it feels like I am missing a huge chunk of life, and in place of that missing chunk is sickness.

Being well was so much fun while it lasted. I thought, *Now, now I can finally make up for lost time. I can hang out with my friends. I can get schoolwork done. I can do things, and* be *somebody.*

Then, communion happened.

It was different this year. Different than it's ever been. I wasn't solemn and serene, humbly thinking about Christ's death. I just wasn't. I was dancing on my way to get the bread. I was happy and jumpy. "I'm well!" I kept thinking, "I'm finally, finally well." And then, something happened that changed everything.

I felt it. The woozy feeling. The funny little headaches springing up the back of my neck. The feelings that *always* precede sickness.

I was sitting in church, and I felt them. I didn't know what to do. I wanted to cry; I wanted to cry so badly. But I didn't.

Then the service ended and everyone was so happy for me. So delighted to see me better. Everywhere I went there were people, people, people. They asked me the same question every time. "Are you feeling better?"

And every time I would smile my fake smile, and say the happy words that weren't true. "Yes," I would say. "Yes I am." I wanted them to be true more than anything. But inside I was screaming "No! The woozy feeling! The headaches! I'm getting sick *again*. What is the world coming to?"

Too many people. Too many questions. Too much pain. I went outside. I climbed into the van, away from everyone. And then I cried as I saw my future go up in smoke.

Handing It Over

SOMETHING JUST HAPPENED TO ME. Something greater than I can even fathom.

I am a worrier. I worry about passing tests, about what my parents will say, about not getting things done. I worry so much I make myself sick, and nothing I do seems to make it go away.

Communion night, when I sat in the van and cried, I was confronted with the greatest amount of worries I have ever had in my entire life. Everything I had tried not to think about came pouring over me.

After a year and a half of virtually no sickness, I began to think I would be okay. That if I didn't eat the foods I was allergic to, I would have a normal life. But now? Three bouts of sickness in a row. What does this mean?

READER/CUSTOMER CARE SURVEY

We care about your opinions! Please take a moment to fill out our online Reader Survey at **http://survey.hcibooks.com**.

As a **"THANK YOU"** you will receive a **VALUABLE INSTANT COUPON** towards future book purchases as well as a **SPECIAL GIFT** available only online! Or, you may mail this card back to us and we will send you a copy of our exciting catalog with your valuable coupon inside.

(PLEASE PRINT IN ALL CAPS)

First Name		MI.		Last Name

Address				City

State		Zip	Email:	

1. Gender
- ☐ Female
- ☐ Male

2. Age
- ☐ 8 or younger
- ☐ 9-12
- ☐ 13-16
- ☐ 17-20
- ☐ 21-30
- ☐ 31+

3. Did you receive this book as a gift?
- ☐ Yes
- ☐ No

4. How did you find out about the book
- ☐ Friend
- ☐ School
- ☐ Parent
- ☐ Online
- ☐ Store Display
- ☐ Teen Magazine
- ☐ Interview/Review

5. Where do you usually buy books *(please choose one)*
- ☐ Bookstore
- ☐ Online
- ☐ Book Club/Mail Order
- ☐ Price Club (Sam's Club, Costco's, etc.)
- ☐ Retail Store (Target, Wal-Mart, etc.)

6. What magazines do you like to read *(please choose one)*
- ☐ Teen People
- ☐ Seventeen
- ☐ YM
- ☐ Cosmo Girl
- ☐ Rolling Stone
- ☐ Teen Ink
- ☐ Christian Magazines
- ☐ Series Books (Chicken Soup, Fearless, etc.)

7. What books do you like to read *(please choose one)*
- ☐ Fiction
- ☐ Self-help
- ☐ Reality Stories/Memoirs
- ☐ Sports

8. What attracts you most to a book *(please choose one)*
- ☐ Title
- ☐ Cover Design
- ☐ Author
- ☐ Content

TAPE IN MIDDLE; DO NOT STAPLE

BUSINESS REPLY MAIL
FIRST-CLASS MAIL   PERMIT NO 45   DEERFIELD BEACH, FL

POSTAGE WILL BE PAID BY ADDRESSEE

HCI Teens
3201 SW 15th Street
Deerfield Beach FL 33442-9875

FOLD HERE

Comments

What about my schoolwork? Will I be able to get it done if I keep getting sick?

What about my plans? How can I take college algebra if I could get sick at any moment? What happens if I get a job and then fall sick for two weeks?

And my future? What about my future? Any option I can think of—getting a job, going to college, doing voluntary service, attending a Bible institute, even becoming a wife and mother—would never work. How could it, if I could fall sick at any given moment and be out for two weeks at a time?

It isn't like this is so far off in the future, you know. This is my senior year. I'll graduate, hopefully. I'll turn eighteen whether I like it or not.

I was worried sick. That was all I could think about. All night. All day. Worry, worry, worry. There was nothing I could do to make it go away.

"I can't handle this!" I told God one night. "This is too much for me. *You* were the one who allowed me to get sick, *you* take them."

I pried my worries out of my mind like old gum from the inside of a trash can. I told God what the worries were and why I had them.

Then I handed them over. "Here God, these are your worries now. Not mine."

And they were gone. Bing bang boom. Just like that.

I thought about school, about college, about a job . . . everything that had caused me to worry before. And I smiled to myself. Someone else was taking care of it for me.

I cannot describe how that felt. Like a cool breeze on a hot day. Like stepping out from a hideously ugly room into an unbelievably beautiful garden. Only a million times better.

Walls

I DECIDED I WOULD do something cool and spin around with my eyes closed, count to twenty-one, and write about whatever I was pointing to. So I did, and guess what? I was pointing at the wall.

Now, there are a limited number of things you can say about a wall. I could say that walls inspire me and make the people who get that inside joke laugh, only it would be a lie because walls don't inspire me. Not really.

A blank wall might inspire me to paint a dragon on it or doodle on it while I'm supposed to be doing my homework, but this particular wall isn't even a nice white inspiring wall. It's painted in a funny print of baby blue and tan.

Amy and Jenny's room also has some random splotches of paint on it. When Jenny was three, she and I shared that room, while Amy had the room I have now. Ah Jenny . . . she ate all my gum, scribbled in all my books, and decorated the walls with any paint she could get her hands on.

But she didn't paint this room. Mom did, all blue and tan with a Peter Rabbit border. I ripped the border down when I got the room, but the blue and tan stayed.

I don't like tan.

There is one interesting thing about these walls. A certain splotch of baby blue paint looks like a mermaid.

That is all.

Analogies

I LOVE COMING UP with analogies. I made up one about my current state of sickness last night.

Imagine you were slowly sinking in a bog. You would have three choices in how you would react:

1. Panic
2. Struggle, hoping against hope that someone will pull you out
3. Resign yourself to the situation

Being sick is kind of like that. At least, being sick for this long without really knowing why, that is.

But what scares me is that I'm not panicking or struggling or hoping against hope that someone, or something, will pull me out of this situation. Slowly, I'm resigning myself to it. I don't know why. I don't really want to be resigned to it, but I can't seem to help it. Plus, the other options don't look too inviting either. I've been struggling, but it wears a person out until they get tired of it. And panicking just makes me feel worse.

It's like my life is on "pause" right now. I don't know what's going to happen to me. I don't know if I have some horrid disease, or if something in this house or Oregon itself is making me sick, and thus, I would have to move.

So here I am, sick, waiting for something to happen.

I don't really want to go back to school right now. I know that is horrible, since I'm so behind and need to get caught up. But that's just it. School for me right now represents a big pile of "behind." Like I'm on the bottom of the down escalator, trying to get to the top. Yeah, I know, another analogy. Analogies are amazing.

Did I tell you that all my test results came back negative? I have no idea where this sickness is heading. None at all.

More Plans

TODAY I FINISHED writing the church play. Finished it for good, hopefully. It's about all these unique characters who are jealous of each other. We're planning to perform it around Thanksgiving. Did I mention that? So the characters learn to be thankful for what they have, instead of being jealous of everyone else. Because someone is jealous of them.

Tomorrow the preachers and their wives are going to anoint me with oil and pray for me as instructed in James 5:14–15.

I was hoping that today I would get better. That's just what I had in my mind. However, I actually felt worse than ever.

I still don't know where I'm going. But I do know this. I'm going to fight like a mad catfish to do the play. I must do it. I have to do it. I am going to do it unless for some reason God doesn't want me to.

So here's my plan: when they anoint me with oil, I'll get better. Doesn't the Bible say that the prayer of the faithful shall save the sick? Something like that.

I don't think I'll get sick again for a while. I'm going to work really hard on my schoolwork and try to get it done early because I often get sick in the spring.

I probably won't be able to get a job, but I really want to do college algebra. I think I could get by if I got sick for a few days because Justin could fill me in on what I missed. And I *will* do the play. I have to.

No Show

THERE IS A POINT when something amazing is about to happen to you that a tremendous fear rises—a fear that something will go wrong, and you won't have your amazing something after all. So you desperately, *desperately* try to correct the kinks and make it happen, and then you fall flat on your face.

I counted on that play. It was going to be my breakthrough. I had it all figured out. Why does everything go wrong when I have it all figured out?

I finished the play. I thought, *What now?* So, I wrote a desperate, long letter to Jeanette, our youth sponsor, asking questions about different aspects of the play, wanting to make sure it was going to happen.

I didn't want it to sound desperate, but I was scared as I wrote it . . . horribly scared. There was always another question, another thing that could go wrong, and I was fervently trying to keep down the "What if I don't get better?" questions that kept popping up inside my head. I wanted her to answer right away with an answer to everything.

She didn't.

It didn't take me long to realize it wasn't the questions I had written down, but the question I hadn't. *If I don't get better, who's going to take the play and run with it?*

The answer to that question is no one. There is no guarantee I will get better and stay better.

I talked to Jeanette about it, and we came to the conclusion that I just can't do it with the way my health has been. The play, *my* play, is off.

The Wish

I HAVE A FUNNY WISH right now that a digital camcorder will mysteriously come in the mail for me. I want a digital camcorder so bad. Every day I check the front porch to see if one has arrived.

I don't dream about being better anymore. Even being better means I could get sick again—falling behind, and failing, and losing all, and clawing my way to the top only to get sick again and plummet to the ground.

And somehow, even getting a digital camcorder from some unknown benefactress seems more likely than getting well does.

The Magic Potion

PEOPLE GIVE ME GIFTS. Cards, mostly. The loveliest one was from all the students at school. Stephy wrote a poem.

Bethany is very loyal. She visited me once last week and brought me a gift from her mother. It was a wonderful gift basket, with crackers and easy cheese (you know, that cheese you can squirt out of a bottle), two white shirts, and amazing markers to use on the shirts, so I can design my own.

Then, Sunday, she came again, bringing a present from herself. This one contained a glass slipper bottle filled with bubble bath, a green fuzzy scarf, and some American Girl lotion.

Phebe had wondered if she could come see me and bring some other girls along. I thought it would be wonderful.

A knock sounded on the door. Was it them? When the door opened, a long line of beautiful young ladies poured in, bearing a gigantic box covered with gold paper. In an attempt to cheer me up, they had filled the box with every wonderful and delightful thing imaginable (except for a digital camcorder). There were clothes and hot pink shoes and tea and a goblet and cards that said the nicest things. There were mountains (okay, small hills) of candy, which was a little unfortunate since Mom had been after me to cut back on sweets to boost my immune system. There were beautiful, inspiring, lovely notebooks. There was a very interesting movie and a very interesting book. But deep in that golden box was the most wonderful thing of all. The thing I've been longing for ever since this sickness started. A bottle of magic potion.

It looked suspiciously like a bottle of Kiwi Strawberry Snapple, one of the few fruit drinks I could actually drink. But the gold label clearly read "Magic Potion."

I didn't want to drink it all at once. I wanted to savor it. So I took a little sip right then, and saved the rest for later.

Every time I thought about it, I took another sip from the wonderful bottle of magic potion. But perhaps I savored it too much. Or perhaps the potion should have had a gold label on it that read "refrigerate after opening." Or perhaps I'm just stupid. In any case, the bottle of magic potion was *not* refrigerated after opening.

I didn't even think about it until tonight, days later, when I again pawed through the gold box of gifts. I was actually looking for a candy fix, but I came across the magic potion. It wasn't quite half-empty yet.

Was it bad? I took a small taste. It tasted a little funny, but not too bad. I decided I had better drink it now, before it got worse.

I took a big swig.

I felt something solid and furry in my mouth.

I spit the big swig back into the bottle.

Then, I sadly poured it down the drain. Such was the fate of my magic potion.

Singing Penguins

HOW LONG HAS IT BEEN? I am still sick. If it were not so, I would have told you.

I am still sick. What more is there to say?

I am still living.

I am still dreaming. Lovely, wonderful dreams. Where would I be if it weren't for my dreams?

As far as how my life is going for real, it is considerably less exciting than my dreams. No singing penguins, no fourteen-year-old friends deciding to get married and live in a yellow and black backpack, no dying from a snakebite while my dad shops around trying to find the cheapest hospital deal.

So my life is slowly plodding along. I'm drinking bottled water and eating pills that are supposed to make me well and waiting for lab tests to come back and reading a book about dragons and arguing with my little sister.

We were having an argument today, and this is how it ended:

Me: That doesn't make sense.

Jenny: Well what you said made sense to me but I want to pretend it didn't. So there.

146

Hobbit Poetry

ONCE WHEN I READ *The Hobbit*, I tried to understand it better by writing down all the poems in my ladybug notebook. I had always skipped the poetry or skimmed through it to get on with the story. But this time I really wanted to absorb it.

Needless to say, after the first three poems, I stumbled upon a long one and gave up. But that is not the point of this story.

One poem was a funny one about breaking Bilbo Baggins' plates and bending his forks. One was a fascinating one that was so much fun to recite, all about "Far over the misty mountains cold/ To dungeons deep and caverns old." I don't even remember the third one, except for the first line, which replays over and over in my head.

"O! What are you doing/And where are you going?" it asks.

I don't know. Seriously, where *am* I going? Nowhere. I should be going somewhere. Sure I'm sick, but I have to be heading down some path. What path am I heading down? Huh? Huh?

And what am I doing? What am I doing at all? I am lying around all day feeling miserable. I'm asking myself where I'm going and what I'm doing. I am lazy and I hate it. But there doesn't seem to be another way.

The Seven Princesses

I'VE BEEN WRITING MORE. Usually when I'm sick I don't write much, since I don't get inspired. But today was different.

I saw a list of the books my sister wants to get someday, and one of them was *The Ordinary Princess*. At least I think that's what the list said. In any case, it reminded me of a book I once read called *The Ordinary Princess,* which was good except for one thing. On the cover, if you looked closely at the ordinary princess's left foot, you could see her toenails were red. So all throughout the book I was waiting for her to paint her toenails red. But she never did.

This inspired me to write a story about a princess who painted her toenails red. However, once I began writing, it quickly turned into a story of seven princesses—Adaline, Brumhilda, Carmelinda, Delphinium, Esmerilda, Fanica, and Grum-ah-lum-ah-tum-tum—who keep drinking forbidden potions that make them do crazy stuff. I probably will never finish the story, but it was fun to write.

I think I'll end up writing for children. I've never really wanted to do anything else. Indeed, I've never really wanted to *read* anything else. Children's books do something for me that other books cannot. They take me places when I want to escape.

Part Positive

ONE BLOOD TEST CAME out part positive. It was the blood test for West Nile fever. Apparently, according to the test, I might have West Nile and I might not. To know for sure, I need to have further, extremely expensive testing.

Wait, how does that work? I might have it and I might not? What kind of idiotic test result is that? I never knew test results *could* be like that.

My mom is all up in the air because West Nile has no cure. I'm more inclined to think I don't even have West Nile. I mean, I get sick all the time and there's never a name for it. It's just another bout of Emily flu. So I have a theory that I'm allergic to something in

Oregon or maybe something in this house, and that's what's making me sick.

When I was twelve, my mom took me to a doctor in Creswell who did lots of allergy testing. I restricted my diet, and it helped a lot with my constant sicknesses. So now Mom and Dad are thinking, *Well, Dr. Hanson helped us so much back then, I wonder if he can help us again now?*

I normally feel very uncomfortable around doctors, specifically male doctors, and don't particularly like visiting them. But I am really looking forward to going to see Dr. Hanson. I want him to say, "You are allergic to Oregon. Go move in with relatives." And then I could go live in South Carolina with Amy or something.

I've always been jealous of girls in books who get to move to a totally new place, but those girls in books never *wanted* to move. I still read books like that and think, *Are you crazy? Why are you so upset about leaving your family and living with your cool aunt and uncle at a super duper cool school in Switzerland?*

Don't get me wrong. I love my family. I love my friends. I love my church. But what I want most is adventure and wellness, and the idea of getting both in one fell swoop by moving somewhere else is my greatest desire right now.

That's why I'm looking forward to seeing Dr. Hanson. If he said "Move," my parents would listen to him.

Insomnia

I ALWAYS THOUGHT staying up all night was stupid. People talk about how much fun it is, staying up all night with your buddies and acting crazy, but I never saw the appeal. I mean seriously.

There are lots of other crazy and fun things to do with your buddies that don't require turning yourself into an annoying grump the next day. And you need to get your sleep sometime, so why not at night, where sleep belongs? Sure, I've had insomnia before. And I do like staying up late, especially at sleepovers, but not all night.

Well look at me now. I just stayed up all night.

It's not like I wanted to stay up all night. I didn't even have buddies to hang out with (unless you count my little sis who got up in the middle of the night to use the bathroom). I just . . . did it. Accidentally.

So now, here I am. 7:57 AM. I have a splitting headache and am as wide awake as a fish.

Stupid insomnia.

The good news is that now I can say I accidentally stayed up all night, which sounds kinda cool.

Random fact: nearly every night, sometime between 11:00 PM and 4:00 AM, my brother Steven bangs on the wall in his sleep.

West Nile

HERE'S THE THING ABOUT high hopes: When you're brought back down to reality, it is such a shocking experience that you cry. You can't help it.

I can't at least.

Yes, I cried coming out of Dr. Hanson's office. Yes I was embarrassed. Yes I wished I could stop. But I couldn't, because Dr. Hanson said none of the things I wanted him to say.

What he said was, "According to the test results and her symptoms, and judging from what I've seen in other people, I think she has West Nile."

Um, hello? The *specialist* thinks I *don't* have West Nile. What about that? Huh? Huh?

When that was brought up, Dr. Hanson said there is a chance the specialist had ulterior motives in saying I didn't have West Nile. Good grief. Why would he have ulterior motives? But of course Mom believes Dr. Hanson over mysterious specialist guy.

Dr. Hanson says I should take fever baths to try and get West Nile out of my system. Basically, he says, when you are sick your body temperature increases to fight the disease. So if I take a long hot bath and force myself to stay mostly submerged, my temperature will rise and help get West Nile out of my system. That is assuming, of course, that I even have West Nile.

Honestly, the idea of taking a long, hot bath didn't seem exceedingly daunting until I took my first bath tonight.

How can I explain the horror of it? Of being submerged in hot water, all but my face, which had sweat pouring off it? It doesn't sound horrible. It really doesn't. But when I think of it, and how weak I was afterward, and having to do it six more times, I think that maybe if I can get through it I'll be able to handle being tortured for my faith someday or something.

Maybe if I do all seven fever baths, and nothing positive happens healthwise, I'll be able to convince my parents that I don't have West Nile, and we need to keep searching.

Practical Jokes

HOW IS MY LIFE GOING? Well, for one thing, I've started entertaining myself by commenting on my mom's blog under a different name. It's so funny, because no matter how often I do it, she never realizes it's me.

Mom: Did you see this comment on my site? Isn't it so sweet? [Looks lovingly at the comment.]

Me: Do you know who Julia Adams is? [Trying hard not to laugh.]

Mom: No, do you?

I burst out laughing.

Realization dawns on Mom's face. She looks startled, then surprised, then she too is shrieking with laughter. "I thought it was some sweet, prim, little, conservative girl from Iowa!" she gasps.

In other news, right now the upstairs hall resembles an obstacle course. And yet, no one thinks to move anything.

One more thing. A recent trip to the doctor revealed that perhaps I should not eat so much sugar. So now my tea is sweetened with honey (which isn't as bad as I thought it would be) and cookies are getting replaced with crackers.

Without Me

I AM NOT GOING TO be in the school Christmas skit. All the casting was done without me. It didn't surprise me, but it still hurt. Like no one even thinks I'm gonna get better anymore.

I think all this is getting to me, all this acting I should be doing but am not. Seriously. Like the dream I had last night.

In my dream, I went back to school. I thought I was better, but I sort of wasn't. And so things went along in odd ways and I tried to push away the bits of lingering sickness.

And then, Harmony Headings asked me to be in a skit that she and some other girls were doing for the Christmas program. I was delighted. Since I couldn't be in the normal play, at least I could be in this one.

I was hoping so badly that I could be the main character, which was a girl. Harmony cast the parts, one by one. She didn't cast anyone to be the girl. I knew it would be me. I was so excited! But she didn't say it was me. She just didn't say anything.

"So what am I, the understudy?" I said, joking.

"Yes," she said.

I was heartbroken, aghast, scandalized. I couldn't believe it. "What?"

I ran out of there, trying not to cry. I woke up from the dream sad. I really, really want to get better. To act. I just want life to stop moving along without me.

Work Craze

I AM ON A WORK CRAZE. I want to make $100 in three days. So I slave away doing odd chores and Mom pays me.

Why am I so desperate for money, you may ask?

A digital camcorder. That's what I want. A digital camcorder that actually has decent sound and picture quality. I want it so much. So now, instead of wishing for one to show up at my door, I am working, even though I feel icky. I wash down furniture and organize books. I sweep floors and do dishes. But vacuuming floors is too hard.

Despite that, Mom is convinced I'm getting better. Dad is too, but somehow Dad always seems to think I'm getting better. It drives me nuts. I am *not* getting better. The fever baths did nothing for me, except make me realize that if I can survive them I can survive doing a couple hours of work each day, as long as I have visions of digital camcorders looming in my head.

However, Mom is so confident I'm getting better she is insisting I go to the Smucker gathering at the coast in four days. Fine. I love hanging out with my Smucker relatives, but I don't love doing it sick.

I suppose, though, if I can survive the fever baths I can survive this.

Smucker Gathering

MY TRIP TO THE COAST started off boring and uneventful enough. There were hardly any people there, and Rosie and Phil, who were supposed to tell us which rooms we were in, were out walking on the beach.

I ended up in a dumb room with uncomfortable bunk beds and no door. Mom and I tacked a blanket over the doorway, but it still didn't offer much as far as privacy goes. Especially since it was kind of in the middle of everything.

I am sorry to say that for most of the weekend, I wandered around not sure what to do. Everybody always seemed to be doing *something* that I was too sick to participate in. Walking on the beach or playing ping-pong required energy, and card games required brain power, both of which I lacked.

I had horrific insomnia that first night, partially because of my uncomfortable bed and partially because I usually have insomnia. Sometimes I zoned out, and later I couldn't decide if I had been sleeping or not. It's hard to tell sometimes when you don't dream.

I heard a rustle. It was some cousins and uncles getting up to go fishing. I thought maybe I would get up and talk to them, since I had nothing better to do.

Well, did I have a time getting out of that stupid bed. It was tucked in so tight, and the bed above me was so low that I was pretty much stuck. That gave me claustrophobia. Yikes. I began to get hot. And desperate. *Calm down, Emily. Think. Move yourself this way, then that way.*

With only a few muscles pulled, I was free of the evil bed. Whew.

After chatting with the fishermen a bit, I stayed awake until other people began to get up, and then crawled into my parents' bed. It was actually comfortable. Somehow, despite that, I still had trouble getting to sleep. But I finally did.

My one beautiful memory of the trip was that evening, when Stephy and I were sitting on a futon talking. Most of the others were watching the movie *End of the Spear*. I could see the left half of the screen, but a pillar blocked my view of the right half. So I started jokingly trying to figure out what was going on by describing to Stephy what I could see.

Stephy, who due to the same pillar could only see the right half of the screen, giggled and described what she could see. Whenever the natives spoke their language, I would read half the English subtitles and she would read the other half. We could have moved, of course. But it was so crazy and fun, exactly what hanging out with cousins should be.

We decided to sleep on that futon that night. The living room had been reserved for the guys, but there were way more futons down there than they needed, while upstairs, where the girls were, bedding was so scarce that Stephy needed to sleep on the floor. Plus, there was a huge lack of privacy anyway. My room wasn't the only one without a door.

I slept so much better that night. We whispered all kinds of secrets and in the morning, when we left, I thought maybe the trip wasn't a total waste after all.

The Vacuum Cleaner

THE SCISSORS SAT on top of my desk in a goblet. The intercom lay on the floor. Only one thing stood between me and them: the vacuum cleaner that was hanging from my hair.

If I reached into the drawer behind me, could I reach the dagger I had gotten in Kenya? I doubted it, and even if I could, the thing wasn't very sharp.

I looked at the intercom again. Could I reach it? I shifted the vacuum cleaner as much as I could in that tiny room, turned my head away so my hair wouldn't get pulled, and reached blindly in that direction. My hand connected with a button of some sort. Hoping it was the right one, I pushed. "Can someone please come help me?" I called.

Steven, who was downstairs doing his homework, heard my desperate cry and came to rescue me. He opened the door and burst out laughing.

"What happened?" he asked.

Sheepishly, I explained my unusual predicament. My room hasn't been vacuumed in a while, so I was trying to do a thorough job. I was sucking ancient dust bunnies out from under the bookshelf with the hose, when I felt a sharp pain in my head. I hadn't thought about the fact that the head of the vacuum cleaner is still sucking, even if you're using the hose. I also hadn't thought about the fact that long, loose hair is never safe around the head of a vacuum cleaner. And thus, the machine managed to grab my hair and wind it tightly around the beater bar.

But it all ended well. Steven fetched the scissors, and I'm not bald.

The Christmas Program

I KEEP HAVING TO go places I don't want to go. One of the big reasons is this thing called the Christmas Program.

I looked at the script for the program once, and it nearly broke my heart. My name wasn't on it, not anywhere. I guess I already knew I wasn't in it, but just seeing those names—Bethany, Justin, Stephy, but no Emily . . . I don't know. It felt like an extra punch in the stomach.

My dad wanted to go over the script with me and have me tell him what needed to be done. Where should the characters stand as they say their lines? When should they enter and exit? I explained it all to him.

My dad also wanted me to help him direct it. But he had an odd way of getting the kids to practice, with no real acting until right at the end. I went to school twice to "help direct," but I really didn't do much.

I went to the big program on Wednesday even though I felt horrible. I didn't want to go, but I did because I realized it was my duty. That's what pushed me out the door.

As soon as we got there, Matt and I rushed upstairs to the balcony. I really did not want to have to talk to anyone.

I watched the play and felt so removed. I couldn't help but think about all the "what ifs." *What if it was me on that stage performing? What if I had actually directed this thing? Think of how wonderful it would be!* I was imagining myself on that bench, waiting for my turn to perform and whispering to my neighbor. Imagining myself onstage and hearing the audience laughing at the funny thing I said. Imagining myself standing on those risers, singing my heart out. It was exactly where I should have been. Where it was normal to be.

I sort of felt like I didn't exist.

At the end of the program, Dad got up and gave a little speech thanking anyone who had helped out in even the tiniest of ways. I had a fleeting hope he would mention me, and I could exist for a little bit after all, but he didn't. I started to tear up. I was barely able to keep from crying, I felt so horrible.

For the rest of the evening, I couldn't think about it or else I would almost cry, and it would take all my effort plus remembering my friend Alfonso trying to do a cartwheel on Rollerblades to thwart it. If you have ever seen someone try to do a cartwheel on Rollerblades, you will understand why it is a funny enough memory to stop tears.

After the program, my friends brought me food and hung out with me, which was wonderful. But I left fairly soon after that.

Coincidences

ONCE, WHEN I WAS YOUNGER, I was eating clam chowder when I saw a funny clam that was black and bluish. I ate it anyway.

Later, I drank some lemonade, and it hurt my throat.

After that, whenever I drank lemonade and it hurt my throat, I thought it was because I had eaten a weird black and bluish clam and it had somehow damaged my throat.

It's odd, sometimes, how when two things happen at the same time it feels like one caused the other, when in reality it was a total coincidence.

The worst, I think, is when I walk into the room and everybody bursts out laughing. It always takes me a bit to realize that no one is laughing at me; indeed, they probably didn't even see me. They just happened to be laughing at some random joke when I walked in.

A Magical Realization

EVERY YEAR, my dad takes us to a football game because he's just so nice, but I've only gone twice. I'm not terribly big on sports. The first year I got a subscription to *American Girl* magazine instead and last year I got a gigantic book. This year, Dad took me to see the play *A Christmas Carol*.

It was a good play. It made me happy inside. We walked back to the car, and the lights of the city, and the crisp, cold air, and being with my dad, who took me to see the play even though he doesn't even really like plays . . . it was all so magical.

We went to Safeway, then, because Dad had to get groceries. Right in front of the door was a display of roses. I said, "Dad, do you ever get Mom roses for no reason?"

"Well, sometimes," he said. "Would you like it if I got you roses for no reason?"

He was seriously offering to buy me a dozen roses!

There, way in the back, were a dozen beautiful, perfect, multicolored roses. And then, as I was standing beside my dad and looking at my beautiful roses, I was struck by a perfect thought.

You see, my family is planning to visit Kenya this spring, and after that, those who had saved enough money were going to take a detour to Yemen before coming home. But oops, my cousin Keith got engaged, and his wedding was scheduled over the time we were planning to be in Yemen. So that part of the trip was canceled, and I, who had been desperately saving my pennies, was very disappointed.

But right then, at that magical moment, standing beside my dad in Safeway and looking at my roses, it struck me. With my Yemen money I'd have enough to buy my digital camcorder, plus extra, for Christmas presents.

I felt like the happiest girl in the world.

It was wonderful.

Randomness

I LOVE MY WATCH. In a book I just read, the characters smashed their watches with hammers, because they were so sick of clocks running their lives. It was cool in the book, but when I looked at my watch, I knew I could never smash it because I love it so much.

I don't know why I keep pens I don't like. I probably keep them because, no matter how many cool pens I get, there is always the chance all my cool pens will end up at school and on my bed and in my purses and in my mom's pen cup. It's happened before. And running out of pens is horrid. Worse than running out of paper, because you can always write on your skin or a napkin or your clothes if all else fails.

I once got a cheap backpack that lasted practically forever, and I loved it more than any backpack I've ever had before or since. I love things like that.

Snail mail is so much more fun to receive than e-mail, but I don't send out snail mail. I would love to be the sort of person who always remembers to write letters to people, but I'm not.

I love reading about characters who are unlike any characters I've ever read about before.

I got a new alarm clock today. My old one has a crack in it, and the second hand fell off and is lying at the bottom of the clock. I used to read in bed with it by holding down on the snooze button, but then the battery would run down, my alarm would go off late, and I wouldn't get up early enough to finish my homework. Maybe I should smash my old alarm clock with a hammer.

Sometimes I wish silver didn't tarnish.

There is a book under my mattress about how God is like an apple. You know, like God the Father, God the Son, and God the Holy Spirit are like the core, skin, and flesh of an apple. But I don't think God is like an apple. I think God is sort of like light. Because light is very hard to understand, if you really think about it. How it somehow contains every color we've ever seen, and yet we can't actually see the colors unless something breaks them apart. There are a lot of things about light I can't understand, and I think God is like that. You just can't understand how he is three in one, because your understanding is limited.

I wonder why everyone loves to give out little wallet-sized pictures of themselves. I have done that twice in my life. I did it because it was the cool thing to do, and then later I thought, *Ugh! I'm doing something I don't like to do, and the only reason I'm doing it is to be just like everyone else!* I immediately stopped. I'm not trying to make fun of people who give out wallet-sized pictures of themselves smiling, by the way. I just wonder why everyone does it. Does everyone else love to have smiling faces of their friends around them all the time, or does everyone just do it because it's the cool thing to do?

The Notice

MY FRIEND Justin Doutrich (who I normally refer to as J. D.) recently posted this on his blog:

NOTICE:

If you are a young lady near the age of twenty years old, one Justin Doutrich has need of your services. The esteemed company, Swartzendruber Construction, is having a Christmas supper, and each attendant is required to bring an attractive date. This is a one-time offer with no strings attached, no long-term relationships hidden in the fine print, truly a free meal for having to put up with the above-mentioned male figure for an entire evening (6:00 PM–10:00 PM). Resumes are not required but e-mails are accepted (use link on this site). Requirements include: the applicant must be alive, at least moderately attractive, have a nice demeanor, and smell pleasant. Submit all applications during normal working hours.

Your country needs you.

I thought it was funny, but of course I didn't apply, being only seventeen and quite sick. But apparently poor J. D. had trouble getting a date, despite his advertisement of sorts (there is a lack of eligible females in our church), because Dad came into my room the other night and said, "Just so you know, J. D. is probably going to call you soon and ask you to his Christmas supper."

I smiled. "So he called you up and asked your permission, huh?"

"Yeah," Dad said. "He wondered if it was okay to take you, since you're only seventeen. But I don't think it counts as a real date."

Because, after all, it is sort of a Mennonite tradition to not date for real until you are eighteen.

I thought it would be fun. I thought I could probably go, even though I was sick. But I also began to think maybe I never wanted to go on a date for real, because despite there being nothing romantic whatsoever about our date, I felt nervous and awkward about everything.

I was nervous waiting for my phone to ring. I was nervous talking to him, which is odd, because I've known J. D. forever. He is my brother's best friend. Talking to him should not be weird.

I was also nervous about what to wear. Was it formal or informal? I decided on a white turtleneck sweater, which was the perfect choice, up until the moment I actually had to wear it.

I was hot and flustered, nervous and scatterbrained, sick and weak. He would be here any minute, and I still needed this, and that, and this other thing . . .

I heard a knock on the door. Oh no! Was he here already? I hurriedly filled my purse, borrowed from Mom, as out of the corner of my eye I saw someone let J. D. in and offer him a seat.

"Emily!" I heard Mom say softly, in her why-on-earth-did-you-do-*that* voice.

Huh? What had I done? I looked up.

Oh duh. I should have been the one opening the door and offering him a seat. I should have at least *looked* at him. What was wrong with me?

Thankfully, it was better once we got on our way, and much, *much* better once we got there.

There were two tables pushed together. J. D.'s boss Ben and his wife Ruth, my cousin Jessi and her husband Kevin, and another couple I didn't know sat at one table, while J. D., Brandon, Phebe, and I sat at the other table.

We had so much fun, us four. We made jokes the whole time, mostly centered around the disgusting orange soup we were served. It was awesome hanging out with them, because, being so sick, I don't get to hang out with my friends that often.

Somehow things were less awkward going back home, and we had interesting conversations about writing and fantasy. And then I was home, and everybody wanted to know how everything had gone.

Despite the initial nervousness, it was such a lovely evening. Just getting picked up at my house, and having my chair pulled out for me, and eating fancy food (and gross orange soup)—the whole thing made me feel so special.

I am happy inside.

Daphne

MY DIGITAL CAMCORDER came in the mail today! Unfortunately I can't film anything yet, because I need to buy tape. But it makes me indescribably happy just to take it out of the box and look at it. It is so lovely.

I named it Daphne.

Still Sick

WELL, WELL, WELL. Christmas has passed, and I am still sick. I always had it in my mind that I would be better by Christmas. Mom did too. Maybe we all did.

But we were wrong.

So now what? Am I going to be sick forever?

On a lighter note, I have decided to become a princess. Don't think I'm crazy. I'm just trying to cope here. If I wanna be a princess, who's gonna stop me?

Amy gave me a very wonderful pair of princess shoes for Christmas.

Yesterday, I got a call from Louise, an older lady from our church. She asked me what color I preferred in dresses: sage green or dusty plum. I said sage green, since I have been obsessed with green of late. And then she and three other ladies from church brought it over. A sage green wonder. A dress. The sort of dress a princess would wear to dinner.

Resolutions

ISN'T IT ODD HOW THE TINIEST, most insignificant things can do the most damage?

Perhaps if I had put on mosquito repellent or decided not to go outside. Maybe if I had swatted it or worn long sleeves instead of short ones, I could be going to school tomorrow, to study some hard, yet surprisingly interesting physics. Then I might head off to community college to take a class of college algebra. Imagine being able to comprehend those complicated math problems.

It's been four months since I got sick. Since then, I've been well for three weeks, near the beginning, but it probably wasn't true wellness. More like an illusion that I was well, though the West Nile was still there, dormant, waiting to attack again. Assuming, of course, that West Nile is what I actually have.

Part of me thought I'd be well by Christmas. The other part of me thought I would never ever get better. I pushed everything up to that deadline. *If I can get well by Christmas,* I told myself, *I'll be able to graduate this year without too much of a problem.* That was the main goal.

But look here. Christmas is gone. School is starting tomorrow. And I'm not going.

I used to have my life planned out. If you asked me, "Are you going to college?" I would say, "Next year I'll probably take a few courses at community college. Especially writing courses."

If you asked me, "Are you going to Bible school?" I would say, "I'll probably go to Biblical Mennonite Alliance (BMA) Bible Institute next year."

And most of all, if you asked me, "Are you going to graduate this year?" I would say, "Yes."

I suppose they weren't definite plans. But they were plans, and now I have no plans. Because now if you ask me, "Are you going to college?" I will say, "Maybe, but I'm afraid I could get sick in the middle of classes, and then where would I be?" or "Maybe, if the effects of West Nile have worn off by then."

Because mostly I don't think anymore. I don't plan. I just exist.

I wonder what my New Year's resolutions would have been if I had never been bitten by that infected mosquito. Would I have resolved to move mountains? To conquer the world?

Because now, all I find myself resolving is to do the two things I would have taken for granted. To get well and to graduate. But what's the point of resolving to do those things? It's not like I can help it if my West Nile decides to stay. What can I do if I open a textbook and find I can't even comprehend what it says anymore? And that is why it's so frustrating. I'm a puppet on a string, totally out of control of my own destiny.

The world would be an easier place if everyone I knew had gotten West Nile in their past, that way I wouldn't have to spend so much time explaining to people what it was like. So maybe someday someone else will have the same thing, and I'll make their life a little easier, because I'll know how to empathize.

Or maybe I'll become a missionary in some exotic place, and I'll get tortured for my faith, but I'll know I'll be able to make it, because I made it through this.

Or maybe I'm just supposed to learn not to worry about my future.

I don't know.

John McCane

SOMETIMES IT SEEMS LIKE I get weaker and weaker every day. First, milk jugs got heavier. Then I started walking slower and slower, and leaning on furniture more and more. They joked about me needing a cane, or a walker, or a wheelchair, and then Mom considered buying me one. A cane, that is.

Yesterday, she actually did it. I now have a cane. And of course it seems crazy for a seventeen-year-old to have a cane, but it's so nice to have it to lean on.

It was boring when I got it—a black, metal cane with a plastic handle. I glued a pink ribbon on it and tied it in a bow. I added fairy-tale stickers: a princess, a prince, a gnome, and a magical bird.

I named my cane John McCane.

I am wondering what will people say? What will they think? To see me, Emily Smucker, with a cane?

Maybe when I go places I can discreetly, you know, lean on furniture or something, and leave John McCane behind.

Maybe I need him too much to do that.

We shall see.

Back to School

I HAVE TREMENDOUS amounts of trouble doing my school-work, and I'm not sure why. I like to blame it on my sickness, but I have a secret fear it's not that complicated and I'm just lazy.

Sometimes, it feels like sickness makes it harder to think, and other times I think just fine. Sometimes I think sickness makes me lazier, and sometimes I think that's a really lame excuse.

It's usually easier to just push it from my mind and think about something else. But right now, school and schoolwork have been on my mind quite a bit, because I went yesterday. I went to school, really and truly.

Not that I wanted to. But I basically had to, because Dad is anxious to start on our senior Bible class. I need that class to graduate. I can't take it by myself later, because a big chunk of the class is discussing things. So now, once a week for half a day I have to go to school.

Anyway, I went to school yesterday, cane and all. I was so proud of myself.

But it wore me out.

And I hated school.

I should have loved school. I loved school last year. The whole student body was like one giant clique, and I was the center of it. I mean, not the *exact* center, but everybody was my friend, and I knew all the jokes and the inside stories and the latest things people had done. And yes, everyone is still my friend now, but I don't fit in anymore.

At first I thought, *Everything is the same. Why don't I fit in?* Then I realized that I've changed. Or maybe just my outlook on life has changed.

Me and them, we have totally different lives now.

More Randomness

IF I HAD ONE WISH, I don't know what I'd wish for.

Had to go to school today. It was noisy. Gave me a headache. Then some kid was scared to sit by me because he thought he could get West Nile. Hello, would I be going to school if I was contagious, potentially ruining everyone else's life? I don't think so.

All right, I'm grumpy. I'll admit it. I wasn't trying to make fun of the kid in the above-mentioned paragraph.

Violets are purple.

Ever since we got home from school, my little sister has been begging me to play Phase 10, our favorite family game, with her. I guess I accidentally promised to yesterday. *Arg zarg.*

A lot of people spell *a lot* as *alot* like it is one word and for some reason it annoys me terribly.

Someday I'll do something more exciting than going to school half the day and watching some kid try to play a board game and work on yearbook at the same time. I can't wait.

Once a girl took a picture of me for the yearbook. Or maybe she took two. Anyway, I think that's the first picture of me for the yearbook, except for the picture of the whole school. I was also making some pretty interesting faces, because it would take her too long to fiddle with the camera and I would get impatient and make an odd face.

Recently, I ate some lima beans. Actually it was before Christmas, but it feels like recently. I always thought I liked lima beans, but I guess I don't after all.

Especially since I once named a cat Lima Bean. Why would you name a cat after something you don't like?

The lima bean is also called a butter bean. Isn't that weird? Why would you call a bean a butter bean? Either it's butter or it's a bean.

However, I normally wouldn't care if someone called a lima bean a butter bean. I'm not always this grumpy.

Reading is fun. I have never understood how someone could not like to read. It's one of the great mysteries of life, way up there with why so many people love coffee.

Once a girl gave me a picture she had drawn. It was lovely. She was very excited to see me in school, I think. But she didn't tell me I looked better like she did last time. Maybe because I was so grumpy.

Actually I probably wasn't as grumpy then. How can you be grumpy when a girl gives you a pretty picture?

There is this thing that people do sometimes, where they hide a message in their writing using the first letter of every paragraph. So I just did it, but I am warning you, it is really lame. But I don't even care . . . so there.

No Sleep

I AM SERIOUSLY IN the most wacky, crazy mood ever. Sort of a cross between someone at a sleepover in the early hours of the morning and someone who has just been on a long, sleepless plane ride.

The cause for my weird mood is that I haven't slept in a long time. Once again I stayed up all night. And the results have been, well . . . strange.

Everything, even the most ordinary things, makes me laugh almost uncontrollably, which in turn is so weird it makes everyone else laugh.

I also have a weird sort of nervous energy. I just feel like tapping my cane on the floor over and over for no apparent reason. Now I'm tapping the keyboard instead. Pretty sweet.

Oh, and one more symptom. Dizziness. Dizziness. Weird.

There was something terribly interesting I was just going to say, but I forgot it so I will think of a new interesting thing to say. Oh, I just remembered the old interesting thing. I answered the phone at the same time as my mom. I did it on purpose too. I'm not sure why I did it. But I did, and it was my dad, and first he talked to me, but then he wanted to talk to my mom about something. I wanted to listen just to, you know, listen. So I listened, but I had a phone in one hand and a cane in the other hand. What does that have to do with anything? Oh yes, I wanted to put a cup in the sink. So I picked it up with my mouth and it fell out of course and banged around. I don't know why I'm saying this. I am not really thinking. I think my brain is half shut down. Maybe now you can feel sorry for my mom, because I already do.

A Real Narnia

YESTERDAY WAS ONE OF the rare occasions that I talked to my sister Amy on the phone. She told me about her students and things, and somehow, in some way, somebody got the bright idea that I could come visit her. I loved the idea of course, and so did she, and as soon as we hung up and Mom came home, I sprung it on her.

"Can I go to South Carolina and visit Amy for a week or so?"

Now I must backtrack and say that Mom has this thing about getting me to ask Dad things instead of asking her, since Dad is the one who always comes up with the best solutions to problems. So she said if I wanted to go, I needed to talk to Dad about it.

Then Mom had a talk with Dad. I didn't eavesdrop or anything, of course, but I'm pretty sure she told him I would love to take a trip to South Carolina, but that she wanted *me* to be the one to officially ask him.

Well, today I finally got up my courage and went into the living room, fully intending to ask Dad if I could. He sat up and looked at me expectantly.

It was weird how I felt then. Like I was staring at a glass box, with words floating and flying around and bumping into each other, yet I had no idea which ones to pull out of the box and use. Meanwhile Dad sat there, knowing the *exact* right words, just waiting for me to say them.

Finally Dad said, "Does it have to do with a plane trip?"

"Yes," I said.

"Does it have to do with a visit to the East Coast?"

"Yes," I said again. And then the words in the box settled down and I was able to choose the right ones from then on.

Dad told me that Mom wasn't sure I should go. He said Mom feels like she always has to push me to take my pills, and get up at a decent time in the morning, and work on my schoolwork. If I went to South Carolina, there would be no one to push me. If I could be responsible in those three areas for two weeks, they would look into sending me to South Carolina for a week and a half.

Wow. So many emotions. So much happiness. I feel like I've been living in a dungeon, and someone gave me a key and said, "Go through that door and down the hall, and you will end up in Narnia."

Narnia. South Carolina. What's the big difference? They both have new things, and adventure, and people I've never met. I want to meet someone new! What is two weeks of being responsible? I can be responsible for two weeks if I have South Carolina dangling in front of me like a carrot on a string!

The only part that troubles me is the "week and a half" bit. I'm afraid I'll have an amazing time and then have to come home again.

But here's the thing. I have a certain feeling that Oregon is making me sick or maybe just this house, and if I go to South Carolina, I will start getting better. Then they'll have to let me stay longer, right?

I know that Dr. Hanson shooed away the idea that Oregon is making me sick and was quite positive I had West Nile. And I believe him, now, I guess. Whenever people ask, I say I have West Nile. Really, if you think about it, it makes sense. But I still cannot shake the idea that if I could just get away, I would get well.

And that is why South Carolina looms in front of me like a Narnia of sorts. That is why I still can't believe I really, truly, might be able to go.

Blessed

I AM BLESSED.

Now I know that is a horribly overused and clichéd thing to say, but I realized today it is true. I am blessed. Even though I'm sick and have no clue when I'll get better, even though I have virtually no social life, even though it's my senior year and I don't even know whether or not I'll manage to graduate, I'm still blessed.

So why am I blessed, you may ask?

I read a blog today, and the girl writing it seemed to be very depressed. She felt like she was lonely, ugly, unable to be herself around people, and without a boyfriend, which upset her greatly. She felt as though life was pointless, useless, and horrible.

This made me realize that although I do feel lonely at times, I get over it. And I can be myself around people. Well, okay, maybe not when I'm feeling horrible or have a severe lack of sleep, but it's not like I'm acting like someone I'm not. And furthermore, I'm not pining for a boyfriend. I can actually say that, at this point in my life, I am glad I don't have a boyfriend. Of course, I am only seventeen and officially too young to date. But seriously, there are lots of seventeen-year-olds pining for boyfriends. Even if they are officially too young to date. And I think the fact that this doesn't bother me in the least is a blessing.

Now I must say that life frequently seems pointless, useless, and horrible. I lie in bed, late at night, unable to sleep, and think about my life. And most often what I think about is how pointless, useless, and horrible it is. But honestly, I think it would be nearly impossible for someone in my circumstances to never get depressed.

The point, the reason I am blessed, is that I can get over my depression. I can wake up in the morning, determined to make the most of my life, no matter how pointless it is. I am sick, and it makes me depressed at times, but I would choose West Nile over being sick with depression. A million times.

Snow Day

I FELL ASLEEP LAST NIGHT to the comforting sound of rain on the roof and woke up to the less comforting but much more beautiful sight of falling snow. Lots of snow. Tons of snow. Mountains of snow. Enough snow that if you weren't too heavy, and if you went to a part of the yard that wasn't under a tree, you might be able to make a snow angel without green shoots of grass sticking up through it and ruining the effect.

And what do you know, it was enough snow that they canceled church. I can't remember the last time that happened.

The snow made Mom happy. Really happy. I don't know what it is about snow that lifts her mood so, because it doesn't really have that effect on me. Rain makes me happy, which is weird, because we get rain all the time and we hardly ever get snow.

So my mom and I were discussing rain and snow and happiness, which led into a discussion about whether we would rather get proposed to in the snow or in the rain. Mom didn't understand at all why I thought getting proposed to in the rain was romantic.

"But Mom," I said, "remember that scene from *Pride and Prejudice* when he proposed to her in the rain? Didn't you think that was romantic?"

Mom shuddered. "With the rain dripping off of his nose? You thought that was romantic?!"

Ben, Steven, and Jenny played in the snow. Mom went on numerous walks, made a gigantic snowman (seriously about as big as the snowmen Calvin is always building in *Calvin and Hobbes*), and just looked and looked and looked at the snow. Dad and I didn't feel like making ourselves cold, wet, and miserable, so we stayed inside.

That evening everybody sat down to play a game of Phase 10.

The game dragged on and on. When we finally finished, we realized it had taken us three hours. Wow.

It sounds kind of bad to say that you're glad church was canceled, but I really am. It's so cool to spend extra time with your family. Singing "I've been waiting for you all my life" from *George of the Jungle* whenever you get the exact card you needed, hearing your dad accidentally say "I think I'll skip my mommy" instead of "I think I'll skip my wife," being constantly accused of being a "Peeker" by your brother after you just happen to see that he drew a wild card—those are the kinds of things that make great memories. Sometimes I think there is no one quite so fun to hang out with as your family.

Still More Randomness

SOMETIMES I THINK I could live off Dr Pepper and English muffins.

I just woke up, and it's 12:42 AM.

Tip for all of you out there who know someone who is really sick and don't know what to get them: get them an amaryllis bulb kit. Those things grow amazingly fast. It's so cool.

Why is it that everybody is always asking everybody else how they are doing? Seriously, the phrase *How are you doing?* is getting to be about as common as *Hello.* And to say *Fine* back is just like saying *Hello* back when someone says *Hello* to you. It's an automatic response. Yet, how many people are actually doing *Fine?* Maybe some, but certainly not as many people as say they are, I don't think.

But what are you supposed to do when the clerk at the grocery store says, "How are you doing today?" Not that I've been to any grocery stores lately, but I remember stuff like that happening after Lenny died too. The grocery store clerk or some similarly out-of-my-life person would say, "How are you doing?" and I didn't know whether to lie and say "Fine," like they expected, or say, "Well, actually my cousin just committed suicide, and I'm doing horribly right now, thank you very much." Seriously. I think we need some new phrases.

Church and John McCane

I WAS RESPONSIBLE FOR two weeks. I also went to church last Sunday evening. It's freaky going to church, because everywhere you go there are people, people, people. They all look at me, and ask questions, and say "You look so great!"

At least that's how I was afraid it was going to be. But I had to go, because it was part of my test. How could I go to South Carolina if I couldn't even go to church?

I was super weak last Sunday. It usually takes me forever to go from point A to point B. Sometimes it takes me forever and ever. Last Sunday was one of those forever and ever days.

It is amazing to me how fast people walk. I never even thought about it until I became a weak, slow walker. But now I'm the first to leave the house and the last to get in the van. As I watch the others whizzing by me, walking at their normal pace, I think, *Wow. I used to walk that fast.* It just about blows my mind.

At church, everybody stared at me and talked to me, but no one said the dreaded, "You look so good!" I probably didn't look too good, shuffling along with my cane. It was a relief to actually look how I felt.

In church I sat, with no place to rest my head, and conversed with John McCane in my mind. There is something very comforting about John McCane. I squeeze him and tell him things (not out loud of course), and then he says something comforting back. It makes me feel like I'm not alone, even if I am.

Sometimes I wish I could forget that John McCane isn't real and actually believe he heard me and was talking back. There are other things I sometimes wish I could believe too, like that I'm a princess. You know, like crazy people in books. What is it like to go crazy? Is it fun? I bet it's not boring.

I can make up a personality for John McCane and pretend to talk to him. I can pretend I'm a princess. I can make up all sorts of things. Pretending is interesting and fun and comforting and perhaps childish, but being childish is better than being bored, I think. But it's just pretending.

But wait! I'm going to South Carolina where it's exciting for real! In just a little over a week! It's hard to believe something so lovely and exciting could actually be happening to me.

Tongue for Dinner

WE HAD A COW TONGUE for Sunday dinner. The thing had been sitting in the freezer for a long time, and Mom finally decided we might as well eat it.

I don't know about you, but to me, the idea of eating cow tongue is, well, revolting. My mom actually felt the same way. "The gross thing about it is that you put it in the frying pan and it looks just like, well, a tongue," she told me, shuddering. I took heart in the fact that I would probably not be forced to eat any.

The family sat around the table facing a Crock-Pot full of potatoes with a huge tongue hidden beneath them. Gingerly, Mom reached in, pulled out a section of tongue, and put it on Steven's plate. Jenny and I politely declined. Matt, however, seemed to think the idea of having tongue for Sunday dinner was cool.

Steven and Matt picked at their pieces of tongue. Jenny, Mom, and I just ate potatoes.

"How's the tongue, Matt?" asked Mom after a little while.

"Mmm-mm," said Matt.

Mom glanced at Matt and screamed. He had stuck his piece of cow tongue in his mouth, so it looked like he had a huge, gray disgusting tongue, and was sticking it out at Mom.

Jenny and I finally consented to trying cow tongue, as long as it was peeled first. If you take off the thick, gray, taste-bud–ridden outer skin of the tongue, it doesn't look much different from a normal piece of meat. But it has a funny texture that I didn't like, so I only took one bite. Mom didn't eat any at all.

Most of the cow tongue got eaten by the dog, I think.

Wheelchair and Planes

JOHN MCCANE AND I flew to South Carolina. Everybody was looking at me as I walked by. Here I was, a seventeen-year-old Mennonite girl with a very bright skirt, a funny prayer veil on my head, and a cane. How often do you see that?

As soon as I was on the plane, I realized something I had never realized before flying with my family. It is extremely awkward to sit by strangers on a plane. You are so close to them, you feel like it is terribly rude not to talk to them. But you have no idea what to say.

I had to change planes in Atlanta. I walked out of that long hall-way connecting the plane to the building, and then just stood there as people surged this way and that, rolling luggage along, chattering on their cell phones, and knowing where they were going. Where was I going? Oh sure, there was a letter and a number on my board-ing pass telling me, but I didn't want to walk there. It was too far.

When we got my ticket we requested a wheelchair for me. Where was that wheelchair? Was it one of the three sitting off to the side with strong-looking guys standing behind them? Was I supposed to just go up to one of them and ask for a ride? Should I ask the lady behind the desk for help?

I was tired. I was hungry. I was confused. I was close to tears. I shouldn't have been close to tears. Stupid, stupid, stupid.

Have I ever told you of my strange fear of asking strangers for help? I wander around stores for ages trying to find things without ever asking the nice people with nametags for help. And perhaps I would have found the gate myself, slowly shuffling along, missed my flight, and burst into tears, if I hadn't caught the eye of one of the strong-looking guys behind the wheelchairs.

"Do you need a ride?" he asked, apparently noticing I was just standing there stupidly with my cane.

"Yes," I said gratefully. I sank wearily into the wheelchair.

And then we were off, pushing through the sea of people, cram-ming onto an elevator, and pushing through more people until we finally reached my gate. I switched from the blue wheelchair to the black airport chair. The strong wheelchair guy ran off.

On my way from Atlanta to Charlotte the flight attendant stood in the hallway, looked around, and said, "Is one of you Miss Smucker?"

"I am," I said.

"Did you request a wheelchair?" she asked.

I said I had. And when I stepped off the plane and into the Jetway, there was a wheelchair waiting for me, right there. But we waited and waited until pretty much everyone was gone before going back to the baggage claim.

And I couldn't get a hold of Amy.

When I got to baggage claim the guy behind the wheelchair said, "Do you see anyone you know ma'am?"

"No," I said, "I'll wait here until they get here."

As soon as he was gone I started crying.

Where was Amy? She didn't answer her phone. I called Dad. He didn't have any magic solution.

Another nice stranger came up to me. "Are you all right?" she asked.

I told her what was going on. She said comforting things to me.

And then Amy was there, telling me how sorry she was, that someone told her it took less time to get to the airport than it actually did, that her cell phone died. I dried my tears and collected my baggage and we were off, with me wanting to tell her all my flying adventures and her wanting me to shut up so she could concentrate on where she was going.

Just like old times.

Valentine's Day

IT SEEMS AS THOUGH every girl in the United States who does not have a significant other hates Valentine's Day. And yet I love it. Today, I got to wondering what it is that I love so much about Valentine's Day.

Maybe it's the valentines. I don't know why I love valentines, as they are never anything more than gestures of friendship, but who cares? I love them. They're so cute, and they indicate that you are special to someone, even if it's not some romantic significant other.

Maybe it's just the memories. It seems as though every Valentine's Day is full of good memories, whether it's making interesting and unique valentines for the whole school, making a valentine for Jesus and throwing it out a window like I did once when I was eight, or decorating heart-shaped cookies.

Or maybe it's something simple, like the fact that by Valentine's Day I am always over my winter sicknesses. In fact, this may be the first year I am sick on Valentine's Day, which is a weird thought.

This year, my Valentine's Day had the potential to be horrible, but in fact it was very lovely. I had an amazingly good day. I got to see my sister again, I met new people, and the weather was beautifully bright and sunny, but still nice and cool. And I did stuff, and while I didn't feel perfect, it was on the better side of things. It was the kind of day that makes me feel as though, maybe just maybe, I'm finally getting better.

Mitch

EVERY STORY AMY TELLS seems to be about her hilarious twelve-year-old student Mitch. Mitch did this funny thing. Mitch did that funny thing. Boy did I want to meet this Mitch. But for the first few days I was here, he was gone.

The day he returned was the day Amy and I did a skit for the students in chapel. Afterwards, they all had to file by and shake my hand. It was kind of weird.

"Did you meet Mitch?" Amy asked when it was over.

"Um, sort of," I said. "I shook his hand at least." He hadn't really seemed energetic and outgoing like I'd expected.

"Mitch! Come here!" Amy called. "Hey Mitch! Do you want to meet my sister?"

"We've already met!" he called over his shoulder and ran off.

He wasn't like I expected him to be at all. I was disappointed.

But wait! By the end of the day he apparently overcame his shyness of me. He sat by me and talked my ear off whenever possible. I loved every minute of it.

There are some people who think in such interesting ways that you can sit down and have a fascinating conversation with them without ever running out of things to say.

Mitch is one of those people.

Blisters and Sisters

A BLISTER HAS APPEARED on the bottom of my foot, making it difficult to walk. It is very odd.

Other than that, I feel better now than I have in months. Since about August, probably. I feel grand. The sun is shining, and the gravel is glittering, and if I don't try to throw anything or open any heavy doors, I can almost imagine what it's like to actually be in good health.

The only really bad day I've had since arriving was the first Sunday I was here. That was really weird because in the morning I didn't feel too bad, but then during praise and worship I got really weak and had to sit down. By the time praise and worship was over, I felt so bad that Amy had to take me home. I had to lean on the wall going out, since I didn't have my cane.

Last night at church this funny little old man came up to me and asked me how I was doing. "Are you better than last Sunday?" he asked.

I assured him that I was.

"You looked miserable," he said. "I thought you were blind."

I'm assuming the reason I looked blind was because I had my eyes half shut and I was leaning against the wall for support.

Anyway, besides that horrible Sunday when I felt sick and the old man thought I was blind, it has been going amazingly. Amy and I are doing all kinds of fun things, like having candlelit dinners with sparkling grape juice, watching movies, and of course talking and talking and talking.

To Leave or Not to Leave

I WAS SCHEDULED TO leave Monday, a week and a half after I got here. But all my theories turned out to be correct. I mean, since I've gotten here, I've felt great. So Mom and Dad will surely let me stay longer, right?

Wrong. It costs a lot of money to extend my stay. As for potentially moving out here for however long it takes to get me totally better or something, I didn't even bring it up.

But I don't want to leave. I mean, hello? *Every day* I go to school with Amy and help teach the kindergarten class. Every day I feel well enough to do this. Do you have any idea how amazing that is? And I get fresh air all the time because you can actually walk to places from Amy's home. Places like this amazing church that leaves its doors unlocked all the time, so you can go in and look at the beautiful green carpets and benches and the purple and yellow stained-glass windows. It is so beautiful and reverent that it amazes me.

And then there's Mitch, who never fails to do something interesting. And Amy, who is super, of course.

But mainly I *feel* so good, and I don't want it to stop. Isn't it worth a little extra money to make me feel healthier and stronger? I haven't used John McCane *once* since I got here!

Boy, was I mad at my parents. I wanted to say, "Hello? Look at me! Don't I look happy? Don't I look well? Don't you want me to look happy and well?"

Then I got the call saying, "Oh, we found a better deal, you can stay until Saturday."

Yay!

Pros: I get to stay longer! A whole week almost! I get to go to the cool February 29th party Amy's students are putting on!

Cons: I still have to leave.

But I'm going to make the most of it. When I get home I'll tackle my schoolwork with a vengeance. If I'm too sick to go with my family to Kenya in April, I'll go to South Carolina instead and hang out with Amy some more. That's two weeks right there.

I'll be back.

The Smart Mouse

ONE NIGHT, AS I WAS calmly standing around in the kitchen I saw a mouse run down the hall.

I shrieked (of course), Amy came running (of course), and we looked for it (of course), but we couldn't find it (of course). The worse part was that it was in one of the bedrooms. I was imagining waking up to find a mouse in my hair or something, but thankfully that never happened. In fact, there seemed to be no trace whatsoever of the mouse.

Ruth, Amy's landlady, set a mousetrap for us in our laundry room (actually it's more of a laundry closet). But a few days went by and not even a trace of a mouse appeared.

Then there came a day when we opened the door to the garbage closet and there were mouse turds on the floor. We got Esther, Amy's roommate, to move the mousetrap from the laundry closet to the garbage closet because we were afraid we would get our fingers snapped.

The next day, the cheese was gone, but the trap had not sprung.

We let it go for a few days, but finally we decided the trap needed some peanut butter on it instead of cheese. So we carefully scraped peanut butter onto the trap using wooden chopsticks, trying not to snap our fingers.

The next day, the peanut butter was gone, and the trap still had not sprung.

"I wonder if it actually *can* spring," I asked Amy.

"I don't know," said Amy. "Why don't you try it?"

I grabbed the broom to spring the mousetrap with, but while doing so I accidentally knocked over the mop bucket, which fell on top of the mousetrap and sprung it.

"Well, I guess now we know it works," I said.

Unfortunately, that knowledge didn't do us much good, as both Amy and I are scared to set the mousetrap again because it might snap on our fingers. Esther and Ruth are gone. And plus, there isn't much point in resetting the mousetrap anyway, because it is obvious the mouse is far smarter than we are.

February 29

PEOPLE SET UP LIGHTS, flowers, tablecloths, and candles in one end of the gym. Students practiced singing and playing their instruments. Everyone was preparing for the February 29th party, which the students were putting on for parents and people in the church as a fundraiser.

I just sat around videotaping and talking to Mitch.

We went home for a bit to change, and when we got back it was totally enchanting. The lights had been turned off, and candles and strings of twinkle lights glittered around the room. Everyone was all dressed up. Mitch had a black tie with little airplanes on it, and suspenders. Everybody loved the suspenders.

Mitch came up to me and bowed. "May I have this dance?"

"I'd be delighted, young man," I said with a curtsy.

The "dance" only lasted several seconds. As you may have gathered from the fact that I said, "I'd be delighted, young man," the only dancing I know how to do is what I've seen in movies and tried to imitate.

At this point I was thinking it was going to be quite the enchanted evening. But I was wrong. Because everyone had something to do except me. The girls prepared food and served it. The guys valet parked the cars except for Mitch, who is only twelve or so. He escorted the ladies inside.

But me? I sat around like an idiot until Shela, the only senior girl, handed me her camera and asked if I could take pictures for her. She was too busy. That was a bit unnerving, because she is a great photographer, and I am a horrible one. But at least it was something to *do*.

Then it was over, and people cleaned up, and we left. Yep, that was it. And tomorrow I'm leaving South Carolina.

But I'll be back.

Right?

Home Again

REMEMBER HOW MY greatest fear about going to South Carolina was coming back? Turns out it was a valid concern.

Nothing is new under the sun. I never thought I had anything resembling seasonal affective disorder (SAD) until I got back. Everything looks depressing. There is no sun, and there is no due west, and there are no breathtaking churches with purple and yellow stained-glass windows and benches covered in green velveteen.

As for the people, there is no Mitch.

I have been so lazy since returning. I had hoped I would be able to tackle working for Mom in full force, but it turns out I am still far too lazy. Laziness is a horrible thing to have. And yet, I didn't really seem to struggle with it in South Carolina.

It seems as though all I have been doing since I got back is complaining. I don't know why. But I just can't seem to get my life together like I had hoped.

Hyperventilating

I HIT THE GROUND RUNNING when I came home. Went to church Sunday, and though I skipped Monday, I went to school Tuesday, Wednesday, and Thursday, getting tests over with and out the door.

Thursday was when everything began to unravel.

Thursday was music class. I didn't wanna go. I haven't gone since September. But I figured now I would have to go back, since I was hoping to be in school pretty much full-time from now on.

The first thing we needed to do, said Jean, the music teacher, was run laps around the church parking lot.

"I can't run!" was my panicked cry. Only I was too embarrassed to make it audible to anyone besides the people right next to me.

"You can walk," said Bethany.

So I walked. I walked slowly. I got tired, breathless, weak, but I wasn't even halfway around. On I pressed.

And when I finally made it I felt a little silly that I was weak as can be from such a short walk.

Then I sat down for music. I was fine. I got over my lack of breath from the walk. And then we started singing.

A verse or two later, I was out of breath again. So I rested, and then I sang again. And I rested and sang. But when I began to feel lightheaded, I stopped singing altogether.

When we switched songs I turned the page, but I didn't sing. The lightheaded pangs didn't go away. They spread, sending secret shocks throughout my body. When we switched songs again, I found I didn't want to turn the page. So I didn't, and then I told myself to, so I did.

By the time we switched to another song, I couldn't turn the pages. My body would not respond anymore.

And there I sat.

Felicia said, "Are you all right?"

I couldn't look at her. I couldn't answer her. I hoped she would figure out that something was wrong, but she didn't.

The clock. I had to see what time it was. Go up, I told my eyes. Slowly, jerkily, they moved upward. Now to the left, I commanded them. They didn't want to obey. But I told them to, and in slow jerky motions, they focused on the clock on the wall. Five minutes. Five minutes until everyone would leave, everyone but me, and they would realize something was wrong.

My heart beat harder, faster. I looked at the other students, and it was as though I was in a bubble. They went on looking and acting and singing like everything was normal, but there in my bubble, nothing was normal anymore. It was like they were in a totally different world than I was—like I was watching a movie about them, and nothing they could do would affect me.

It was all so scary and sad that the tears I was trying to hold back slipped down my cheeks.

I breathed in, but no air came.

I gasped in desperation.

At that moment, the bubble burst. People turned around, and began yelling, "Open the window! Go get Mr. Smucker! Get her outside!"

Someone hauled me outside. Someone else got a chair. And whether they hung around for a while or went back to the classroom, I don't know, because all I could think of was the fact that I could not breathe.

Slowly I calmed down, and began to breathe more easily. My palms tingled. I began to tremble. I needed to get back to the classroom and finish my test. I was better now. Slightly weakened, but better.

I slept as soon as I got home. All evening and all night was spent on the couch with a small blanket, in my clothes, sleeping, then waking up, then sleeping.

And ever since then, I've felt horrible. It's like I took a gigantic step forward when I went to South Carolina, and then when I hyperventilated I took another step the same size, only it was backwards.

Strange.

The Dream

I JUST HAD A DREAM (I woke up in the middle of it, and now I'm writing this) that I will share with you.

Everything was going wrong for me. I was sick and weak—seriously, why can't I be nice and healthy in my dreams?—so weak that I collapsed onto the floor and couldn't get up. Then all of a sudden I realized I was wearing very little clothing. I was so embarrassed that I threw a blanket around my shoulders and ran.

There were a bunch of people outside, and I was so upset that I started singing to them. First I sang about how I always stood out in the crowd because I'm a Mennonite girl. Then I sang about how boring and bleak and horrible my life was because I was so sick, and how going to this youth retreat (so I guess I was at a youth retreat, though I had been hanging out with Tinkerbell in my dorm, so I'm not sure . . .) was supposed to be all wonderful and exciting, but more horrible things had happened there. My point was that I was running away from it all because I was so tired of it.

But the awesome thing about it was that it was just like I was in a musical or something. You know, background music mysteriously appeared, and I had a good voice all of a sudden. I've made up songs as I went along in real life before, but I don't think I've ever done it in a dream.

Anyway, I was running away as I sang, since that's what I was singing about. I ran and ran, but it was too good to last. I collapsed, of course, but at least I got to run. I haven't been able to do that in real life for about six months. Anyway, the last verse of song was all about how I was out of breath and was probably going to hyperventilate. I was lying on the ground, exhausted, but there was a small group of people who had followed me, all strangers, and they gathered around me. I had the feeling they really cared about me and were going to help me. And then I woke up.

Going Nowhere

AM I DESTINED TO go nowhere in life?

I did get to go to South Carolina. But there was another thing I was looking forward to, and all of a sudden I can't go. My Sunday school class was going to go to Eagle Crest for the weekend. I haven't hung out with my friends in ages, and Eagle Crest sounds like an awesome resort even though I've never been there. But now there's too much snow in the passes. We can't go.

That, by itself, I can get over. But pair that with the Kenya trip and am I destined to go nowhere in life?

I was thirteen when we went to Kenya the first time. Unfortunately, it was during one of those weird lulls where I didn't keep a diary. But I remember feelings I had while I was there, and read odd bits I scribbled down in notebooks, and it is fascinating. I want to go back. I want to experience it again.

Our family has all these plans to fly to Kenya again this April. We weren't sure we could, for a while, because there was all this fighting over there. But then the two guys who both wanted to be president signed some sort of agreement, and everything is fine and peachy. So we're planning to go after all.

Everyone but me.

My dad has this idea there's a chance I'll get a little better and be able to go. But not me. Or my mom. Because going to Kenya is a big trip, not a little one like going to South Carolina. And even if I could somehow handle it, there is so much disease in Kenya. I mean, what if I got something else on top of West Nile? What would it do to me?

I thought maybe Amy wouldn't be able to get off school for two weeks to go to Kenya, and I could stay with her over that time. But it's not gonna happen. She got off. Everyone is going but me.

Pink Jelly Beans and CPR

THERE IS ONE THING I don't understand about life, and that is jelly beans. Especially pink jelly beans. How can something look so cute and have such a cute name, and yet taste so gross?

I guess it's just one of those things that looks good and tastes awful, like lipstick or daffodils. I don't know of anyone who's ever eaten lipstick before. And I guess I don't actually know what daffodils taste like, only that they are poisonous. I heard about a lady who decided daffodils were so pretty that she was going to make a soup out of them. It killed most of her family, including herself.

That story was told to us as a cautionary tale in the first aid/CPR class we had to take today. So besides knowing never to eat daffodil soup, even if all your friends are doing it, I also learned to do CPR on a dummy I named Christine.

We also learned mouth-to-mouth, which wasn't as weird as I thought it was going to be. The dummy didn't really have a face, just a hole in its head that you stuffed a plastic bag into for a lung. Then everyone had their own personal rubber dummy face that snapped on, as well as a breathing barrier, so you weren't breathing directly into their mouth but into the breathing barrier.

But I still find the idea of mouth-to-mouth gross, so if you're planning on having a near-death experience any time soon and want me to rescue you, I would rather you be choking.

Day

I WENT TO CHURCH ON Sunday, but in the evening I did not feel up to par. *Should I go to the youth group thing? Should I go home?* The questions reverberated in my head.

Justin walked in. "What's up?" he asked.

"I'm trying to decide whether or not to go to the youth thing," I said.

"Hmm," said Justin, "let's list the pros and cons." He started listing all sorts of pros, but whenever I mentioned a con he tried to shoot it down. Then others started gathering around. J. D. offered to wear his red shoes if I would come. Heath offered to take me home. So finally I said, "Okay . . . fine."

"Come with us. We're leaving right now," said Justin, pushing me forward. I had to go tell Mom first, but once we were on our way, Justin, J. D., and I had a great time chatting.

The party was horrible and wonderful. My headache was brutal and the noise was overpowering, but everyone was so nice and funny. I was glad I had come. Sometimes excitement is worth pain.

I have been doing lots of stuff lately, it seems, like going to school every once in a while, or church or a youth thing, but I still feel sick. Sometimes I wonder if those feelings will ever go away.

I guess if I can live in the moment and trust in God, everything will be fine.

Night

I AM SUCH A LOSER.

Look at me. Look at my life. I'm graduating. I'm turning eighteen. I'm sick. Nothing is sound anymore. I can't just live anymore. I can't just make the best of what I have because I don't have anything anymore.

I am losing the chance to go to Kenya, losing it every day. And every day I think of new things, things I did and saw when I was there last time that I may never do and see again.

I want someone to tell my troubles to. At night, when everything rushes down on me, I know I must tell someone. But there is no one to tell.

Is all lost?

Right now I'm thinking maybe I should learn to do that cool thing they do in movies where they scream so loud all the glass breaks. Or maybe they sing really high and screechy but I don't feel like singing high and screechy. I feel like screaming so loud all the glass breaks. How awesome would that be?

Day and Night

EVERY DAY I CAN shove my problems aside and enjoy the good things life hands me, even if I am in pain.

Every night I cry in anguish because life seems so hopeless. It seems to never end.

Sinking Down

I AM ON A SERIOUSLY annoying downward spiral. I feel icky all the time again. Really icky. So all I do is sit at home all day watching movies and surfing the Internet on Mom's laptop for excitement, occasionally dreaming up things or watching rainbows dance in my eyelashes.

For about a whole week I cried every night. Deep, deep into the night when no one is awake, I would sob to myself, because life was horrid. Pointless. Insanely pointless. Nothing I did mattered. Nothing. And I couldn't go anywhere because of how horrible I felt. But I don't cry at night so much now.

I began writing simple blog posts about how I felt like screaming and stuff, because I was so mad at life but couldn't bring myself to out-and-out complain on my blog.

Then one night I went to bed early and woke up at one in the morning. I got on and what do you know—Shelley, my cousin Randy's girlfriend, had written me a comment asking what I felt like screaming about. Which was exactly what I was hoping someone would ask.

I wrote her a big, long, complaint-filled message. After all, she had *asked* why I felt like screaming. Then I sent it and went to sleep feeling much, much, better.

She replied saying wonderful things. All the nice things I hoped she would say and more. After that I didn't cry to the night nearly as much. But I began to feel sicker and sicker, which could be part of it, because sometimes my brain is too shot to even despair.

So here I am. It is late, and I feel horrible, body and brain. It feels like this setback is here to stay. And I will lie in bed forevermore.

Sometimes it feels like when my brother stomps up the stairs singing "When I was sinking down" in his really loud, low dramatic voice, he is personally tapping into something in me that is very raw. I want to shut out the world while I sink down. I want to lie still and dream of the beautiful things and the confusing prospects of life. I don't want anyone to talk to me, and the light needs to be turned off. I wish it was later, and no one would invade. No noise. No movement. And I could look out the window at the stars and sing the song in my heart, and no one would ever know.

Nothing at All

I DIDN'T WANT TO STAY HOME while my family was in Kenya. I wanted to have a mini-adventure, like going to South Carolina with Amy, only of course that didn't work out. So Mom posted about it on her blog and called relatives, and somehow we worked out this complicated plan.

First I'll be spending several days with Uncle Fred and Aunt Loraine in Oklahoma. The rest of the time I'll be in Kansas.

Wait, Kansas? Who do I know in Kansas?

Well . . . no one. But a friend of Mom's thought I should stay with Mom's aunt and uncle (whom I've never met) who live there. Only that didn't work out, so she found alternate housing for me nearby, with families from the church who have daughters relatively close to my age.

One of the families I've never heard of before. The other family is, of all things, the Mast family. The famous Mast family.

What makes them famous? They're just an ordinary family from Kansas, but my mom reads their blogs and is intrigued by them. She talks about them like she knows them. That's why the idea of meeting the Masts seems like meeting someone famous, because I hear about them all the time but never expected to meet them.

So how do I feel about the trip? Of course a small part of me is disappointed. I should be going to Kenya with my family and the other seniors in my class. Kenya is certainly more exciting and exotic than Kansas, that I am quite sure of. But it is also more disease-ridden. That is the last thing I need right now.

I should be scared too. I'll know my relatives in Oklahoma of course, but in Kansas I will know no one. What if they have a depressing house with dark walls, dead animal heads everywhere, and hardly any books? What if the people I stay with get on my nerves? What if I feel horrible and don't have anyone I know around to comfort me? What if the house smells weird? But for some reason I'm not scared anymore. I was, but now I'm not, and I'm not sure why.

But most of all I really should be excited. My life is so lifeless and boring; something like this should send me into frenzies of elation. When I heard I was going to South Carolina, I could hardly contain my joy. So why am I not more excited than I am?

I'm feeling nothing at all. It's weird to feel nothing when you should be feeling something.

Never Mind

OKAY, I'LL ADMIT IT, I didn't want to go. I don't know why, but I didn't want to. I didn't want them to go, either. I wanted everyone to stay home and wait for me to get better, and then we could go to Kenya together.

Well, all I can say is, be careful what you wish for.

One hour before we were going to leave, I checked my brother Matt's blog. Matt isn't going to Kenya with them. Did I mention that? He's away at school.

"Pray for my family," Matt said on his blog. "They are on their way *here*." I clicked on the indicated link and up popped an article about more violence cropping up in Kenya. Apparently, thinking we were already on our way, he hadn't bothered to call us about it.

"Mom," I said running downstairs. "Mom, I have to show you something."

She read it. She called Dad. Dad called people.

The verdict? No Kenya.

Which also means no Kansas. As soon as I heard that, I desperately wanted to go. Especially when Heidi Mast, the middle child of the famous Mast family, commented on my blog and said:

> *Emily, I was really sorry to hear that you aren't coming here after all! I'm Heidi from Kansas, and you were gonna stay with me for a few days and then with one of my friends for a few more . . . and lol, I can assure you that we don't have dead animal heads decorating our house, and I hope it's not dark and depressing! My sister is addicted to books so that shouldn't have been a problem . . . I have some food allergies myself, and when Mom was reading me yours I was thinking how much fun it would be to make you special meals. =) There's a group of us girls out here that were eagerly awaiting your arrival and think*

you sound like a blast! We were planning for a while all the amazing things we were gonna do while you were here—if you're feeling good enough. We had a drama picked out to do, parties in the hayloft, reading some of our favorite books out loud to you, etc. I think you're hilarious, and I love reading your posts! Anyway, us girls would love to have you come sometime anyway, even if your family's not going to Kenya . . . just want to let you know you're always welcome!

Of course I wanted to go more than anything after that, but it was too late.

And now, everyone is so disappointed about Kenya and I'm thinking, *Why did I wish for this? Am I crazy?* It's one of those times when it's really nice to know that somehow God has a plan all figured out. Seriously.

Every Ant Must Die

I WAS IN MY BEDROOM making tea. Everybody else was asleep. Blindly, I reached down to get a sugar cube.

I pulled out the box of sugar cubes. It was swarming with ants. Now I don't hate ants like I hate moths, but when there are ants swarming over something I just can't stand it. They simply must die.

Normally, I could bribe my brothers to do such a task, but my brothers were currently sleeping away.

The annoying thing about ants is that they are hard to kill. Seriously. You can squish them, of course, but then they stink and several ants might crawl up your arm by the time you have squished one. And it takes forever to drown an ant.

I sprayed the whole box liberally with all-purpose cleaner from the bathroom. Some of then shriveled up and died, while others walked around like nothing had happened. And still more ants kept climbing out from between the cubes.

Well. Back to the bathroom I went, this time getting the old plastic container that the toilet brush sits in and filling it with water. The whole box of sugar cubes got dumped into this. Then I carried the whole contraption back to the bathroom, where I squirted little piles of lotion over any ant that dared to climb to the top of the box, out of the water.

That'll show those ants who they're messing with.

And by the way, mint tea really doesn't taste that bad without sugar.

Alternate Vacation

THERE IS NOTHING QUITE LIKE cramming six people into a pop-up tent-trailer for a weekend. For one thing, everybody pretty much has to go to bed and wake up at exactly the same time, because the slightest movement vibrates the whole flimsy contraption and wakes up everyone else. I got around this rule by reading with the light from my cell phone after hours and going back to sleep every time someone woke me up the next morning. But the latter gave me strange dreams, all about my mom yelling at me to get up, chasing me all over the bed trying to whack me with a folding chair, and telling me I had hairs growing on my chin. I was so mad I woke up yelling, causing everyone else to laugh. It turns out that in reality Mom had been telling Ben that hairs were growing on his chin.

Most of the meals were eaten outside, due to the nice weather and the cramped living spaces indoors. But breakfast was eaten inside, with everyone stepping over boxes, trying to convert the bed into a table, dipping tea out of a pan into ugly plastic cups with a ladle that tended to drip.

But even with everything so cramped inside, it was really beautiful outside. And there is something adventurous about spending time camping in a little trailer with your family.

The reason we went camping was to have a little fun, even though Kenya got canceled. And it worked. It wasn't amazingly adventuresome, as I spent a lot of time just lying down in the camper, but it was still fun.

Like, that evening I followed the sandy trails all the way to the end, at the outskirts of town. I walked to the bridge, and then sat there, amazed I had walked so far. When did I get so much energy? I haven't used John McCane since I got home from South Carolina, but I still haven't been particularly strong.

I called Dad. He picked me up. I think he was annoyed with me for not coming back before dark but at the same time proud of me for walking so far.

All in all it was a lovely little vacation. It felt great. I read good books. I hung out with my family. What more could I ask for?

Three Quirky Habits

1. I have a habit of sitting in church and trying to position myself exactly right so it looks like the preacher is in the ear of the person in front of me.

2. Usually when I settle down to read I take my hair down to

get more comfortable. Then I take whatever was holding my hair up and fiddle with it while I read. I use my hair chopsticks to poke myself with, and if they are translucent I place them over the line I'm reading and try to read through them. I clip hairclips onto the book and onto each other and onto my fingers.

3. I tend to do a lot of strange things to occupy my time when I'm in the car, since I'm usually not driving. Since before I can remember I've always imagined a long knife jutting out from the side of the car and cutting down all the grass and trees and bushes and signs along the road as we drove along. Sometimes I just pretended that the car's shadow was a knife. Whenever I'm seated just behind the driver and it's dark, I try to situate my head so I can't see the oncoming car's headlights. They are always blocked by the driver's head. Then, when the driver's head starts to glow, I try to time myself exactly right so I quickly close my eyes, the car zooms past, and then I open them without ever seeing the car's direct headlights.

So there you have it.

Unmentioned Amazingness

THERE ARE THOSE WHO are so wonderful, so self-sacrificing, yet I never mention them. Why? Every day I should write of their amazingness.

How can I even begin to describe how beautiful my mom is? I complain, and she listens. Weeks go by. Months. Years could pass, and she would not change. She would still bring me tea on lovely little trays. She would still feel sorry for me when I complained. She would still do anything in her power to help me. Can you imagine a more beautiful soul?

And my dad. He always says, "Emily! You look so well!" It's quite discouraging, until I look in his eyes and see how desperately he wants me to get better. Normally he is very careful about saving money, but I believe he would pay anything if it would help me feel better. He pays for countless blood tests and doctor visits. When our family went to the coast for the weekend and I felt good, he was talking of taking me to the coast *every* weekend, if it would help.

But most of all it's God. Why does it feel like it would cheapen an unbelievably beautiful relationship if I blabbered on and on about Him? Yet why does the single most important thing in my life get left out of my writings so often?

How can I describe what God does for me? How can I explain the cold and lonely nights when I have nothing, nothing at all, but Him? When he says, "I have a plan," how can I describe the hope it brings, even though I can't see a faint semblance of anything good ever coming from this?

Yet I know He is telling the truth.

I trust Him. How can I not? He took my worries away.

Prize Capsule Machine

REMEMBER HOW I TALKED ABOUT the Mast family? It turns out that the oldest one, Hans, is currently in Oregon. He came to a church potluck, and we stood in line together. "Where are your brothers?" he asked.

You know those things at stores that look like gumball machines only they have prize capsules with interesting things in them, but when you put the quarter in and turn the handle, out pops a prize capsule with some cheap plastic doohickey in it that you don't even want? That's how my brain was right then. There are a million interesting answers to "Where are your brothers?" You could say "They flew off to Neverland," or "They ate too much food, grew two inches, and now they're hiding because they're embarrassed about how short their pants are" or even "I think I saw the Pied Piper go by a few minutes ago, maybe they followed him." But of all the interesting answers to pop out, it had to be, "Oh, they died."

I'm serious. That's what I said. "Oh, they died." He snickered slightly to be polite, since I was obviously trying to be funny, but I wanted to sink to the floor. Because, if you think about it, it was not interesting or funny at all. It was actually rather morbid.

Stupid prize capsule-machine brain.

May 2008

Skip Day

EVERY YEAR THE juniors take the seniors on a surprise overnight trip, skipping a day of school. Only this year the sophomores took us, because there are no juniors.

I always imagined my skip day to be like this: Me, Justin, and Bethany walk out of school, suspecting nothing. All of a sudden the sophomores go, "Hey guys, guess what, it's Skip Day!"

"Skip Day?" we gasp in surprise and astonishment as our moms drive up and hand us bags of clothes they packed for us. Then we all pile into a van and drive to some exotic place we never would have imagined going, where we have so many fun times it is impossible to count them.

Wanna know what really happened?

A week ago Mom said, "Emily, you don't know this, but you might want to pack your bags."

Sure enough, last Friday I was lying in bed feeling awful when Stephy called. "Hey guess what? It's Skip Day!" she said. "We'll pick you up at your house soon."

I waited and waited. Then they arrived and Ben came running upstairs, frantically throwing things into his backpack. I went to the van. Turned out the reason they got here so late was because they

210

also had to pick up Justin and Bethany. Bethany was at work. Justin was sick too. It was the first Skip Day ever that none of the seniors were in school.

Everything was wrong. I was sick. Justin was sick. The whole trip yielded only one halfway interesting conversation. I shot a decent movie with my video camera about monsters in closets, and did a funny acting game with the other girls. Other than that? Sickness. Headache. Watching other people have fun. I mean ick.

Most of the day I spent lying down at the beach house, while everyone else ran around in the sand and played football, and went shopping, and did all sorts of fun stuff. I mean, I sort of feel like I was cheated out of a decent Skip Day, you know?

The Room

EVER SINCE MATT moved out, his room has just been sitting there empty until Dad has enough time to redo it into a marvelous paradise for me. I've been waiting for that day since I was thirteen, and soon it will be here!

Dad drywalled it and hired a guy to come spread this white stuff all over the walls to smooth them out. I picked out the most enchanting green paint called "Shimmering Lime," but I wasn't strong enough to paint it myself, so we asked a lady from church who loves to paint if she could do it for us.

Now it's painted and all it needs are finishing touches and furniture and things like that. Steven finally started working on the ceiling today, filling the holes with something white. He stood on boards, which rested on sawhorses. Jenny loved the boards, riding them like horses and naming them horse names. I don't know why she called the boards her horses instead of the sawhorses, but then again, who can know the ways of Jenny?

I can't wait to move in! I've been trying to think of a good name for my new room. I considered "Tara" from *Gone with the Wind*, but it's too short and abrupt and not quite lovely enough.

Yearbook

ONE OF THE SEVERE DISADVANTAGES of being sick for the entire school year and being editor of the yearbook at the same time is that, as you may guess, it is very difficult to get the yearbook completed on time. Justin is the only other one who really knows how to do anything, and he can't make any final decisions without me.

Yesterday, Bethany, Justin, and I worked on the yearbook, staying after school and actually working a total of eight straight hours. Today it was only four. We got it done. All the yearbook pages are put together!

Tomorrow I will graduate. Mom bought me silver pumps. I can't decide if I like them or not. But I suppose I will wear them anyway. My silver dress is done, and so is my green jacket.

I finished my speech tonight. I have a distant pleading hope that it will be something lovely people will remember, something that will touch people, something that will make people see something, I'm not sure what. But I want *something* to come out of this. I mean, I'm not even really graduating.

I suppose since I was such a unique case, being sick the entire school year, the school board was lenient on me. I'm graduating, getting a fake diploma, and then finishing up the rest of my stuff at home.

So here I am, graduating, leaving school forever. And yet it doesn't feel like I'm leaving school forever because it feels like I already left school forever, a long time ago. For the first two weeks of school, between West Nile's first kick and his second, I felt like I was a part of school. Ever since then, every time I've gone back I've felt like I was just a visitor.

I peeked into the fellowship hall this afternoon. Shiny silver tablecloths with black graduation hats printed on them covered the tables. A huge poster was hung over the ugly window between the fellowship hall and the old kitchen, with something graduation-like written on it. And there were white and green daisies in pretty vases.

I hope that graduation will turn out well.

Graduation

GRADUATION WAS LIKE I ordered a chocolate cake and got something else instead, maybe a pickle. A really good, fat, juicy pickle. It wasn't chocolate-cakelike at all.

The auditorium was unbearably hot. The whole time J. D. was up there giving us an amazing speech about holding onto our dreams or something, I was afraid I was going to hyperventilate. I barely heard any of it. Amy brought me a glass of water and Bethany fanned me, and then went out to tell someone to turn the thermostat down.

Then it was time to give my speech. I was seriously freaked out about it. I mean, I was talking about my sickness because I couldn't very well talk about the school year, since I hardly was in school. The problem was, there is no good ending to my story.

My mom helped me write it. I told her all about the frustrations of being sick, missing out on life, and being uncertain of my future. She took notes. Then I stopped talking. I had no more to say.

"However . . ." she prompted.

Then I burst out with the main thing that was wrong with my story. "There are no howevers! I feel like everybody will expect me to say, 'However, all these wonderful character-building things came out of this so it was all worthwhile.' But in my mind there are no howevers yet! I still feel sick, and I don't think I've changed into some sort of wonderful patient person or anything like that. I don't understand why I have to go through this!"

"Then say that," my mom told me.

So I did. With everybody watching me, expecting me to talk about the special grace from God I received during my time of sickness, or about the amazing things I learned from it, or about something good that came from the pain, I told them the truth.

"I always believed before this sickness came that God would never give me more than I could handle. But I realized during this time that the big flaw in that is we can handle anything if we're not given a choice. We think there are things we can't handle . . . we'd just go crazy. But if something is handed to you, you just get through it if you think you can or not, because going crazy is a lot harder than it sounds.

"I can't say I ever got mad at God, or that I ever felt like He deserted me, I just don't understand, I still don't understand, so many things. I don't understand why I had to get sick in the first place. I don't understand why it had to be my senior year. I don't understand why it had to last so long. But most of all, I don't understand why I didn't get this outpouring of grace to go through this hard time like it seemed all those other people who have gone through hard times got."

My speech ended. I could see people, and they looked moved. Bethany discreetly brushed tears away. Justin told me, in a serious voice, that he thought I had done well. It gave me a fluttery feeling of happiness inside.

Afterwards many people told me just that. They loved my speech. They also congratulated me on graduating, which I didn't understand, since all I got was a fake diploma.

I opened piles of presents and talked, and opened more presents and talked, and finally, I was exhausted. I went home then. And that was it. The end. I left so early that no one even got a picture of the complete graduating class.

It was a nice enough graduation—I got presents and people liked my speech. But it was pickle nice, not chocolate cake nice.

Epic Randomness

SO FAR, THE MOTHS have stayed pretty much out of my way this year. I was beginning to think with some happiness that perhaps I had killed them all off last year. Not so, apparently. I saw a moth yesterday, but unfortunately I lacked the strength to go chasing after it. Steven, the moth rights activist around here, would be so proud.

I am tired of pills, pills, and more pills. Why does everyone think they have the magic pill that will cure me? Why do I have to try them all out?

Amy is home now, which means I have to move from her couch to my bed. Sometimes I wonder why couches are so much more comfortable than beds. But anyway, it's super having a big sister again.

Colorado

IN THE BOONDOCKS of Colorado, five-and-a-half hours from the nearest reasonably priced airport and somewhere around twenty hours from here, my cousin was getting married. Matt, Mom, Dad, Jenny, and I crammed in the car and drove to the wedding, every seat filled. Needless to say, it was a little squished.

We left at 3:30 PM, drove through the night, and arrived around noon. It seemed like all anyone wanted to do the whole trip was sleep. And somehow, none of us could. It was particularly hard for me, Mom, and Jenny, in the back seat. After all sorts of maneuvering and whining, Jenny finally put her head in Mom's lap and her feet in mine, and slept like a baby. But Mom and I, with our laps full of Jenny, couldn't get into a comfortable position to save our lives. And every time I shifted around I seemed to stick my fingers in someone's hair or poke someone else's toe.

Finally we arrived in Colorado, took nice naps, and then went to the rehearsal dinner. It was a strange rehearsal dinner. Neither the bride nor the groom were there.

The next day was the wedding. Matt got bored and drew the back of Grandma's head on his bulletin. I briefly met the bride's sister, who had candida for almost a year and so knows what it's like to have a long prolonged sickness, but I didn't get to talk to her much. I left the reception early since I wasn't feeling well, and the rest of the day I just hung out with my family and my Aunt Barb and my cousin Stephy.

Sunday morning, we all piled into our car to come home. Jenny was in a singing mood. She sang "How much wood would a wood-chuck chuck" over and over, and when I asked her to stop she sang

"Goo goo ga ga goo ga goo" to the same tune. She sang "If my brother told a lie, I could see it in his eye," which is a silly song I made up, only she sang it wrong, which drove me nuts. Then Mom bought her a cowboy hat at a gas station, since Jenny is all into horses, and after that Jenny attempted to sing Patch the Pirate songs with a country twang.

Nothing would make her stop. She would feel bad for annoying everyone, stop singing for about five minutes, and then start up again, repeating the song she'd been singing for the last two hours. Finally Matt decided to let her listen to his iPod. He was quite proud of himself, wondering why he hadn't thought of that solution earlier. But then Jenny started singing "mmm mmmmm in Texas, you gotta have a fiddle in the band." She mumbled the words she didn't know and sang some notes way too high and others way too low. Needless to say, it didn't exactly solve the singing problem.

This time, when we got to Salt Lake City, we dropped Dad off so he could fly home. That gave us much more room.

Slowly it got darker and darker, and Mom and Jenny fell asleep. I stayed awake to help keep Matt awake and to watch for deer. We drove and drove, and talked about Bigfoot in whispers, scaring ourselves good and proper. The desert road at night is a truly enchanting thing. And then we began seeing less and less sagebrush and more and more trees, and we were in the beautiful part of Oregon again, and I dropped off to sleep.

One More Test

I HAVE A SECRET WISH that there is something in Oregon's environment that's making me sick. I want to move and get better, and have an exciting life somewhere else. That's what I've wanted ever since I first got sick.

On June 10th I am getting a blood test. That blood test is supposed to tell me if Oregon is making me sick. I mean, I felt good in both South Carolina and Colorado. So what if there is some, you know, mold or something that I'm allergic to? One that only grows here?

There is no right answer. Who wants to be allergic to the place they live? And yet, if it promises excitement, that is what I am wishing for in my heart. There are things I don't understand, and this is one of them.

It is nice to know, though, that God knows what is going to happen and why it's going to happen. And that whatever happens I can know it was the best thing. Or at least the right thing. The thing that was supposed to happen.

Holding My Hand

I GOT BLOOD DRAWN again yesterday. As the doctor prepared the vials for the blood and the big ugly needle and all those sorts of things, my mom looked at me and said, "Do you want me to hold your hand?"

"Yes," I said, like I always do.

About halfway through the filling of the second vial, the doctor made some sort of comment that I just wanted a hand massage, and

I really didn't need my mom to hold my hand at all. I was a very brave girl, he said.

Yeah, yeah, doctors are supposed to say things like that. But seriously, I normally shrink away from touchy-feely things, and getting blood drawn doesn't really hurt very badly.

The thing about getting blood drawn, I realized, is that I hate the idea of it more than I hate the pain of it. Yeah, it hurts somewhat, but it's a pain I can stand. Because even if it doesn't really hurt, you can still feel that needle there, poking into you. And if you happen to look at it, even if you try your hardest not to, you can see that vial slowly filling with blood. Your blood. Something about knowing that gives me the chills and makes me want my hand held.

I'm not sure why I needed three vials of blood just to see if I'm allergic to Oregon, but that's what he took.

I Wish . . .

I WISH I COULD GO somewhere far away and meet someone new and do something exciting, even if it hurt.

I wish I could magically find a place to put everything.

I wish I could figure skate.

I wish bugs would sense my presence and flee. I saw a moth in the Honda today. I screamed, and Amy got scared. It died very easily. Then I came home and there were little bugs on the toilet paper. Ugh.

I wish everybody would say "pol-ka dots" instead of "poke-a dots."

I wish I would never accidentally be rude.

I wish I could wear costumes everywhere without being embarrassed.

I wish the doctor would just call and make an appointment for me to come see my test results already. I don't like waiting.

Tea Party

TODAY I WAS INVITED TO a tea. I love tea. I love dressing up. I don't understand why people stop dressing up and having tea parties when they grow up.

So I was all decked out in a silky pink dress, a floppy pink hat, white gloves, silver shoes, the whole nine yards. The other girls came dressed normally, and then changed into old bridesmaid dresses there.

We all sat around a beautifully decorated table and chatted about the dashing princes of our acquaintance.

We went on a walk, then, in all our fluffy pink attire. It was great to see people's expressions when they drove past us, and we all waved to them.

Dressing up, pretending, and drinking tea. What better way to spend your time? Unfortunately, it seemed to exhaust me a great deal, and, though there was a sleepover tonight that I was invited to, I did not attend.

No Go

I HAVE THIS LITTLE sick feeling growing in the pit of my stomach. And I am also feeling frustrated. And mad.

I am not going to the BMA Convention in South Carolina. I am upset. I really, really, really wanted to go. I was counting on going. Because I am longing for adventure, and I wanted to see Mitch again.

And there is more to it than that. I thought maybe if I went back to South Carolina I would feel well again. I want to feel well so badly.

But no, I need to stay home and watch over things here.

Sigh.

Lists

FIVE THINGS I DON'T understand about life:

1. Why everyone always seems to be bored and/or dissatisfied with their life.
2. Why you have to add sugar to applesauce but not apple cider, even though they are both made by just squishing apples.
3. Why people don't like to read.
4. Why I'm still sick.
5. Why I can only think of four things right now even though I'm always thinking of things I don't understand about life.

Five things I've learned because of my sickness:

1. No matter how many blood tests I take, they're all going to come out negative.
2. It's easier to lie when random people ask, "How are you?" than it is to explain the truth.
3. The whole idea that "God is never going to give you more than you can handle" is silly because you can handle anything if you are forced to.
4. I am going to be sick forever.
5. No matter how bad it gets it could always get worse, but somehow that thought isn't comforting in the slightest.

Five things I wish I was able to do:

1. Like every type of food.
2. Always have something clever to say.
3. Not be afraid to do things unless they are actually dangerous (like jumping off a cliff or swimming with sharks).
4. Read slow-moving classics without getting bored.
5. Make the most of life, despite my illness.

Five things I wish I had:

1. Picture frames to fit all my lovely fairy-tale pictures.
2. Better video editing software.
3. A place in my room to set my dressmaker's dummy, which I got for graduation.
4. Magic potion.
5. Some of that BBQ pork from that Chinese restaurant in Junction City—the place with the really gross water and the waitress who gives out back rubs.

Five weird things I've fallen in love with in a dream (or at least had a crush on):

1. A bird that was sometimes called a firebird and sometimes called a snowbird.
2. John Travolta's character in the movie *Grease* (I don't remember his name, probably due to the fact that I've never even seen the movie. Just read about it.).
3. This guy who was in this Christian band that had one song called "Eva Was a Mermaid." Only each time they sang it they made Eva a different thing (such as, "Eva was a cheeseburger," or "Eva was a mouse.").
He also worked in a mechanical pencil factory.

4. This guy who controlled (and lived in) the clouds, had really powerful black hands, wore silver earrings that were actually little scissors, and reattached his hand to his arm after it came off when I tried to climb up to the clouds with a rope tied around his wrist.

5. A clothespin.

Manderly

MOM AND I WENT "shopping" for bedroom furniture, checking out stuff we'd seen on Craigslist. I've always secretly, in the innermost depths of my heart, wanted a canopy bed. Well what do you know, some girl decided her canopy bed was too babyish for her a couple weeks after she started sleeping in it. She's getting a new bed, her dad told us, complete with Hannah Montana sheets.

Hmm . . . I wonder how long it will be until the bed becomes too babyish for me, and I beg for a new bed and some Hannah Montana sheets.

I named my bedroom "Manderly." I got the name from the book *Rebecca*, which is an amazing book. Only I spell it "Manderly" instead of "Manderley" because when I printed the sign for the door, I didn't realize it was spelled with an extra *e*.

Manderly will be a lovely paradise. I am currently in the process of moving in.

I have so much stuff it's crazy.

Staying Home

THERE IS A SMALL TOWN called Winston a couple of hours away. There is a little Mennonite church in the town of Winston, and every year they have a Vacation Bible School for the kids in town. Lots of kids come. The church is small. They need help. So last year Amy, Stephy, and I went to Winston for a week to help out. I can't even describe how much fun it was.

They're going again this year of course. They are but not me, and somehow that really hurts.

Not only that, but my family is taking a canoe trip again this summer. It's an annual thing. Matt and Mom aren't interested, but the rest of us like to go. We swim, camp, and paddle down the beautiful Willamette River. It is beyond lovely.

Canoeing is sort of my thing. No one else in my family can paddle a canoe as well as I can, except for Dad of course, and maybe Matt, but Matt lost interest in canoeing a while ago.

This is the way it usually is for me: I can spend all day learning to do something, like skateboarding, or playing a video game, or using a pogo stick, and Amy or Ben or Steven will come along and, in five minutes, be better at it than me. But canoeing is different. Canoeing is my thing.

And besides, there is nothing more lovely than paddling down the river at dusk, laughing with your siblings, and smelling the unbelievably beautiful smell of the river.

By now you may have guessed that my weak little arms can't paddle a canoe, and my weak little self can't sit in a canoe all day with no place to rest my head. You may have guessed that missing Winston, the canoe trip, and the BMA convention has me feeling much like I felt last March when I couldn't go to Eagle Crest or Kenya. And your guesses are right. That is exactly how I feel.

Only there is one more thing. The doctor called. I am not allergic to Oregon. So all my distant dreams of moving somewhere else, and meeting people and getting better, are dashed to pieces.

Good Lives

SOMETIMES I THINK my life is pretty good. I have a new, big-but-not-too-big room filled with wonderful fascinating things. I have a canopy bed. I have my own computer, my own video camera, my own dress form. Sure, I don't have a lot of money, but I don't have anything to buy, and I never go shopping anyway. Everybody keeps giving me wonderful things.

Every day I wake up in my beautiful canopy bed, with a satin bedspread covering me and a fuzzy orange pillow under my head. Sitting on a tray by my bed, there is always breakfast and Kenyan tea prepared by my dear mother.

I can sleep in as late as I want. I can go to bed as late as I want. I don't have to help with many chores, and if I am working and don't feel well because of it, Mom or Amy will usually be lenient. If I ask someone to do something for me, they will usually do it. I can read books or surf the Internet or watch movies or hang out with my cool, interesting family. I can write stories or read stuff I've written years ago or go into my amazing closet and become any character I feel like being.

Sure I feel sick all the time, but if I'm not really doing anything, it's easy to ignore it, and life just goes rolling right along.

In other words, I have a very easy life.

But sometimes, I visit random blogs and see people who, in their "about me" section, write "I am just one of the 'runners' in this crazy race we call life!"

Or "I love life and making new friends."

Or "I'm on the ride of my life and am hanging on for dear life!"

Or I go on Facebook, and my friends' status updates say things like "Susie Smith is aching from a long day at work . . ." or "Jessica Miller is going to the lake."

Or I go on virtually any young person's blog and read, "Sorry I haven't written in so long, I've been so busy . . ."

In those moments, that's when I tend to get jealous and hate my easy life.

If you would have asked me a year ago if I wanted a normal life, I would have said, "No way!" But back then I wanted an extraordinary life, not what I've got.

Now I just want a normal teenage life. I want to ache from a long day at work. I want to be so busy that I don't have time to post on my blog. I want to be on the ride of my life, you know?

I feel like someday I'm going to wake up and realize, *You know what, I've never really done anything in life. Why haven't I ever done anything in life?*

Sometimes I forget what it's like not to be sick.

Eighteen

I AM GOING CRAZY. I don't want to see anyone. I don't want to talk to anyone. All I want to do is lie on the floor and thrash around and make it all go away.

Today is my birthday. I feel horrible. I wish I could say it's the worst birthday of my life but it isn't. My worst birthday was the one I spent in the funeral home two years ago, when my cousin Lenny committed suicide. This is just a plain old horrible birthday.

I am eighteen but I don't believe I am eighteen. I can't make myself believe it. When my grandpa died I didn't believe he was dead until I saw him in the casket. I knew it but didn't believe it. That is how it is now.

How come I keep thinking about people I loved who died? Why don't I believe I am eighteen?

I don't want to be eighteen! Why? Because I was never seventeen. All I ever was, was sick. My last year of school, my last year of being dependent on my parents, my last year of being a kid, and I never got any of it. Now it's gone and I don't want it to be gone. I want it to come back.

I just decided that seventeen is the perfect age to be and I want to be seventeen forever.

I feel so horribly sick. I don't want to talk to anyone. I want to pull the covers over my head and make it all go away.

Allergies

YESTERDAY, A WEEK AFTER my horrible birthday, I woke up feeling odd. Oddly good. Not even close to totally better or anything, but good enough that it felt odd.

Wednesday, I'm getting lots of blood sucked out of my arm. When I was twelve, Dr. Hanson gave me a blood test, and figured out what foods I was allergic to. I still don't eat those foods, even though I probably got over those allergies.

After the blood test results come in, I may be able to eat chicken or cranberries or goat cheese again, but I also may find new things I'm allergic to. Still, I think I might like to have new things to be allergic to just to mix things up a little. Then again, I sort of lost my taste for apples and oranges and ice cream, and I never did like olives or goat milk or tin. Who eats tin anyway?

Ha! That reminds me, once my friend Preston told me that he and Justin figured out why I was so sick. Their theory was that I was building a tin shed and got really hungry.

But I would love to eat chicken and drink cranberry juice again.

Something Happy for Once

WELL . . . I WENT to the doctor and they stuck a needle in my arm, and lots of blood pumped through the needle and through a little tube and into these glass vials, and Mom held my hand and joked about how this is the one time she gets to hold my hand, yadda yadda yadda.

After that was all taken care of, and there was a cotton ball and a Band-Aid on my arm, Mom asked the doctor if there was anything she should know about the results from the previous blood test I had taken.

The doctor looked over my records and informed us that, when I got tested way back in November, my West Nile count was 57. When I got the last blood test, on June 10, it was 39. Normal is 30.

Okay, yeah, I was a little confused about what exactly those numbers mean, but I got the gist of it.

I am officially getting better.

It was very, very encouraging. He said that if I was tested again in six months he would almost be positive it would all be gone. I could have cried for joy.

I want to go to Bible School next year. Oh, and Kenya? Is it possible that I'll be able to go to Kenya too? My family is thinking about going around Christmas, you know, and if I could go along . . .

Of course Kenya and Bible School are months ahead, but honestly, this is the first time I've actually thought I might be well enough to go both places. I don't know, I just seriously think sometimes that I'm gonna be sick forever.

Somehow, the idea that I could still have months of sickness ahead of me doesn't bother me. Just so I can get well. I just want to know that I'm actually gonna get well.

The doctor also seemed to think that once I have an update on what foods I'm allergic to, that will help me feel better and get well faster. I certainly hope so. That would be amazing.

Lovely Thoughts and Things

MY LIFE HAS BEEN just right recently, and not just right as in perfect but just right as in right now, at this recovering stage.

And yes, it appears I am recovering. I keep having good days, pretty much ever since that Sunday I woke up feeling oddly good. I hang around, drinking tea and writing and just enjoying being in Manderly. It's nice, really, loving your room.

I don't go many places and do many things, mostly because harvest is on and everyone is working, but I like the whole thing of just being calm in a beautiful place while I dream of Bible School and Kenya.

I wonder what percentage of songs are about love.

The color silver is just shiny gray, but is gold shiny yellow or shiny brown? I asked Jenny that and she said that gold was shiny yellow. I argued with her, and then she said gold was shiny tan. But that was kind of silly because when I had said "brown" I was thinking "light brown," which is pretty much the same as tan.

My cousin Jessi just came over to chat with me. It was a lot of fun. I made her some tea. I wish more people would just come visit me randomly and I would make them tea.

I like my life right now.

Wake-Up Call

TODAY WAS SUPPOSED TO be the day when I would go in and get the results of my blood test, but in typical Emily fashion, the blood test "didn't work."

This morning Mom came into my room with my tea. "Are you awake enough for me to talk to you about something?" she asked.

I grunted.

She looked around the room, fiddled with this, fiddled with that, looked up, looked down . . . I wanted to scream. I have this weird pet peeve about people doing that, but have you ever noticed that when you have just woken up, your pet peeves turn into something more like torture? I couldn't stand it. "What are you doing?" I asked her.

"Looking for your sugar and a spoon, so you can drink your tea, so you'll be awake enough to talk."

Oh great.

"Just talk to me now," I said.

"Okay." She sat down. "It turns out the reason the blood test didn't work is because your white blood cells died out too quickly!"

"What does that mean?" I asked.

"I don't know," said Mom. Then she went on and on about how she looked up all this stuff online and she e-mailed Aunt Barb, who is a doctor. Mom was all worried because she was going on a trip and wouldn't be able to talk to Dr. Hanson about my poor white blood cells very soon.

"Why can't we just wait until you get back and then talk to Dr. Hanson?" I asked. "It's not like I'm dying or anything."

She gave me this look of astonishment and then laughed. "I never even thought of that," she said.

But she's still worried anyway, even though both Dr. Hanson and I told her not to worry.

August 2008

Saturday Cleaning

IF I WAS AT THE BMA Convention with my mom and Amy, I would have something of substance to write about. As it is, I am stuck home with the daunting task of keeping the whole house in order. Hello? I have trouble just keeping Manderly in order!

And, as today is Saturday cleaning, there's a good deal of vacuuming and washing and sweeping and dusting going on. And even worse, I need to try to motivate siblings.

Oh! I do have one thing to say. The other day I did something I never before realized I could do.

It started when I was looking at some flyers for the store Fred Meyer. There were these short little vests, and I couldn't decide if they were cute or weird. They were the sort of thing I might buy if they were for two dollars at Goodwill, but not twenty dollars at Fred Meyer.

Then I got a crazy idea.

I started pinning newspapers to my dressmaker's dummy, and made myself a pattern for a short vest. Then I found some black denim on the shelf of fabric that I'm allowed to use without asking, cut out the pieces, and sewed them together. I now have a cute little vest that fits me perfectly!

Now before you start thinking I'm some amazing seamstress, I must admit that I had to sew the whole thing with the serger because I couldn't get the bobbin in the sewing machine correctly, and Mom couldn't help me, of course, being gone. Furthermore, since I wasn't sure how to put seam allowances in a pattern, I just traced around the pattern with chalk and cut an approximate half-inch around that. I was planning on following the inside edge of the chalk with the sewing machine needle, which would probably have worked, but unfortunately that is difficult to do with a serger. As a result, I had trouble getting things to match up.

But I totally love it, even if one strap is a little wider than the other.

Stinkerbell

I WANT TO GO to BMA Bible Institute so badly. A year and a half ago Amy went, and the year before that Matt went. Both of them had incredibly good times. I am old enough now, and if I can just get my schoolwork done, get my diploma signed, and get well, I can go. Dr. Hanson says I'm getting better, plus I have been having good days ever since that Sunday in the middle of July I woke up feeling oddly good.

Of course there is the tuition factor, which is getting paid partially by the church and partially by my parents, but some of it I have to earn myself. Seeing as how I'm too sick to have a job, I have to resort to other means.

Enter Stinkerbell.

Stinkerbell is a character I made up, a fairy who stinks and tends to shed a lot of pixie dust. Orlis Avery is a garbage truck driver. I made up a story about them, painted pictures to go along with it, and spent hours on the computer making it into a little book. Mom took several copies to the fair with her when she went to sell her book, and nearly every one sold.

Yay!

I also wrote a story for these Sunday school papers our church gets. They accept almost anything according to my mom, and they pay well. I've sold them a couple of stories before, but as a general rule, I would much rather be writing stores about fairies drinking coffee than children learning lessons.

But like I said, they pay, and I need money.

Morning Person

EVERY MORNING I get up and drink my tea and sit at my window seat and watch people ride bikes or drive cars below my window. I get lots of stuff done then. Lots of schoolwork.

Then I get tired and am tired for the rest of the day. If I take a nap I will get enough energy to perhaps take a walk in the rain, and then I will be tired again.

It's odd to find yourself go from a night person to a morning person.

Ten More Random Facts About Me

1. I'm scared to look in the mirror when it's dark. It always feels like something horrible and freaky will look back at me.
2. I have a wart on the second toe of my right foot.

3. When I was little, I used to think high notes were low notes and low notes were high notes. When I took piano lessons I was very confused. (I didn't take lessons for very long.)

4. If someone gives me something and I hate it, I feel horrible, so I usually try to pretend it's magic, and then I can make myself love it.

5. If I was like Jerry Spinelli's *Stargirl* and didn't care a hoot if people thought my clothes were weird, I would wear costumes all the time—pretty costumes, not Santa Claus costumes or anything.

6. I have a habit of imagining amazing stories in my head, but when I write them down I realize that they have virtually no plot. It is very frustrating.

7. I used to write a random fact about me on every blog post, but then I realized they all had to do with food. Like how I don't like eggs except for the yolk of soft-boiled eggs, or how I like to eat pie dough, or the way I like mustard but not ketchup, or tea but not coffee. It was embarrassing. So I stopped putting a random fact about myself on every blog post.

8. I have two pink hats. I am wearing the one I got for my graduation right now. I got my other pink hat in Mexico. As soon as I put it on my head, I knew it was just right.

9. I've always wondered what it would feel like to faint.

10. I have a stuffed frog named Professor Dough-Head.

The Results

APPARENTLY I AM ALLERGIC to caffeine and cane sugar. What? No more lovely black tea in the morning? With sugar? I suppose now I can eat apples and oranges and cranberries and poppy seeds and carrageenan gum and even goat cheese, but still . . .

Cane sugar is in everything. Seriously. Tortillas, clam chowder, you name it. Everywhere I go, I have to read labels. It's a good thing I'm sick and don't often go to friends' houses or out to eat because what would I do then?

And caffeine, I mean, I'm tired enough as it is.

I'm also still allergic to chicken and some other things with odd sounding names. Like dibutyl phthalate. I mean, what is that anyway?

One more thing. I have now been sick for an entire year. I'm glad I didn't know it would last a year when I first got sick.

Application Fee

THINGS WERE GOING SO GOOD. The doctor predicted I would be well in time to go to Bible School, and my parents and I figured out a way I could actually conceivably do it, financially and all. First term would start just after Christmas, and I would go with Amy, Bethany, J. D., and Brandon. But I would go second term too, and the other people from my church would go home. Just me against the world.

Suddenly, I had a renewed ambition to get my schoolwork done, because I obviously can't go to Bible School without a high school diploma. And even though my life was boring, I could stand it, just dreaming of what was to come.

I filled out the forms that were for me to fill out, and gave reference forms to different people I knew. Everything was ready. I carefully sealed the envelope and proceeded to the mailbox. The whole world seemed full of promise.

But wait! I had forgotten the stamp. Back inside I went, rummaging around in the office.

"Do you have a check in there?" Mom asked.

Oh, duh. The application fee, $150 per term. "I forgot," I said. "Can you make out a $300 check?"

Mom was hesitant. "I don't really feel comfortable putting a $300 nonrefundable check in there without asking your dad first," she said.

"But Dad already said he'd pay the application fee!" I said, starting to panic. It felt as though my dream of going to Bible Institute in 2009 would vanish before my eyes if I didn't get that check in the mail in five minutes. But my earnest begging and pleading amounted to nothing.

It turned out that Dad thought the entire application fee was $150. So he had to e-mail the headmaster and ask if I could have the application fee for second term be refundable if I felt too sick to go.

By the time the headmaster replied, I realized that there is no way I can know now where I'm gonna be in January. Who can know if I'll be better or not? There is no guarantee. I could be sick forever. I am not going to Bible School, and I am terribly depressed about it.

Why I Feel Depressed Today

1. I didn't get much sleep last night because there was a moth in my room that wouldn't die.
2. I had a horrible dream that made me wake up feeling sickish.
3. I spent all morning cramming on schoolwork since I've been slacking off, on account of not having any Bible School motivation.
4. I am still far behind on schoolwork.
5. Remember the story I sent to the Sunday school papers our church gets? Well they rejected it. The rejection slip said, "Thank you, but I do not need this story." What does that mean, anyway? That my story was horrible but they want to let me down easy, or that they have enough stories and don't need anymore, thereby ending my get-rich-quick-by-writing-stupid-stories plan?
6. I worked on a Xanga message off and on all day and then somehow erased it.
7. Facebook acted all weird and goofy today.
8. My room went from being a little messy to a huge mess.
9. I am not going to Bible School.
10. I can't have caffeine or cane sugar.

The Day I Would Just as Soon Forget

THEY ALL WENT TO Justin and Stephy's house to play volley-ball. Not me. I was sick with sadness and depression.

I lay in Manderly all alone. *You can't let it beat you,* I told myself. So I took a shower and dressed in a funky outfit and started walking to Stephy's.

I saw the youth group in the yard playing volleyball. But just as soon as I sat down to watch and catch my breath, they were done, and standing around talking. I went over to stand around and talk with them.

"Shall we do something?" they asked each other. "We could, you know, go out to eat."

Going out to eat seemed a good plan to them. Not to me, of course, but I wasn't about to spoil their fun. They discussed where they would go and what vehicles they would ride in. I tried to swallow the lump in my throat, but it just got bigger.

What was I supposed to do, go and drink water? Send the waitress back into the kitchen countless times to see if certain foods had sugar in them? Is this stupid sugar thing going to ruin my life? I started walking home. I burst into tears.

Halfway through the first field I saw headlights, and my friend Lyndon's blue rig bouncing through the field. He stopped in front of me and rolled down his window. "Want a ride?" he asked.

It was pretty much dark already. I squeezed in along with all the other people Lyndon was taking to whatever restaurant they had decided on. I just sat there, staring out the window, tears streaming down my face. It was embarrassing, but I didn't even care anymore.

"Do you want me to take you home?" Lyndon asked.

"Yes please," I said.

Now I'm alone in Manderly again. And I wish I could just forget today, you know?

A Job

I GOT A JOB, SORT OF, driving our van full of kids home from school every day, and dropping them off at their houses. I also have to help out in the classroom some. Since there were a lot of students who had things they needed to read out loud today, I spent a good deal of time there listening to them read.

Josh is one of the younger kids, and he cracks me up so badly. He had a bit of a hard time reading, but acted like he really wanted to learn. He paused in the middle of the passage he was reading and said, "How about you read a word and then I read a word? That's what my mom does."

"I would," I said, "except it wouldn't be fair, because all the other kids have to read everything."

Then he started fake crying, so I started fake crying too . . . "Boo hoo! I just want to be fair!"

He laughed and laughed, and then sat up straight and finished reading the page without a problem.

Later, in a story we were reading, there was a character named Ace talking to Baba, his pet lamb. Every time Josh came to the letter *I* he thought it was *L*.

"No," I kept explaining, "it's *I*, not *L*, because sometimes they leave the little marks off the top and the bottom."

"There are lots of *I*'s," he said. "I want to count the *I*'s."

So he counted them and then started reading again. I think there were ten.

Soon he came to another *I* and again thought it was an *L*. When I explained it to him again, he said, "Bike. Is bike an *I* word? Can you say some *I* words?"

So I said "dike" and "spike," and he laughed. "Let's say some *I* words every time we come to an *I*," he said. But then it was break time.

The whole ordeal wore me out terribly, though. I came home and took a four-hour nap.

Unfortunately, as a whole, life still feels pretty pointless. I mean, I have nothing to look forward to. I guess I should just be glad I have a job and good days. That's what I wanted, right?

But there is nothing new on the horizon at all. Even our Christmas/Kenya plans seem to be backfiring.

Just Ask

TODAY I PRAYED WHILE taking a shower in the dark, and that's when I decided something. I need to talk to my dad about this. I have no inspiration to do my schoolwork anymore . . . no inspiration to make money, really, and no inspiration to go through life happily, because all I have to look forward to is endless bleakness.

I've told my mom about this before and she feels sorry for me. But my dad is more of an answer man.

If I do my schoolwork and try to pay half, is there any way I could go on a vacation somewhere?

Please?

I just need something to look forward to.

I must ask him. He can make things better, but he can't make things worse.

Not Living

TODAY WAS A HORRIBLE BEYOND HORRIBLE day in terms of how I felt physically.

My cousin Justin got video chat on Instant Messenger. I've never video chatted before in my life and it was fun, only we couldn't actually talk to each other . . . just see each other.

I am not living life anymore. I am dreaming it. I am so sick everything is like a dream. Who in real life would do a video chat without sound and be beyond amazed?

I don't know what to do now because I know I can't sleep and I am so hot and miserable, and, if you can believe it, still trying to wrap my mind around the wonders of video chat.

I can't read. It hurts my head. I could watch movies endlessly, but hey, that is what I was doing, and I can't do that all night because, seriously, that would be pretty crazy.

I never did talk to my dad because I got so sick and you can't talk things through in a rational undreamlike manner if you are crazy sick.

I spent a good deal of time today trying to rationalize what keeps trains from running into each other.

Dad

STILL CRAZY SICK.

Oh, I talked to Dad today despite my horrid sickness. He was beyond amazing, and approached it with all his problem-solving skills. I was crying and carrying on like a crazy person because I am sort of, well, crazy right now, and he made all these plans. And I might go somewhere someday . . . like Kansas to see the famous Mast family or something. I am so relieved. I have something to live for now, so that is amazing. I should have talked to Dad about that problem ages ago.

Everything is not so hopeless after all.

The Shower

I HAD A LOVELY SHOWER in the dark and was sitting on the floor (still in the dark) thinking about guys who hate cats, and the door started to open. Like someone's coming in!

I screamed. Loud. Gut reaction, hello?

Oh yeah, did I mention it was three in the morning?

It was Matt. He wanted to turn off the fan, and my scream totally freaked him out. He didn't think anyone was in there, you know, since the light was off.

Helminthosporium

HELMINTHOSPORIUM SATIVUM is currently voted "most likely to rock my little world." I didn't even know what it was when it showed up on my allergy test along with cane sugar and caffeine and whatnot. So I just sort of ignored it.

It's a major reaction though. The others—cane sugar, chicken, locust bean gum, whatever—they are all minor reactions. So Mom has been doing research on helminthosporium.

Turns out that it is some mold that grows on grass in mild wet climates. Well, what place has more grass and mild wet climates than here? The main crop is grass for Pete's sake!

I don't know why this *helminthosporium sativum* didn't show up when I got tested to see if I was allergic to Oregon. But if this brings me excitement and wellness, I'll take it. I really like the idea of moving and then getting better. I always have.

The Coast

I DECIDED TO GO TO the coast with my older Smucker cousins. I still feel horrible. But all I was doing all day was watching movies and knitting. Everything else was hurting my head. It's beginning to feel like I live in a movie instead of in real life. So maybe a change of pace will be good for me.

Everyone is having so much fun. Everyone but me. I lie upstairs in bed watching movies or knitting like always. Sometimes I make my way downstairs and try to find something to eat, something I can have. It is terribly, terribly hard.

I haven't gone to the beach yet. I probably won't at all. I am too sick. I can barely make it up the stairs sometimes.

People talk to me. That is fun. It makes me laugh.

Then I lie in the dark, hearing everyone else laughing and having fun, and I feel so absolutely alone. That's when I cry. It is so much easier to have no life when I'm alone in Manderly. It's so much harder when I can hear the laughter and none of it is mine.

I wonder if the good points of this trip will outweigh the bad— if it is worth it to laugh if I am also going to cry.

More Helminthosporium

HELMINTHOSPORIUM SATIVUM. That's what we talk about these days. Where could I go to get away from it? Will I get better if I get away? How can we know?

I want to get away so badly. I want to have an adventure and get better. I don't want to leave my beloved Manderly forever, but I would rather have wellness than Manderly. No question.

October 2008

Redmond

IT IS 3:16 AM, and for the life of me I cannot get to sleep. Under normal circumstances, this would not bother me. I would just read or write or twiddle my thumbs until I did fall into restful slumber, and sleep in as late as I wanted the next morning. But as it is, I am currently sharing a hotel room with my parents, and they are both sound asleep. I tried reading with my cell phone for light until I ran out of battery. I tried going to sleep several times but it never worked. Now I am trying to type while sitting in the bathroom so the light and tapping sounds won't wake up my parents.

We are in Redmond, Oregon.

I am hungry. So dreadfully hungry. I could eat an apple, but even though I am apparently over my apple allergy, homegrown apples still tend to give me stomachaches. I could eat saltine crackers with peanut butter, but how messy would that be? In the dark and all? And plain saltine crackers are drier than dry, and I am already feeling dry. My eyes are dry. My lips are dry. The inside of my nose is dry. There is no wetness here in eastern Oregon like there is in the valley.

Tomorrow we are going to look at apartments. I may move here.

This bathroom floor is not a comfortable place to sit. Maybe I'll sit in the bathtub. Ah, much better. Yes, I am sitting in a bathtub in a hotel in Redmond writing at 3:30 AM. That sounds very interesting. The thought makes me a little happier.

I want to get better so badly. You have no idea how badly. I can hardly imagine myself better. I remember a time I played volleyball over and over, or a time I partied all night and how much fun I had, and I think, *How could I do that? Didn't I get tired? Didn't I get a headache? What was it like to feel so wonderful all the time?*

I need my sleep. I can't drink caffeine so I am bound to be tired tomorrow.

Ten Reasons Why I Am Moving to Redmond

1. Redmond is one of the driest cities in Oregon. If there is no moisture, helminthosporium can't grow.
2. If helminthosporium can't grow, my terrible immune system can improve.
3. If my terrible immune system improves, perhaps I will finally be able to push West Nile from my system.
4. Redmond is only two-and-a-half hours from home, so someone in my family or one of my friends should usually be able to stay with me.
5. After an extremely annoying wild goose chase involving a studio apartment, an office in a closet under some stairs in an obscure building in Bend, and weird complications involving the fact that I am living in the apartment but Dad is paying, we finally found a suitable place. It's safe. It's close to important things like the library. It has a bathroom, a kitchen and living room, and a bedroom. Plus it has beautiful windows.

6. I need adventure. I need something new. I've wanted it ever since I first got sick. Actually, I've always wanted it. But not desperately like while I've been sick.

7. The sky is beautiful. Well, okay, technically that played no part in deciding to move, but it is definitely an added bonus. I mean, I knew western Oregon was wet and eastern Oregon was dry, but I never made the connection in my head that dry equals beautiful cloudless sky.

8. There is a good Mennonite church a half hour away that I can go to. The people there are so nice and welcoming. Unfortunately, there isn't a youth group. But it is still a great church.

9. I need to be tested, you know? Because while I am convinced that moving here will make me better, based on things like South Carolina and going to Colorado for the wedding and feeling better in the dry summer months, Dad is still a tad bit skeptical. He wants to see if I improve over several months and then arrange for a more permanent place to live.

There is no tenth reason. If there is I can't think if it. But it looks dumb to talk about nine reasons for something.

10. I thought of another reason! Redmond was founded on my birthday.

Okay, that was a pretty lame reason.

Wide Awake

I'VE BEEN DOING SOME weird half-sleep thing for the past five-and-a-half hours, and now I'm awake and tired and hot and stressed out because I have a gazillion more things I need to pack before I leave in twelve hours. I am so hungry. My head hurts so badly. I am wide awake. I don't know what to do. It's one in the morning.

A New View

I'M HERE, SITTING AT my new window, looking out over Redmond, my new home. It is lovely outside. The sky is dusty blue, and there are pink clouds.

I love this window. What will my life be like while this is my window, my view of the world? What will happen to me? Will I be happy? Will I be sad?

I don't know. I haven't the faintest clue what the future holds, and I love every minute of it. Anything could happen! Anything but lying on my old bed in my old house facing the same thing day after day like I have for the past year.

Do you understand what I'm saying?

There is hope.

Epilogue

I have a job.

I have a cute little motor scooter to get places on.

My new window and view of the world is in the tower room of a very old Victorian house in Colorado.

And while some would look at the above statements and say, "Yay! It worked! She is all better, and now she has a perfect life," the truth is, I am not all better. But I am some better. And Redmond did work.

Unfortunately, while Redmond did amazing things for my health, there were things it lacked, too. For instance, as it turned out, the Mennonite church was far away enough that it was too hard for me to build relationships with the people there and really feel like a part of the church. In Redmond, I also had to do without a youth group to hang out with and a place to serve. Colorado has all those things, plus a dry, helminthosporium-free climate. It also is the home of a family that has been friends with our family for ages. They treat me like I belong to their family, since I am so far from my own.

The Mennonites out here have a mission: raising babies born to ladies in prison. When the mother is released, the baby is given back to her. If it weren't for the mission, the babies would go into foster care, and the mothers would never be able to get their babies back. I find it so beautiful and self-sacrificial.

The mission also runs a couple thrift stores that help support the mission, and they gave me a job at one of them. A job with a totally flexible schedule. If I feel icky I can go straight home. If I feel great I can work a couple more hours. It is amazing. Totally amazing.

All I can say is that somehow it all worked out.

And every day I get a little bit better.

Book Club Discussion Questions for EMILY

1. Much of *Emily* is based on the author's blog, which she writes primarily for friends and family. What did you find unique or interesting about Emily's writing style and voice throughout the book?

2. Emily is a Mennonite, and her religious affiliation is a big part of who she is as a person. What kinds of things did you notice in Emily's social, school, and family life that reflect her Mennonite background? How do these things differ from your own experience? How are they the same?

3. How do you think Emily's overall outlook on life is based on the way she handled the challenges of West Nile?

4. Put yourself in Emily's shoes. How would you feel if you were diagnosed with a rare and incurable sickness such as West Nile? Who would you turn to for help? How would you cope?

5. Emily goes to a Mennonite school with thirty-two students. How do you think the social scene would differ at a school this size versus your school? Do you think it would be easier or more difficult socially to attend such a small school as compared to a more typical-sized high school?

6. When Emily is at her lowest point and is feeling like life is hopeless, she often turns to God for comfort. Have you ever felt

this way? What kinds of things do you do to find comfort and solace when you're struggling with feelings of hopelessness?
7. *Emily* takes place over the course of a year and a half. Did you notice any changes in Emily's maturity and perspective as the story progressed?
8. Emily shares her unique quirkiness through her writing, such as her habit of naming inanimate objects. If you were to write a memoir of your life, what quirky things would the reader discover about you?
9. Did you learn any surprising or interesting facts in the course of reading this book?
10. Is *Emily* a story of hope? Why or why not?

About the Author

Emily Smucker loves to write. She keeps a regular diary and takes a notebook with her everywhere she goes. Emily is a Mennonite and born-again Christian, and considers her heroes to be Peter Parker, Hadassah, and Luke Skywalker, because they made the right choice and it changed the world. She loves dreams, Dr. Pepper, badminton, watching people, making movies, and unlike 99.5 percent of Mennonite girls in America, not coffee or scrapbooking. Her online blog can be found at http:///www.xanga.com/SupergirlEmzel.

Marni

Chapter I

I HAVE A TON OF IRRATIONAL FEARS. I refuse to cross streets without a clear sign that it is my turn to walk. I am afraid of driving because I have trouble telling my left from my right. I am scared of snakes, spiders, beef jerky, unnaturally colored foods (like Jell-O), and technology in its many forms. I also fear spandex. Don't ask me why. What I try really hard not to fear is the truth. I always want to know who should be held responsible, even if it's me. And a lot of the time, it is me. Sometimes I don't even realize that until years later, when I wake up and think, *Wow, how lame am I for trying to blame someone else for that?* Answer: exceedingly lame.

So I don't blame anyone else for my hair pulling. I refuse to bore you by wailing about how if it hadn't been for my dad, or my sister, or our beauty-obsessed consumerist society, my life would have turned out differently. Partly, because it just isn't true. All of those were factors (maybe even large factors), but they don't explain why I have an insistent craving to reach up and pull out my hair. Why I long for the rip and relish the sensation. And I suspect that blaming my love of pulling on other people is just as fruitless as blaming Toll House for my love of raw cookie dough. There are times when people need to stiffen their spine, nod their head, and admit they do it to themselves. For me, that's pulling.

It didn't start out as this big convoluted heap of ugliness in my life. It turned into that, sure, but at the beginning it was something much purer. I wasn't doing it to be mean to myself, or to punish myself, or to abuse myself. It wasn't nearly so dramatic or masochistic. I honestly thought I was beautifying myself. A little part of me even thought that pulling might make my life better. Maybe if my eyebrows were more attractive, people would notice me as being someone special. Maybe then I wouldn't feel like I was always being passed over and slotted in the role of the understudy sidekick who would only be in the play if something happened to someone else. I honestly thought that if I were prettier (and had the self-confidence that goes with it), maybe my life would be better. I thought pulling my eyebrows was one way to get there. It didn't work out that way.

Instead, I found myself clutching long strands of hair I had ripped from my head, unable to stop myself from reaching up and wanting more. My pulling was never supposed to take on a life of its own—it was never supposed to take over mine. I knew it had, though. When I stared at the mirror and tried to recognize the girl without eyebrows, eyelashes, and bangs as myself and failed, I knew something had gone horribly wrong. It's hard to recognize yourself when you've pulled at your eyebrows so consistently that there is almost nothing left. It's hard to believe you could have done something so destructive to your face, and that tomorrow you have to go to school pretending nothing is different.

At some point in my life, I stopped being Marni and instead turned into an addict who ravaged her head when she didn't think anyone was looking. I pulled during breakfast, lunch, and dinner. I pulled at school, in restaurants, in grocery lines, in my room, in the bathroom. If I were in a Dr. Seuss book, I would pull in a box, I would pull with a fox, I would pull here and there, I would pull most everywhere. There was no way to escape it. Hair has a tendency to travel with a person—it's even more persistent than a shadow that way—and mine came with an incredible temptation to zone out and lose myself in the soothing rhythm of my plucking.

How did I get this way? I still wonder that sometimes. How is it possible that I am so consumed, so obsessed, with something that brings no real comfort to me? Why can't I stop? Why must I make a New Year's resolution to kick the habit, only to end up hating myself even more when I am at it again the next day? Why am I so ashamed of something I don't feel I have control over? How did I go from a happy-go-lucky kindergartener who believed in fairies, to a teenager with the urge to yank, pinch, and pull until there is nothing left to grab? Some of these answers I just don't have. To be honest, I don't know if anyone has them. How did I get here, though? Well, that I should be able to tell you. All we have to do is go back to my childhood and my very first lie.

Chapter 2

I CAN'T REMEMBER A TIME when I couldn't read. I took to it so naturally that I never needed an adult to help me sound out the words. Assistance of any kind was quickly deemed completely unnecessary. The librarians readily handed over the more advanced books and wracked their heads for a series that would engross me long enough until they came up with something else. I happily spent the majority of my childhood curled up on the nearest couch, lost to my surroundings. In elementary school, I read during lunch, through recess, while walking home, after school, and before bed. My best friend, Gwyn, would shake her head with a mixture of amusement and disgust when I'd nearly walk into parked cars and trees because I was focusing solely on a book. Gwyn let everyone know I was one strange kid, which didn't exactly come as a shock— they knew it already.

Not that I was some prodigy who only found comfort in the complete works of Shakespeare. If someone made me pick between a book and an ice cream cone, I would be biting into the crispy crust before the question was finished. In many respects, I was painfully normal. I had a normal fear of phys ed class (especially anything that involved tumbling, running, rolling, climbing, jumping, or coordination of any kind) and a strong sense of self-preservation. I didn't read everywhere to prove I was special or different. I did it because, even at the age of five, I knew I wanted nothing to do with reality. It was *way* too messy.

In the imaginary world I refused to leave, I wasn't the runt of the family, pushed around by my older siblings Jordan, Jonathan, and Shayna. I didn't have to listen to the constant bickering and fighting that comes with sibling rivalry. My own mother never cried in any of the stories I read. My world was contained in a bubble full of mystery and freedom. I couldn't understand why anyone would want to join "reality" when they could have amazing adventures with King Arthur and Merlin. So, I would grab a book, peer inside, and escape. It soon became the easiest, most natural thing in the world.

Reading was by no means my only method of evasion. I also used GRS (Golden Retriever System) to romp fearlessly around the neighborhood with our family dog, Rusty. Since Rusty always found his way home, I had more faith in him than a map or a compass. I reasoned that if I stuck by his side, nothing bad could happen. Together, we frolicked all over the neighborhood, returning to find the police and a frantic mother waiting for us. All the warnings in the world wouldn't have made much of an impression on me.

No matter what anyone said, acorn caps were really fairy boats and trees were really magical giants who guarded me while I slept. Mythical beings and magic were barely out of my reach, and I was certain that if it hadn't been for my birthday, I would have been happily whiling the days away with the fairies. My birthday was the one thing I knew had gone horribly wrong.

I should have been born on Halloween. All the rules of magic and nature agreed *that* should have been the day. Instead, due to an incompetent doctor who showed up several hours late, I entered the world in the wee small hours of the morning on November 1st. I blamed my lack of magical powers entirely on this birthing misfortune. The Disney Channel movie *Halloweentown* didn't help improve my spirits. The main character, Marnie, was born on Halloween, and she could cast spells and visit a magical world where Halloween never ended. Our almost identical names and birthdays were undeniable similarities and informed me of the truth: my birthday was a mistake that a magical being (aka my elusive fairy godmother) needed to remedy. She never showed up though, and I learned rather bitterly that fairies weren't to be depended upon. If my special powers had arrived, I would have consoled myself by reflecting that being born on the Day of the Dead was still interesting. Since they didn't, however, and I was likewise cursed with muddy brown hair, equally dark eyes (which my brother Jonathan kindly described as dog-poop brown), and a well-padded stomach, I refused to be soothed.

Just because my magic powers didn't show up didn't stop me from reading about them. I soaked in everything I could find on heroines and heroes, dwelling in particular on King Arthur. I loved that the scrawny underdog pulled out the sword and emerged triumphant. Happily ever afters in any story made me feel euphoric. I felt so strongly for the characters I would cheer and moan and rejoice for them. Sometimes, I would sit happily under a bush listening to a book on tape and wonder whether life would work out perfectly for me. I also wanted to know if I could train a bird to carry messages to Gwyn. To be honest, I still have no idea. Not about the bird—that question was firmly negated.

Reading became my life, and my life became reading. It was also the subject of my first lie. Long before I turned five, I had convinced my dad that I didn't know how to read. This wasn't exactly a difficult feat to accomplish. My father's life was based in his accounting firm in Los Angeles; mine, in a messy room in Ashland, Oregon.

Given that my parents' marriage was still intact at the time, this living arrangement might appear strange. Whether or not it was conventional, it was still highly agreeable to everyone. My father could work without giving his family a second thought and visit when it was convenient, while my mom could raise her four children with little interference. The only reason my parents were able to stay married for so long was because they didn't share a house (or even a state). This arrangement also made it pathetically easy to convince my dad of my illiteracy.

Looking back, I can make a pretty good guess as to why I pretended I couldn't read. It wasn't because I didn't want my dad to think of me as intelligent. I wanted him to be impressed with me. I wanted him to love me. I lied because I knew that intellect wasn't the way to his heart. After all, he didn't like my sister Shayna, and she read voraciously as well. Since he wasn't impressed with that, I thought maybe illiteracy would do the trick. I didn't realize at the time it was a desperate ploy for attention. My four-year-old self couldn't grasp what was going on. What I could understand was its immediate success. All I had to do was feign ignorance around my dad, and I was in. So, I stuttered and bumbled through picture books I could have read upside down with one eye closed and felt rewarded with his attention. My dad had no idea I was acting, which is no compliment to his intelligence as I have always been a lousy liar. He just didn't know me well enough to tell. My plan worked; I became Daddy's little girl. He chose me to be his favorite child. And for a while, that was all I could ever imagine wanting.

Chapter 3

THE DIVORCE DIDN'T COME as a surprise, as the marriage had always been more fiction than fact. When my dad did come home to visit, the quality of life deteriorated for everyone. He spent the majority of the time on the telephone making angry business calls. The rest of his time was spent pressuring Jordan, dismissing Jonathan, reprimanding Shayna, and doting upon me. I have to admit that back then, from where I was standing, things could have been considerably worse. I could do no wrong; Shayna, no right. I think my dad sensed from the beginning that Shayna possessed a strength of will and conviction that I lacked. He was looking for someone who was easy to manipulate, and there was no one with less resistance than me.

In the movies, being the favorite child always comes with benefits like bigger weekly allowances or later curfews. For me, there weren't any perks except the assurance that Daddy liked me. We didn't really do anything meaningful together in Ashland. My dad never quite understood the concept of "special time"—ultimately it was all about him. If I suggested we go see a movie, I would find myself watching an artsy Nepalese film about Sherpas. The film made up with subtitles what it lacked in plot. Not so much fun when you are seven years old.

My most treasured moments with him were fairly indistinguishable from his work. The proud owner of the local Laundromat, my dad would take us down to the store every time he came to town. We were then granted the privilege of entering dark, lonesome, tunnel-like rooms behind the rows of machines. That was where the real excitement hummed; it was a miniworld composed exclusively of cement, canals, and soaking treasures. The machines thoughtfully dumped money left carelessly in pockets into the waterways before me. I spent hours in the detergent-scented tunnels searching for a prize, lost in mystery and darkness. It was an alien place unlike any other, and I loved it. It never occurred to me to be upset my dad was always busy arguing with one of the managers and ignoring all of us. As much as I enjoyed going to the Laundromat, it wasn't enough to make me wish he visited more frequently. Most of the time, I wanted him gone just like everyone else. The house never felt right when he was in it.

So, when my parents led me into their bedroom and explained that the marriage was over, I didn't really care. I don't think I really understood what it meant. Sure, I knew the concept of divorce: two people no longer together. What I couldn't see was what difference that would mean for me. Nothing seemed to change in the slightest. My mom still loved me, and my dad still visited when it suited him. The only real contrast was that instead of visiting the Laundromat, he was dragging my mom through an ugly divorce. My mom did her best to hide this from me. She didn't want any of us to feel stuck in the middle. In my case, she was entirely successful because I felt no urge to pry deeper. Divorce didn't belong in my imaginary world, and I had no intention of incorporating it.

My nonchalance about the whole thing concerned many parents at my elementary school. Polite, perpetually upbeat, and charmingly innocent, I was an easy kid for people to worry about. Mothers in particular hated the idea that I was being ripped apart by the strain of divorce. They would approach me, eyebrows furrowed in unease, and ask deep, probing questions.

"Are you all right?"

"How are you hanging in there?"

"And how does that make you feel?"

They never expected my answers.

"Everything is great. I feel fine. He visits all the time. Never been better. We're all okay. Really. Thanks for asking."

I honestly thought I was telling the truth. As far as I was concerned, everything continued without a hitch. In fact, things only got better, because at that point, I had also discovered the first Harry Potter book. I felt an instant connection with the "Boy Who Lived." We were both spending our formative years surrounded by Muggles who couldn't understand that we were just plain different. My mom had read the first one aloud to us before it was popular, and I was instantly hooked. By the time my elementary teacher agreed to read it to the class, I had it memorized. I mouthed all the words in perfect time, not caring that my classmates were staring at me instead of the teacher.

Immersed in the world of Harry Potter, I was sheltered from the divorce. When my spirits dragged, I concentrated on writing a sequel to the first Harry Potter book, divining things in my crystal ball, using a quill and ink, and building a hammock outside my room. All that I was able to create was a few sloppy pages of writing (my one attempt at fan fiction) and a large blue stain on my carpet where the ink spilled. Still, I was diverted from the battle that was raging around me. I didn't have to worry about any of the big questions: *Who gets the kitchen table? The cabinets? The kids?*

I was oblivious but not stupid. Eventually, I noticed the change. It wasn't hard to figure out once my dad stopped visiting. He disappeared from Ashland and only set foot in the town a handful of times once the divorce was finalized. Years later, he told me it was because it was "too hard . . . emotionally." I don't believe a word of it, especially since it took him so long to come up with that excuse. In the beginning, he just demanded we fly down to see him.

Since all of my relatives, from my grandparents to my cousins, lived in Los Angeles, flying to see him wasn't that unreasonable of a request. In fact, it worked out pretty well for everyone. We usually spent the first night at my grandparents' house before Dad would collect my siblings and me. My mom stayed with her parents until we were ready to go home.

The best parts of those trips were the times I spent with my grandparents. We'd watch old movies, do the morning word jumble, feed the squirrels, and tell stories together. Their house was on the short list of my favorite places in the whole wide world. It was neat and clean without feeling sterile. Better yet, it was filled with decidedly unusual purchases from their travels. Colorful rugs entertained me for hours, and I carefully traced patterns in them with my feet. More than the objects, I loved the people inside the house and the relatives who visited.

Visiting my dad wasn't the highlight of those visits. I felt obliged to spend time with him, but I doubt I felt real happiness. Seeing him was sort of like applying for a job. I paid so much attention to being on my best behavior (all smiles and enthusiasm) that I couldn't really relax. My grandparents didn't require that type of effort. I could be me. Once I left the safety of their house, however, that wasn't the case anymore.

I don't know why he wanted us to come in the first place. In the movies, the dad always misses the children horribly and does anything to see them. My dad didn't belong on the Disney Channel. If he missed us, he sure had an odd way of showing it. As soon as we got to his home, we were piled into his car and then dropped off to see his mother, our Grandma Joyce. The only time we actually spent with Dad was limited to the car rides back and forth and an occasional museum outing. Even when we were in the same city, I hardly saw him. So much for bonding.

He came up with a way to explain the situation: it was my mom's fault. If she just allowed him more time, then he could spend a few days with us after our stay with Grandma Joyce. Of course, if he hadn't dumped us at her house, he could have done that anyway. My dad didn't see the logic behind that simple idea.

What he did see was the opportunity to create a convenient system for himself. He thought he fulfilled his paternal responsibilities by picking us up, dropping us off, and going back to work. Blaming the arrangement on my mom was just icing on the cake. If anyone asked how we were doing, he could shake his head mournfully and say that he hadn't seen us lately because of the divorce. Meanwhile, at Grandma Joyce's house, the four of us were waiting to go home.

Her house was the complete opposite of my other grandparents' home; it was an unmitigated disaster, with gargantuan piles of junk everywhere. The only area where a clumsy girl could walk without fear of tripping was in the garden. That was where my siblings and I were soon put to work. No visit was complete until we had done our share of manual labor. We had a complicit understanding that boiled down to "You scratch my back, and I'll scratch yours." In this case it was "You pick up disgusting rotten fruit, and I'll take you to a museum." All things considered, this was not a bad deal. Sometimes it came with smoothies and *Doctor Dolittle*. Most of the time though, our reward was listening to her complain.

Everyone has different talents, and Grandma Joyce has a natural gift at whining. If she was forced not to complain, I suspect she would become a mute. Very little was agreeable in her eyes. Things she approved of were limited to:

1. Her son
2. Her garden
3. Discounts

And for a while, she approved of me. Probably for the same reason my dad did—because I was eager to be loved and easy to control.

Her favorite topics to moan about were my mom, the divorce, and Shayna. This didn't change even when Shayna was in the room. In fact, that was when Grandma Joyce encouraged me to tell Shayna what I really thought of her. Grandma Joyce even made me practice ordering an imaginary Shayna to back off and leave me alone. Since Shayna hated me and tried to walk all over me, I can understand why Grandma Joyce thought I needed protection. Unfortunately, she was just making a bad situation far worse.

Shayna had plenty of provocation to hate me. My spineless, bobble-headed submissiveness to Grandma Joyce was just another complaint to add to the list; it wasn't the real reason for her enmity—that had begun long before Grandma Joyce ever contributed to the problem. As soon as Dad decided to love me over her, I had become the enemy. As far as she was concerned, I was the devil in sister's clothing.

Dad's preference was too marked to be a matter of opinion. It was a fact. I was his favorite child and had been since before I could even walk. It wasn't a position I competed for, but one I heartily accepted. I loved being loved. Shayna hated being hated. It's not hard to guess which one of us got the short end of the stick. Dad and Grandma Joyce had trouble even tolerating her.

After stewing over what happened for years, I think I understand how it all fell apart. Once my dad realized Shayna could not be manipulated, he cast her aside. She in turn cast me aside. This left me at the mercy of my father when abroad and at the mercy of her when at home. Shayna's contempt for me only became more pronounced over time. She hated me with an intensity she didn't even try to conceal. We fought over everything and nothing.

I desperately wanted Shayna to love me, so I hatched a plan. I thought if we could bond over something, she would learn to like me. It seemed like a sensible idea, so I waited for an opening.

Everyone believed Shayna was the writer in the family. She fit the bill perfectly, especially considering the notebooks she perpetually carried around. Our family predicted Shayna was an Emily Dickinson in the works. Without having read so much as a page, I was positive her writing was brilliant. Shayna had a way of speaking that with each syllable proved her intellectual superiority. I couldn't imagine her writing would be any less intense, and I bowed before her acerbic tongue and sharp wit. Secure in my inferiority, I decided to write something of my own so we could bond over writing. Everyone loved it. Everyone except Shayna, that is. According to her, it was a shameless imitation of one of her stories I had overheard. What's worse, she saw it as an artless, calculating ploy to get attention.

My protests and apologies were flatly ignored. What I had intended to bring us together only drove us further apart. Shayna banned me from reading her favorite books and swore that never again could I read her writing, since I would just try to copy it. Her rants about plagiarism cemented in my mind, and I began to fear writing. I was afraid that maybe she was right about all of it.

So I took a lesson from the ostriches and hid my head in the sand (or in my case, books) until the danger was averted. Like the ostriches, I soon learned my approach wasn't the most effective way to handle problems. There was no way to escape my family life, be it my dad or my sister. The divorce made neutrality an illusion and impartiality a farce. I had to pick a side. The question was . . . *whose?*

Chapter 4

MY REALIZATION THAT I HAD no real relationship with my dad came about through a series of small epiphanies. I began to notice things I had missed before. Slowly, I discovered ulterior motives everywhere I looked.

When he didn't dump me with Grandma Joyce, my dad either took me to his office or to museums. Of course, I preferred the museums (with the notable exception of a Holocaust exhibit that haunted me for months) since there was always something to look at. His office, on the other hand, afforded no entertainment. I was so bored, I actually gave his assistant free back massages. At the time, I would have paid her for helping, ever so slightly, to relieve the interminable dullness.

Then there were the few solo trips I took to see him. Instead of curling up next to a fire with hot chocolate for some good old-fashioned bonding, we went to parties. Not fun parties. Nope. Bar and bat mitzvah parties of distant and unknown relatives, because nothing says togetherness like a roomful of strangers. In many ways, I was arm candy. Or arm bubblegum to be more precise. Dad picked me up in my brand-new velvet dress and then set to work parading me around. He saw me as a way to make himself look better. More impressive. He wasn't just an accountant if I was around. Suddenly, he had the title of "father" as well. I was just tossed around in his

quest for admiration. "This is *my* daughter," he'd proclaim obnox-
iously, "Isn't she great? It's such a pity about the divorce. I miss her
terribly." All of these dramatics were performed while I was stu-
diously ignored. The events felt so contrived and fake that I wanted
to rip up my dress and curl into a ball. Instead, I was serenaded by
"Baby Got Back." Listening to a song devoted to the wonders of big
butts at a stranger's bar or bat mitzvah with my dad was too uncomfortable for words.

Nevertheless, I discounted my feelings of insecurity and kept
suppressing myself around him. I thought the parties would make
him love me more. I hoped that, somehow, my dad would care about
me the same way my friend Gwyn's dad loved her: unconditionally
and wholeheartedly. It didn't happen.

Slowly, painfully, I realized my dad and I would never have that
sort of connection. This became a fact, not merely an unwanted
thought, during what I dubbed the Vacation of the Music Man. It
was to be an experience of a lifetime. My dad invited me, and only
me, to be his companion on a trip to Costa Rica. I was thrilled to
go, and the timing seemed impeccable. I was about to enter middle
school, which meant that I was ready for anything. I imagined it as
a spectacular adventure (which only proves, once again, that I never
got the magical power of predicting the future).

The plan was simple. I would spend a week with him in Los
Angeles (without Grandma Joyce for a change) before we left the
country. Once we returned, I'd go back to my mom's. I thought the
week in Los Angeles would be more than long enough to fulfill my
daydreams of long conversations and good-natured laughter. I envisioned the two of us playing cards for hours.

Instead, he merely substituted Grandma Joyce with his girlfriend. He dumped me at her house and, with a pat on the head,

went to work. Andrea, who I never heard of until we were introduced, was a kind and attractive woman. A single mother with two sons, she was also a lawyer who looked more than capable of handling herself in court. Her smile was warm, but a rather cross default expression made me fear she was secretly displeased with me. We did have one thing in common though: we both deserved far better than my father.

Andrea and her boys were perfectly wonderful to me. It wasn't their fault I was miserable. The only serious flaw I found in Andrea was that she didn't confront my dad about leaving his daughter alone in a strange house for a week. To be fair, I suppose that might not be the best thing to do when you are trying to keep a boyfriend.

I became the California version of fictional recluse Boo Radley and morphed into a complete shut-in. I didn't know the neighborhood, so I couldn't leave the house. I didn't want to risk losing my way and having no one to find me. Since I couldn't escape the house, I did my very best to disappear. I hadn't packed sufficient reading material and was thus reduced to watching *Free Willy* and *The Music Man* multiple times each day. In between screenings and chocolate chip cookies (which served as my breakfast, lunch, and snack), I read *FoxTrot* comic strips. Up until then, my experience with cartoons had been limited to *Garfield*, and my introduction to *FoxTrot* couldn't have come at a better time. I sprawled out on the floor in the boys' room and read comics until they began to blur.

I realize that in many ways my vacation sounds great. Comic strips? Check. Movies? Check. Massive amounts of sugar? Check. I should have been happy. That's what I kept telling myself anyway. *I should be happy right now.* The thought helped me slap on a brave face and pretend to be cheerful. Once again, my dad didn't see past my truly awful acting. I guess he didn't care enough to look deeper, which just made me miss my mom dreadfully. She could tell something was up just by the strain in my voice over the phone. I even missed my dad—not my actual father so much as the fantasy of him I constructed. I wanted that back. The mythical world I had created wasn't as protective anymore. Reality was creeping in.

In many ways, Costa Rica was even worse. The flight in particular stands out, thanks to all its awkward glory. My dad had complained his way into getting us adjacent seats in first class, which would have been exciting if it weren't for the fact that he had nothing to say to me. After being in a state of solitary isolation at Andrea's, what I wanted most was a little human interaction. I got zilch. *Nada.* Nothing. So, we just sat next to each other in silence and waited for the in-flight entertainment.

If I had known that *Edtv* was the movie, I might have refused to board the plane. Okay, I'm exaggerating. I just would have made arrangements to parachute off the damn thing when my dad began slobbering over a half-naked woman who filled up the screen. His greasy hair only helped illuminate his expression as things got increasingly . . . intimate. I was repulsed. Absolutely grossed out. Even today, the memory makes me wrinkle my nose and grimace. At the time, I just hoped things would improve once my feet were on the ground. Frankly, not a whole lot changed.

Sure, we were in Costa Rica, but we *still* had nothing to say. Maybe part of the problem was that my dad saw me as the innocent bobblehead he taught to read: Daddy's little girl. But, I didn't feel like that girl anymore. Reality had intruded, and now I noticed things like a lack of birthday presents, telephone calls, and visits. He'd say he missed me, but he never tried to change things. He didn't even know how to hug me. I wanted a real relationship, and he didn't know what that meant. Maintaining the appearance of the good, All-American Dad was the only thing he understood. The silence between us was deafening, so I tried to stimulate conversation. The only foolproof topic I could think of was the divorce—I knew he could talk about that forever. The price I had to pay for conversation was listening to him insult my mom. What confused me most was that I hated talking about the divorce, yet, I was the one instigating it. This left me with a very important question: *what the hell was I doing to myself?*

I had no answer and returned home thoroughly confused. My dad and I were still strangers. Somehow, our trip to Costa Rica hadn't been enough. Staring into lush forests, horseback riding up a volcano, flying through trees on zip lines . . . none of it had been enough. We still had nothing to say. What I didn't know was that all too soon I would have plenty to say—and none of it good.

Chapter 5

I HAVE NEVER UNDERSTOOD BOYS. Or men. The male species in general. My dad is an excellent example, as he made absolutely no sense to me when I was growing up. He'd say one thing and do something completely different. I couldn't just pretend it was opposite day, either. It wasn't that up was down with him. Instead up was actually down, reversed, and to the left. Confused? So was I. In fact, there were only a handful of truths I knew for sure:

1. I didn't want to give up on our relationship.

2. We had almost nothing by way of a relationship.

3. I couldn't stand to hear him criticize my mom.

This last truth was probably the most important. My mom had always been the very best thing in my life. Growing up, one of the reasons I craved my dad's affection was because my mom's was never denied. The two of us had a habit of cuddling on rainy days and playing the "I love you more than . . ." game.

"I love you more than all the socks in all the world," I'd tell her as I snuggled deeper into her side.

She would stroke my hair comfortingly. "I love you more than all the stars in the sky."

"More than all the socks and shoes," I'd proclaimed earnestly.

"More than all the grains of sand."

I never had to wonder if she really meant it, either, which was why seeing my dad tore me up inside. He vilified her, blaming the divorce, our infrequent visits . . . everything on my mom. He verbally cut down the woman who had single-handedly raised me. And I would listen, grin, and bear it.

My mom, on the other hand, never said a word. She never criticized my dad, and she never discussed the divorce with me. Trashing my dad would have hurt us, and she wasn't willing to have her ranting come at the price of our happiness. Her primary concern was keeping the four of us emotionally safe. She did everything she could to ensure our preserved peace of mind, including going to therapy.

I think she would have gotten a whole lot more out of her sessions if it hadn't been for Richard. After the divorce, my mom reunited with her ex-boyfriend, and soon there was yet another male in my life (and house) who I didn't understand. While my mom didn't regret marrying or divorcing my dad (she said her four children were worth every minute of it), she certainly regretted Richard. He was the biggest male mistake of her life. He was one ex who should have remained an ex.

Richard was an "artist" and just as moody as the term vaguely implies. He believed the definition of a true artist was one who suffers greatly. In order to fit this description, he took to haunting the house in a foul mood. Whenever he couldn't sleep, he stationed himself in the living room, glowering fiercely at the television through the night. Richard prided himself on feeling everything intensely. Accordingly, when he wasn't happy, everyone knew about it. His mood swings scared me. He pretended they were normal and proudly discussed his time in therapy. He thought it was amazing that he'd been transformed from a mess into a true artist. I doubt the transformation (if any had even occurred) really stuck.

Long story short, my mom wasn't happy, my sister wasn't friendly, my oldest brother Jordan left home early (because of Richard), and my other brother Jonathan spent all his time locked up in his room. I lived in a house full of people who weren't really there. It was a lonely world and I was armed with just my books to ward off depression.

In the middle of this mess was my dad. He just sort of molded in California while things got increasingly worse in Oregon. He didn't call, and we didn't talk—not because I objected to it, but because there was nothing to say. I didn't stop visiting him, but my trips became less frequent. They were limited to bat and bar mitzvah parties. I guess having an escort was losing some of the appeal. I didn't enjoy the trips but still looked forward to the possibility of connection with my dad they offered. I continued to hope that someday we would have the real father-daughter experience.

Eventually, however, I just couldn't believe anymore.

Things changed during my first solo trip to Los Angeles. I'd become accustomed to traveling with someone older and wiser and felt very important flying as an unaccompanied minor. I was also terrified of the Los Angeles International Airport. Everyone was wheeling luggage and rushing off to unknown destinations while I stood outside the terminal utterly confused. I didn't know who to follow. I had no idea what I was supposed to be doing. Several hours later, my dad collected me from airport personnel, and I felt like a princess who had just been rescued. I also felt a little cranky that it had taken him so long to do it. Still, I was relieved to be under my dad's watch. For a little while, anyway.

This trip included another infamous bar mitzvah dog and pony show. "*Baby Got Back*" still wasn't comfortable—no matter how many times I had heard it around my dad, it was to remain perpetually awkward. Actually, everything about the parties felt awkward to me. My dad always urged me to join in the dance where the family was supposed to circle the person being celebrated, so I would end up doing the grapevine around a complete stranger (second cousin once removed or some such thing), feeling completely out of place. The celebrations were always over-the-top, with glass-blowing stalls and other extravagant projects I couldn't imagine people affording.

This particular event was memorably lousy. For the first time, someone (I believe one of my unknown cousins) was being friendly. He gave me a sailor's cap, we danced around, and, for a brief second, I had fun. For some reason, this made me want to cry, and I fought back tears all the way to my dad's apartment. I probably sound ridiculous. I enjoyed a party and therefore wanted to bawl like a three-year-old. I think it was mainly because I didn't expect it. I was so used to being ignored and awkward that inclusion felt odd. The worst part was that it had been fantastic, and I doubted it would happen again. My dad never noticed any change in my mood.

My visits in California were always brief. I guess my dad didn't need an escort after the event was over. The whole thing felt devised to be as impersonal as possible. I went to a party, saw a museum, and flew home. On this trip, my dad took me to the library the same day I was scheduled to leave Los Angeles. *Why*, I wondered silently, *is he doing this? Does he want to spend as little time with me as possible? Surely that's crazy though, right?*

The weather matched my mood. Sunny California had been replaced with bitterly cold wind, thick fog, and sopping wet streets. Winter had set in with a vengeance and had no intention of relinquishing its hold on the West Coast. Still, my attention wasn't on the temperature or the road conditions as my dad drove to the airport. Instead, I was preoccupied with replaying the visit and panning it for memories. I searched for something that was worth telling my mom, but came up empty. I wanted more time. I wasn't ready to go home yet. I needed one real moment with my dad first.

I got my wish. In a really sick, twisted way I received exactly what I wanted. As a result, we had a moment that changed our relationship forever. There are thousands of clichés (at least) about how things change so quickly . . . *in a snap, on a dime, in an instant.* Well, sometimes that's how things work. In flashes. They seem like they should be small, insignificant little things, but they're not. Or at least they aren't to me. Whether I made too much out of it, I'll let you decide. Regardless, my life was never the same again.

We arrived at the airport and discovered my flight was delayed and I couldn't leave until the next morning. Suddenly, time wasn't an issue anymore. I turned to my dad with a goofy grin on my face. I was ecstatic . . . for all of three seconds. Then I saw his expression. He looked like he'd been told he had a cavity or a button had popped off his favorite suit jacket. Mild annoyance set in to his weak jaw and disappointment settled in his eyes. There was no wild hug, no profession of happiness at this unexpected bounty. Was I hoping for too much? I don't think so. A little enthusiasm was more than in order, right?

In that moment, that instant, all his former declarations of love felt hollow and empty. The car ride back to his place passed in silence. There was only one question on my mind: *had he* ever *loved me?* I was too afraid of the answer to ask. When my dad finally spoke, it was only to say we needed to return to the airport the next morning early enough to buy breakfast with my vouchers. Upon arriving at his apartment, he turned the couch into a makeshift bed, gave me a hug goodnight, and disappeared into his room.

I didn't sleep that night. Every time I closed my eyes, I saw my dad's face as he realized my flight was delayed, so I burrowed deeper into the blankets and read. Books had always helped me escape before, and I hoped they wouldn't fail me now. I underestimated the power my dad had over me. As the hours marched on, my eyes began drifting from the pages, and his expression came crashing back in flashes. It was like a twisted version of Morse code that brought nothing but pain. Disappointment. *Keep looking at the words.* Never loved me. *Turn the page, Marni. Just flip it over.* What did I do wrong? *Don't think, Marni. Just read.* How can I make it better? *Read!* When had it changed? *READ, MARNI! JUST READ!*

Shadows fell in the room by the light of a single lamp. Everything felt gloomy and dark. I had always loved the rain and considered it the coziest form of weather imaginable, but alone in my dad's living room that night, it just made me feel insignificant. I started having strange, uneven thoughts. Death was on my mind, hazy and nebulous. Always the flashing continued. I began to cry, quiet tears at first that I hiccupped into the scratchy blankets while I hugged my books tighter. The flashes were undeniable, and the disappointment irreconcilable. My crying grew louder. Hesitantly, I called out for my dad. I wanted him to do everything he hadn't before—to place his arms around me and never let me go. Tears streamed down my face as I called "Dad?" plaintively into the silence. I was afraid to move from the couch. The shadows were too ominous for me to risk it. So I continued calling into the darkness for him.

I don't know how many hours I spent that way, terrified of the dark, and the truth, and the shadows, calling for my father. When he did come at last, I was exhausted. What he said, what I said, I can't recall. I know I didn't ask him if he loved me. The dream was better than nothing at all.

My dad's actions had troubled me for years but had been a jumbled puzzle before that night. I knew I had the pieces, but I hadn't been able to see the big picture. His disappointed look made everything click into place. I didn't like what lay before me, but at least I could recognize what I was up against. I waved good-bye to him as I boarded the plane, unaware of just how differently I would think of him the next time we saw each other.

The flight back home was a disaster. The plane sat on the runway for hours, waiting for the fog to lift. I munched on pretzels and tried to stop the flashing. It was only when I was well into the flight that I finally found relief through sleep. When I woke up, my personal issues were eclipsed by confusion and disorientation. The fog that had kept me in Los Angeles was still thwarting my journey home.

"So, the weather condition on the ground is preventing us from landing in Medford," the pilot announced calmly over the speakers. "We are circling above the airport right now so we can land if the fog clears. If it doesn't, we will have to land in Eugene. We apologize for this inconvenience and hope that the rest of the flight will be as pleasant as possible."

I felt nauseous. The pretzels I had consumed earlier were not agreeing with me. The plane continued circling while I kept flashing. I wanted to be home with an intensity I had rarely felt before. I needed my mom. I needed her to tell me everything would be okay. And she was just out of reach.

The fog didn't lift. By the time we landed at the Eugene airport, I was feeling more than a little loopy. The flight, the salt, the fear . . . it had all left me befuddled. Fortunately, I had the airport staff to take me under their wing and propel me behind closed doors. I was frog-marched to a small waiting area where I sat while my travel arrangements were made.

It wasn't a pretty room. The fluorescent lighting was obnoxious and made everything look unhealthily pale. I remember fake potted plants that I tried to avoid throwing up on. The room did have one considerable distraction: Snickers. There were shelves full of them, box upon box of the delicious substance. I considered crossing the room and popping the treat into my mouth. *They wouldn't miss just one,* I rationalized, but I couldn't bring myself to do it. Instead, I kept hoping they would offer. In my head, it played out like this:

ME: Thank you so much for all your help.

AIRPORT PERSON: No problem. Is there anything we can do for you? Would you like a Snickers bar? They're really tasty.

ME: Are you sure you wouldn't mind?

AIRPORT PERSON: Absolutely.

[Camera zooms in to a close-up of the candy bar being unwrapped before focusing on my expression as I take a bite. My entire face relaxes as I enjoy the chocolaty goodness. Eyes roll back in appreciation.]

That didn't happen. Instead, I was hustled away from the room and loaded onto a bus with the other people from my flight. My queasiness refused to ease up, and it was only when a nice man noting my tense shoulders and worried face gave me half a croissant that things began to get better. I spent the rest of the bus ride peacefully watching the animated *George of the Jungle.* The movie did what the books had not: paused the flashes.

Three-and-a-half hours later, I was in Medford, where my mom scooped me into her arms and hugged me every bit as fiercely as I hugged her. In that moment, I knew everything would be okay. It didn't matter that my dad didn't really love me, that he didn't really want to get to know me, or that Richard was in the house. I had my mom and, as far as I was concerned, that was pretty damn good.

Chapter 6

MIDDLE SCHOOL IS HELL. Actually, that's a lie. It isn't hell. It's far worse. After all, no religion sentences people to a sinkhole where *hormones* run rampant. I'm not the only one who feels this way, either. It's one of those universally acknowledged truths. In middle school, the popular kids seem to float effortlessly while the dweebs (aka me) just struggle to keep their heads above water. I hated everything about the place, from my locker, which had been cleverly designed to never open for me, to my teacher, who had no sympathy for those of us who happened to be mathematically challenged. Everything felt painfully mediocre. My brown hair felt browner, my stomach rounder, and my sweatshirts uglier. It just sort of happened.

The only thing worse than my first day of sixth grade was the second day, which confirmed my suspicion that it wasn't going to get any better. My teacher, Mrs. P., was insane. Not "ha-ha, you're so eccentric/unique/charming" insane, either. Nope. She was a staunch believer in "tough love" who had declared war on all forms of "coddling." In actuality, she was annihilating all displays of understanding and empathy. To that effect, she devised a system. Whenever someone needed help, she would listen without eye contact before she produced one loud, crisp, humiliating, mortifying word: *bummer*. That single word took up the space of thousands and gained extra syllables as it reverberated around the room. Somehow, it became *BUM-MMM-ER!* One woman alone could never create the necessary force for this to happen, which is why the whole class joined in. Humiliation really isn't complete unless everyone is actively involved.

Middle school did help me develop one magical skill. That was the power of invisibility. Considering I practiced disappearing every school day, five days a week, my success isn't all that remarkable. Once I mastered the technique, it wasn't as difficult as I had anticipated. I just kept my head down, avoided the girls' locker room, had minimal social interaction, and hid in the library. This kept me shielded from Mrs. P., but didn't exactly make me popular. In fact, I became "that girl." You know, the one who eats lunch in the library every day in her bulky sweatshirts. The one who only expresses herself in stilted sentences. Yeah. That was me.

I didn't even have Gwyn to lean on anymore. The two of us had a falling out right before we entered middle school and weren't on speaking terms. Actually, that isn't exactly right. I wasn't speaking to her. Not because I didn't miss her or still like her. I just felt like with all her popularity, she didn't care about me. I didn't want to be clinging to someone who didn't value me. That isn't all that happened between the two of us to end the friendship. I had a flash with Gwyn too. I was on the ground, having just managed to fall off a low tree branch, and Gwyn looked at me with complete unconcern. Instead of thinking her reaction was because I wasn't hurt, I took it as a sign that she didn't care about what happened to me. That's the problem with flashes. When they are right, they are convenient, but when they are wrong, they bring about horrible misunderstandings. Luckily, I was able to figure out this particular error of mine before it was too late. Unluckily, I was out of middle school by the time I did.

Without Gwyn, my life was seriously lonely. She had been my best friend for as long as I could remember, and I felt lost without her by my side. Trying to make sense of a Gwyn-free world that included Mrs. P., the middle-school social scene, my inability to understand math, and my family problems, I ended up in therapy. In hindsight, I am only surprised it didn't happen sooner.

Deep down, I think I always knew the decision to seek professional help was the right one. It took me awhile to work up the nerve to explain it to my mom. I didn't come right out and say, "Hey, Mom, guess what? My life sucks, and I need professional help so I can stop living like a social pariah. Oh, and so I can figure out how to deal with Dad. How was your day?" So instead, I just told her the truth about how I was feeling. I explained that I went around empty inside, like somewhere along the line the ability to love had been sucked out of me by an enormous vacuum. Coming from the mouth of a sixth-grader, my mom found it disturbing enough to take action, which is how I landed Carrie the Therapist.

I'm not ashamed of my time in therapy anymore, although when I first started going, I was embarrassed about it. I thought it was humiliating to be just starting middle school and already have a shrink. That's how I saw it, anyway. *I'm hardly here a week, and already I need a professional to fix me.* I couldn't bring myself to tell anyone but my mom about my sessions. The whole family knew I was going, but I still wanted to keep it quiet. If anyone asked about my plans during a therapy session time, I casually said I had "an appointment," before scurrying away. Despite the fact that I thought therapy consigned me to a lifetime of loserdom, I kept going regularly because I knew it was good for me. I *had* to talk things out. My only regret is that my therapist was Carrie.

Carrie was nothing if not consistent. She always brought her clients into a small, windowless room with two chairs and a sandbox. She settled down in the one chair that was remotely comfortable before telling me to "express myself" with the sandbox, which is far more difficult than one might expect. I was instructed to "transfer my emotions" onto figurine animals that I then placed deliberately in the sand. Carrie watched all this and nodded her head expertly from time to time. Right before my mom was scheduled to pick me up, she examined the scene to interpret my inner angst.

"Are you the bird?" she asked me. "Does the fox represent your father?"

I replied that it did.

"See how the fox is creeping up on the bird? I think you're worried your dad is going to hurt you out of the blue."

I was amazed because she was right. I *did* worry that my dad would crush my heart. I already felt so empty. I was afraid that if I suffered any more pain, I'd be impossible to put back together again. So I nodded and stewed over my relationship with my dad until our next session. In hindsight, I can recognize that Carrie was not a good therapist. I never felt like she actually cared about me. I was sure if she did, she would have occasionally let me sit in the one non-lousy chair. I sort of resented that.

I don't think Carrie deserves credit for my growth—I never would have improved if it hadn't been for my mom. The best part of my therapy sessions, the only part I looked forward to, was the drive to Carrie's office. It took well over a half an hour, and my mom and I were the only people in the car. I never went through a "rebellious teenager" phase that made me shun my mother. In fact, middle school just made me want to open up to her more than ever before. The best part of my day was always retelling it once I returned home. We discussed everything, from the boys I was crushing on to my inability to comprehend basic mathematics. How I hated Dad. How I missed him anyway.

My mom didn't try to be my therapist. Maybe that's why she was so helpful. She didn't need to look into a sandbox to understand what was going on. Instead, she listened, laughed, commiserated, and gave me advice. Talking to her gave me more peace of mind than any session with Carrie. When it was just the two of us, we were free. I didn't have to try to make a good impression or disappear. She didn't have to worry about Richard and keeping everyone happy. It was a chance to let go of worldly pressures.

Our home certainly wasn't a refuge from trouble and stress. Especially not with Richard trying to be a combination of therapist/friend/father/role model. He saw me as a challenging puzzle that he wanted credit for putting back together. Richard decided the fastest way for me to become self-actualized was to concentrate on my relationship with my dad. He prodded me until I cried. Richard believed tears were the only reliable sign that therapy was working. Obligingly, I wailed and moaned and felt like a complete and total fake, which only made me feel emptier in the end.

Not that I didn't have plenty of provocation to cry over my dad. Our relationship had disintegrated to the point of nonexistence. I wasn't cute anymore, which meant I could no longer squeeze into little velvet dresses and go to bar or bat mitzvah parties. My inability to turn down chocolate chip cookies meant that he no longer wanted to parade me in front of strangers, which was fine by me since I'd always hated the social awkwardness and pageantry. The awful part was that he just sort of . . . left. We never spoke on the phone and we never e-mailed. He wasn't necessarily trying to cut me out, but he didn't care enough to keep me.

I tried to stay connected with him and overlook the truth. I remember receiving a letter from him on my birthday. I was bursting with excitement because I hadn't heard from him in ages. Smiling broadly, I tore open the letter expecting to see well wishes and proclamations of love. Even if I knew they weren't real, I could have pretended he still loved me. What I found inside was a magazine clipping about inventions made by kids with a hastily scribbled postscript that just said "Happy Birthday." There wasn't even a card inside. He called that night and asked if I had gotten his letter. For a second, I hoped he was going to tell me he had sent two letters and the other one had a card with a bear holding a birthday balloon. He didn't. Instead, he chatted about the stupid inventions before hanging up. I remember turning to my mom and bursting into tears. There was no real card, no real call, and no real present from Dad that year. That became the birthday trend.

Still, I did everything I could to preserve what little we had. After discussing it with Carrie, I called up my dad and let him have it. I told him how hurt I was and how much I wanted him to be in my life. I pleaded that he do the flying for a change and come see me. I flat-out begged. He turned me down. He said he couldn't come back to Ashland because of "all the memories it brought up." I pointed out that since I was there we could create new, happy memories. He still refused. I gave him an ultimatum: either he hop on a flight within the next four months or I wouldn't speak to him. I thought for sure that would propel him into action. Once again, I was wrong. The months passed with no sign of him. I was rejected by my own father. It wasn't to be the last time he broke me.

Chapter 7

THE BEST THING ABOUT Richard was that suddenly I had a male figure in my life. I had someone to take me fishing. I didn't even like fishing, but that didn't matter. I had a fishing buddy who wanted me to be out on the lake with him. Someone besides my mom was telling me that I was a great girl. I couldn't really believe it, but I never minded hearing him say it.

History does repeat itself. Or at the very least, it echoes a lot. Once again, I was the favorite. Like my dad, Richard preferred me to my siblings, and he wreaked havoc with the house. This time, Jordan got the brunt of it. The two of them jockeyed for alpha male position until Jordan up and left. I understand why he moved out. In his position, I would have done the same. Jonathan, Shayna, and I could cope with Richard by staying away from him when he was feeling moody. We didn't need Jordan to protect us. I'm not so sure Jordan realized that—I suspect he felt like he was abandoning us. I could be very wrong, but I do know that ever since then, Jordan has tried to act like a father to me. He counsels and advises until I want to smack him and demand he be my brother for a change.

None of that mattered at the time, though. Jordan was gone, and Richard ruled the house. The other problem was that my mom wasn't happy. Richard kept her emotionally stifled and artistically repressed by critiquing everything she did, searching for flaws. He pretended this was to "help her grow." I suspect he was afraid of what would happen if my mom reached her full potential, that she would realize she didn't need their relationship and leave him.

Even if Richard hadn't been there to put a damper on my home life, I probably still would have been depressed. Therapy can't fix everything, and my loneliness persisted. My school life was miserable, my social life nonexistent, and my family falling apart at the seams. I hadn't been able to make things better with Shayna—she still hated my guts. The rift between us was too deep and old to be overcome. It didn't matter that I understood Dad now too. Nothing changed between Shayna and me, even when I officially severed all contact with Dad. The two of us had been raised as rivals, and the presence or absence of Dad couldn't change that.

I didn't know who I was. My mom pointed out that she was in her forties and was still puzzling it out. This fact didn't strike me as comforting. Middle school was supposed to be a magical time when your true identity could be uncovered. That isn't how it actually worked. The only thing I knew was that I repulsed myself. I hated everything: my antisocial ways, my body, even my hate. I walked around the halls of Ashland Middle School with a pool of venom inside. I didn't know where I belonged, so I holed up in the school library and focused on reading books. It seemed like the safest thing to do.

I don't think I was ever truly suicidal, although there were times when I thought death might be preferable to the emptiness of my life. At those times, I'd walk into the kitchen to look at our knives. There was something coldly appealing about the shiny, black handles that jutted out of the rack. The knowledge that I could end it, make all of it disappear, sank in as I stared, transfixed by the possibility in the flashing metal.

I only came close to taking action once.

I've never been much of an artist. Not in any one field, anyway. I sort of dabbled in one thing before I checked out something else. Consequently, there are only a handful of art projects I've ever made that are anything special. In fifth grade, I created something spectacular. It came out of nowhere. One second I was making a pastel drawing of a toucan, and the next, a bird was knowingly looking back at me. He (the bird was very clear on the matter of his gender) was an unexpected present. He was also one of the few things that Shayna complimented, which in my eyes instantly propelled him to *Mona Lisa* status. I lovingly posted him to my door so we could look at each other every day. My toucan became a daily reminder that I hadn't always been in middle school. He pointed out that I had actually enjoyed school once before and could do it again. He was far more to me than paper and pastel—he was a friend. One of my only friends. It was the attack of the toucan that almost drove me to kill myself.

Shayna was mad at me for some reason, which was nothing new. I was always doing something to set her off. Just breathing appeared to be enough to send her into a rage. This made it hard to know if I had screwed up or if Shayna just felt like yelling at me. Shayna and I also had very different perspectives on right and wrong. Leaving a bowl to soak in the sink a little too long wasn't a big deal in my opinion. For her, it was a hanging offense. Anyhow, she confronted me late one night about my most recent transgression. She was ranting about something I had failed to do while I tried to tune her out. I remember thinking it was one of those times where she just felt like screaming. I knew it'd be best to nod and wait it out, but for some reason, I couldn't. It was late, the house was silent (with the exception of her ranting), and I just wanted to go to sleep. I flat-out didn't have the energy for an emotional roller coaster. So, after she had gotten most of the rant out of her system, I asked her to leave.

What happened next, I'd like to forget. Shayna became livid and continued yelling until she stalked over to my door. Whipping it open, she clenched her hand into a fist and proceeded to mutilate my toucan. She beat upon the door, smudging the bird with the single mechanical purpose of a semi-automatic: to destroy. For me, it was the shot heard round the world. It brought me to a level of hysteria.

I scrambled to rescue my toucan. Pastels are designed to smudge and create a blending effect. While his eyes didn't stare at me as brightly, he wasn't completely ruined. His long shapely beak, brightly-colored plumage, and sturdy torso all remained perfectly preserved. None of that struck me as important, as it was a mere technicality. I was staring at a bird of a different feather. My toucan had never known hate or anger. He had been raised in a happy bubble world just like me. Shayna's fist had destroyed that, and there was no going back. My toucan was gone forever.

Shayna's icy gaze never left my face. I remember wondering vaguely how eyes could turn so flat and cold without creating frostbite. Maybe she was protected from the chill by the seething hate that burned in her throat.

"When you die, Marni," she said deliberately, "no one will come to your funeral."

She left after that. I don't think she could have invented a harsher parting shot. At first, all I could do was stare at the toucan and apologize to it. I told him that I had wanted to keep him safe. I never meant to put him in harm's way. That wasn't enough to distract me from Shayna's final words. In fact, the toucan only seemed to confirm that I wouldn't be missed. I let everyone down. I couldn't even be trusted to keep an inanimate object as a friend. I wracked my brain for names, for faces, for anyone who would care if I were to disappear. The list I produced was pathetically small (with no birds). It didn't even include my dad. I figured he couldn't miss something that wasn't in his life. He'd be able to move on without too much trouble. My mom would have a harder time dealing with the loss. "But what would she lose?" I wondered aloud. "What on earth would she miss? Shayna is smart. Jordan is charming. Jonathan is athletic. What do I bring to the table? Nothing." I spiraled downward, lost in self-loathing and pity.

I started talking to God that night. Don't worry, he didn't answer. I didn't find religion in my moment of crisis. That only happens in movies. I don't even know if what I was doing could be considered talking. I was muttering accusations and demanding answers. I threw out all my questions to the silence. I asked whether it was better to be entirely dead than to keep living with death inside, whether an empty heart trumped a broken one.

I went to the kitchen and forced my shaking hands to pull out a knife. Spoiler alert: I didn't do it. I guess that doesn't come as much of a surprise. Instead, I had a miniature epiphany. Not a godly or a magical one. There were no celestial choirs instructing me. It was a very down-to-earth, well-isn't-that-obvious moment of enlightenment. As I held the glittering knife, I suddenly realized the magnitude of the act . . . there were no do-overs. I couldn't die, realize my mistake, and rejoin the land of the living. Once I used the knife, it was game over. I would have my funeral and probably prove Shayna right. That's what made me stop. I needed to make sure her prophecy never came true. I needed to find people to attend my funeral.

If this seems petty and small, all I have to say in my defense is that sometimes that's how life-altering epiphanies work. That night, I resolved to change other people's lives. I wanted to be on the dedication page of someone else's book. I wanted to be the I-couldn't-have-done-it-without-you person. The one who made all the difference. If that could be me, I decided, they'd have to buy Kleenex in bulk and airlift it in for my funeral.

I never really considered suicide again. Not just because of my determination to fill my funeral with mourners, but because I realized that I'm worth saving too. Sure, I make a lot of mistakes (and have a tendency to humiliate myself), but that's part of my charm. That's what makes me Marni. That's one thing I should never change. Life is just more interesting with me in it—especially when I've got no idea what I am doing.

Chapter 8

I LOVE MY SISTER. I know it sounds like I don't (or perhaps that I shouldn't), but I love my sister. I always will. This doesn't mean I don't realize we have a twisted relationship. It'd be great if we could see each other without descending to snarky comments and back-handed insults. Somehow, I doubt it's going to change anytime soon. The crazy thing is, despite our inability to express our love, it's still there. Under all the anger and frustration is a whole lot of love. I had a hard time believing that as a kid. I understood the concept of a loving relationship and a hate-filled one. I just didn't get that something could really be both. I never realized that when Shayna yelled at me for talking to strangers it was because she was horribly afraid someone would take advantage of me. It wasn't until years later that Shayna confided her biggest fear was that I would be raped. *That* is caring. That is part of the reason I will love her no matter what she says or does (although I might not like her a lot sometimes). It was fortunate for me that situations arose that revealed true affection. Our trip to Costa Rica was one such occasion.

Grandma Joyce invited all of us on a trip to celebrate her birthday. I wasn't sure I wanted to go. I didn't know if I was ready to deal with my dad. I'd come to the conclusion that he was a lousy human being, and I didn't want that confirmed again on the trip. The idea of going back to Costa Rica was very enticing, however. I thought that maybe if I went with all my siblings, it would work out all right. I figured it would be a lot harder for my dad to mess with my head with Jordan, Jonathan, and Shayna present to set the record straight. Part of me was also hoping that with my therapy, I was mature enough to form a connection with my dad. I wanted to be able to deal with him like my brothers did—in a sort of cool, professional manner. A relationship based on an impersonal exchange of niceties sounded like a great solution to me. Maybe it would have been, if I hadn't hoped for more. As it was, I overestimated my ability to remain detached.

The first bad omen was the rental car. Technically, there was nothing wrong with it. It started, stopped, and turned. It behaved like a perfectly normal, nonpossessed car. The problem lay in its size, which, for the record, matters. It might have been perfect for an intimate honeymoon trip, but for a large family vacation it was a nightmare. My dad tried to argue his way into a bigger one, arms flapping and head bobbing in his best chicken impersonation, but failed.

There was really nothing for me to do but sit in the sweltering heat. I had nothing to distract me from the sensation that the plastic seat was melting into me. My mom thought it would be best if I didn't lug my CD player to Costa Rica. Meanwhile, Jonathan and Shayna had their headphones on while Jordan tried to sort out the problem. Not that Jordan had any luck, since my dad refused to listen to him. Everything (even the arrangement of the suitcases) had to be done my dad's way. So, there we were: squeezed and squashed within an inch of our lives in the rental. The heat made everyone surly and smelly as we bumped along the road to our hotel.

This is a good time to point out that many roads in Costa Rica aren't so great. They come with potholes. Lots and lots of potholes.

Our suitcases served as seatbelts, but made me feel like an arcade game pinball being buffeted from all sides. Even so, driving in Costa Rica would have been bearable if it hadn't been for the orange juice.

We were a day into our trip when the OJ came up in conversation. Grandma Joyce wanted to know if we wanted anything from the all-purpose convenience store. Her timing couldn't have been worse, since we were in the middle of a particularly uncomfortable meal. My dad was sulking about something—possibly his inability to get a bigger car—and was in no mood to be pleasant. He was glowering at the table when Grandma Joyce broke the silence.

"So, does anyone want anything special for the morning?" she asked.

My siblings and I traded looks. All we wanted was to go home. Or keep traveling without the two of them.

"I think we're fine," said Jordan, taking on the role of spokesman.

"Are you sure?" she pressed. Grandma Joyce, like her son, was primarily led by what was in her best interests. In this case, she wanted to buy juice but make it look like she was doing us a favor.

"We're sure," Jordan assured her.

"What about orange juice?"

None of us really liked orange juice. We never drank it at home. We had some in the refrigerator, but it was used primarily for my mom's sludge-like concoction of orange juice, ice, and Diet Coke.

"We don't want orange juice," Jordan replied politely.

"You say that now," she wheedled, "but tomorrow you'll be saying you want it and complaining that we don't have any." She said the last bit like she understood fickle teenagers better than we did. But she didn't know us. She didn't have a clue as to what we were really like. If she had, she wouldn't have asked us about orange juice in the first place. It was therefore up to Jordan to try to educate her.

"We don't want orange juice," Jordan repeated. There was no way to make our position clearer. We were anti-orange juice.

"But . . ." was as far as she got. My dad, who had been growing increasingly angry as the conversation progressed, had reached his limit.

"They said they don't want orange juice!" he barked.

Silence descended.

Grandma Joyce muttered a few choice words about kids' inability to make up their minds. She mumbled that soon, very soon, we would have a change of heart. The meal ended with the tension more palpable than the food.

The orange juice incident would have ended there had she not bought a whole carton. As expected, she was the only one who wanted to drink any of it, which only led to more juice-related conflict the next morning. She tried to convince everyone that we were secretly craving orange juice. If drug dealers guilt-tripped and pressured people the way my Grandma Joyce did, the streets would be a lot more dangerous.

We declined the orange juice. It felt like a matter of principle. She thought she knew us better than we did, and the only way to prove her wrong was not to drink it. All of us ignored the orange juice. This left her with an almost-full carton to transport via pathetically small rental car to our next hotel in Costa Rica, which is where the real trouble began.

I didn't actually hear the conversation between Grandma Joyce and my dad. I'm guessing she told him to be careful of potholes so as not to spill the juice. That's mere conjecture though. It was hot in the car—a steamy, sweaty hot that left me feeling languid and tired. I rested my head against the window and wished myself somewhere else.

WHAM!

My dad slammed on the breaks, and we were thrown forward onto suitcases. The jolt was followed by cursing and sharp intakes of breath. I gasped and rubbed my stomach where the corner of something had jabbed me. Jordan, Jonathan, and Shayna repositioned themselves beneath their loads, muttering darkly.

I stared in disbelief at the back of my dad's head. He hadn't stopped because there was some rare lizard crossing the road or anything. He had done it because of the orange juice. More specifically, because he was mad at Grandma Joyce for mentioning it.

He yelled something and started the car again before any of us had even caught our breaths. The car had just started moving steadily when Grandma Joyce opened her mouth. She just couldn't resist.

WHAM!

The second lurch sent Jordan into action. He shoved the boxes off him, wrenched open the door, climbed out, and marched over to my dad in the driver's seat. Leaning past him, Jordan snatched up the orange juice, opened the carton and deliberately poured every last drop onto the nearest plant.

I think everyone has moments in life when they get to show what they're really made of, and that was one of Jordan's. He refused to be tossed around in the car over orange juice, so he ended it. As I watched him dump out the juice, I saw an act of rebellion every bit as big as the Boston Tea Party. It was comforting watching Jordan take care of everything, especially since I couldn't count on my dad to do the right thing.

Believe it or not, the orange juice helped me bond with my siblings. Adversity either brings people together or wrenches them apart. Stuck in a foreign country with Grandma Joyce and my dad made Shayna and me closer. It created a truce between us while we focused on making it out of there with our sanity intact. Presenting a united front was the only way to survive. It also proved once and for all that we loved each other.

I remember one night in particular when the love wasn't hidden between us. It started with my dad giving Shayna an extra hard time. We finished eating, and Shayna was ready to return to the hotel. Dad refused to give her the room key, saying she wasn't mature enough to handle the responsibility. This was ridiculous. Walking a few blocks to a hotel doesn't require much maturity. What it does need is a level head and a sense of direction. Shayna had those qualities, as well as his required maturity, in spades. Everyone tried to explain the idiocy behind this position, but he remained firm. It was only when Jonathan announced his intention to join us that he budged. He handed the key to Jonathan, and the three of us marched out of the restaurant.

It was dark and quiet as we walked along the street. It felt good to move and hear the sound of my footsteps reverberating with theirs. We felt so close, so united, that nothing could tear us apart. Jonathan took out the room key and awkwardly offered it to Shayna. Jonathan was interesting like that—he could be a major pain, but when someone was hurt, he'd always try to fix it. He wanted to show Shayna that he trusted her with the key—that *he* knew my dad was wrong. Shayna didn't take the key. I think it was sort of her toucan. If my dad had just handed it to her, that would have meant something. Now, it was just a reminder that she was still untrusted and unloved. This time she wasn't alone in her anger at Dad. Jonathan and I were just as sick of his self-centered ways and commiserated as we walked shoulder-to-shoulder. That's when I began swearing.

I started with the classics. I used every word I'd heard in the middle-school hallways that I'd decided never to repeat. I loved it and felt a surge of power as the words rolled off my tongue and filled the chilly night air with nothing but the dulcet sound of my profanity.

Shayna and Jonathan were shocked. They'd never really heard me swear before. In fact, I'm not sure I ever had. My mom had kept me sheltered as a kid, and that had lasted longer than she probably expected. Growing up on happy-go-lucky musicals like *Singin' in the Rain* had made me a stranger to the world of profanity. The words felt strange on my tongue, and I was caught by surprise at the hatred that spilled out. That night, my dad became an infection and swearing the only possible antidote. There was a sort of poetry to it too. It wasn't elegant or profound, but it was beautiful.

The walk back to the hotel that night was one of the best strolls of my life. Sure, it felt like the world was in cahoots with my dad, but I had my siblings on my side. I wouldn't have traded teams if he offered me the world. I sensed Jonathan's concern for me. As a little kid, Jonathan used to be my protector. I was too young to remember, but apparently he guarded me from the others and watched over me diligently. I wish I could recall those times. Even though he had moved on to spending all his time either closed up in his room or on the tennis court with his friends, I guess some things don't change. Not that he would want to own up to his softer side. He was always secretly sweet and guarded his kindness fiercely, as if afraid someone would catch him in the act and tease him about it. At the end of the day though, I knew we still had a connection. I could hear it in his voice when he called me a "dorkus maximus."

Alongside Jonathan's concern was something akin to appreciation coming from Shayna. In that split second, it was as if our history didn't matter, as if I was forgiven for being his former favorite. We were no longer rivals but allies. It was partly born out of necessity, since we had both agreed to spend a few extra days in Los Angeles with him after Costa Rica. I think there was more to it than a survival instinct, though. We had a moment, and that was what mattered to me. My favorite memory from the trip wasn't swimming with dolphins, or river rafting, or any of the things that fill up travel brochures. It was the memory of an empty orange juice container and a night of swearing with my siblings at my side. They weren't traditional Kodak moments, but for me, they were better. So I sort of have my dad to thank for that . . . and nothing else.

Chapter 9

COSTA RICA WAS GORGEOUS, and even the presence of my dad and Grandma Joyce couldn't diminish it. Everything was lush and green and overflowing with life. Ironically, it sort of reminded me of Ashland. Or maybe I just thought that because I was homesick. I missed my mom, and after the heat, the insects, the crabs running under my bed, I felt like I'd had my share of the exotic. I was ready to return. Unbeknownst to me, we were going to be taking a lot of Costa Rica with us.

My dad decided to bring coffee back to the states for his clients, which sounded reasonable to me. The last time we had gone to Costa Rica, my dad had been excited about bringing home coffee. He had dragged me to a place where they roasted it right in front of the customers. The smell of coffee was so strong it stung my eyes, and I had to wait outside to catch my breath. So, I didn't think it was unusual in any way that he wanted to get some coffee this time too. Frankly, I wouldn't have cared, had he been able to restrain himself. He purchased 100 pounds of it.

There is really nothing you can say when someone does something like that. One second, we were all waiting in the rental car for him and the next he approached with a stranger wheeling 100 pounds of Vanilla Blend, a big, foolish grin plastered all over his smarmy face.

Our first question, quite naturally, was *What was he thinking?* There wasn't enough room in the rental car without the coffee—the last thing we needed was more cargo. When we pointed that out, he just shrugged his shoulders (still grinning) and said, "You'll have to make more room." Gee, thanks.

By the time we reached the airport, none of us ever wanted to see our father again. We were at the point of mutiny when we boarded the flight. The boys were lucky enough to be going straight home, which left Shayna and me wishing we'd never agreed to stay a few extra days in California. For once, Shayna wasn't my biggest problem. Until we were out of enemy territory, the truce had to remain intact.

This might not be fair, but I would like to blame *The Far Side*, *Calvin and Hobbes*, and Richard for the next disaster. I'm sure this has a fancy clinical name like blame transference, and that a therapist would point out it is not a particularly productive way of dealing with things. Still, it would be nice to have someone other than my dad to hold responsible.

Dad took Shayna and me to a used bookstore under the pretext of "bonding." He wasn't fooling anyone. Once inside, he went straight to the geology section and never left it. Shayna checked out their selection of romance novels, and I decided to examine the comic books. Richard loved comics, so I thought buying him a few might make a nice present. Of course, this unselfish little act helped me out quite a bit too. When Richard was happy, he didn't sulk around the house like a peevish ghost. So, I approached my dad a few hours later with several books tucked under one arm. He was carrying a stack that was as enormous as it was impractical. He had geology books written in French, a language he couldn't speak or read. Yet, for some strange reason, he felt compelled to own these books. I decided not to comment on it and instead added my comic books to the pile.

My dad could never pass up a deal, and apparently the bookstore had a promotion—an extra discount for purchasing 100 dollars worth of books. In order to reach the magic number, he harassed me into grabbing a few more comic books. He kept telling me what a good deal it was, which would have been nice if he were footing the bill. He wasn't. He fully expected me to pay him back for every penny. Back at his house, we realized that was a problem because I didn't have the cash. Jonathan had offered to transport most of my money back to Ashland for safekeeping. So, even after I'd checked every pocket in every article of clothing I owned, I still had a five-dollar deficit.

Five measly bucks. Less than a tall Mocha Frappuccino and a pumpkin loaf from Starbucks, and my dad wouldn't let it go. Instead, he demanded I mail it to him from Ashland. *Seriously.* When I told him that wasn't going to happen, he took to bugging Shayna. Why didn't she loan me the money? She was my sister after all, it was only right that she look after my debts. He even started making bargains in my name, offering to exchange cash if I did her chores for a week or more.

Shayna refused, while I watched him in disbelief.

"Dad," I pointed out reasonably. "You haven't sent me a birthday present, a Hanukkah present . . . *anything,* for years. I haven't even gotten a *card* from you! Why don't you put the five dollars towards that?"

He rounded on me.

"I take you to Costa Rica, and the first thing you do is hit me up for money! I'm not made out of it, you know!"

This coming from a man who bought 100 pounds of coffee and dozens of geology books written in French.

"Grandma Joyce paid for the trip," I countered. "And we're talking about five dollars here. I haven't seen you in well over a year. This shouldn't be a problem!"

But for my dad, any money not in his bank account was a problem.

"I paid for half of that trip, and I am not giving you the money," he insisted.

We parted ways with a lackluster good-bye, and I took the comic books and the five-dollar debt home with me. Leaving was a relief, and the only sad part was the way my solidarity with Shayna crumbled the second we landed in Medford. I was back to being the little sister she wanted to avoid. Still, at least I had my mom. Much to my surprise, I also had Richard suggesting a way to exact payback.

He got the whole thing set up for me. It didn't require much equipment: wood boards, strong glue, sandpaper, and 500 pennies. The rest was up to me. Painstakingly, I sandpapered one side of each penny and neatly glued them in sets of 100 to slabs of wood. It was supposed to be the ultimate slap in the face. I owed him five dollars, and this way he would get every single penny of it back. The only catch was that it, rather like him, would be absolutely worthless. The whole act was rich in symbolic meaning, and I knew I could never have thought up such an intricate way to say "screw you" on my own.

I would love to think of my pennies as a huge success. In a movie, I think it would have played out really well and been very dramatic. I would've waited to deliver the pennies in person. Around midnight, I would've walked the handful of blocks that separated my grandparents' house from his and leaned on the doorbell until he showed up. Then I would've shoved the boards into his face and told him what I really thought—that he was a lousy father who had put his children through hell. That I wouldn't cry at his funeral.

In reality, my life wasn't quite that dramatic. Or maybe it was, and I was too much of a chicken to go through with it. I couldn't even bring myself to face him.

The next time I was in Los Angeles, I stayed in the safety of my grandparents' house and refused to see him. My brothers went instead and played basketball with him. That was the easiest way for them to spend time with my dad without becoming irritated by him. If they were concentrating on dribbling, guarding, and shooting, they didn't really have to talk. I chose not to talk at all and just enjoy spending time with Grandma and Grandpa. The pennies were burning a hole in my suitcase though, and I knew I had to send them to him. I didn't want to owe my father anything. I wanted to pay up, close shop, and walk away.

I considered dropping the pennies off at his house in the night and just leaving. In the end, I took the wimpy way out and asked Jordan to deliver them for me. He didn't really want to do it. He looked me squarely in the eyes and with brotherly concern asked if I knew what I was doing, if I understood the message I was sending. He was concerned I wasn't prepared to deal with the consequences of my first act of teenage rebellion. I replied confidently that I knew exactly what my pennies were saying. In hindsight, I think perhaps I was mistaken, not for sending the pennies, making the pennies, the sentiment behind the pennies, or my ability to deal with my dad's reaction, especially because he saw it as one big joke. No, I think it might have been a mistake because it wasn't about my father or me. It was all about Richard. He liked dramatic acts of vengeance, and I knew he would be proud of me if I did it. Once again I was pandering to the man in my life. My declaration of independence from my father didn't prove a thing. I still craved attention and love and was willing to sandpaper my hands to get it. I had a long way to go.

Chapter 10

I WISH I COULD SAY that middle school improved. However, in most respects, it didn't. I returned from Costa Rica to the same social problems I had left behind. I did, however, become craftier. I slowly figured out there are some areas only elite nerds (including myself) have access to that can be used to their advantage. Granted, this was behind the counter in the school library, but still, it came with perks. I could read all the newest books, check out tapes that weren't typically distributed, and turn in books late pretty much hassle-free. I saw this as a huge success. I was also invited to join the prestigious, if somewhat unknown, Ashland Middle School Book Club. I didn't care if this certified me as a dork. I was discussing intense novels like *Icy Sparks* (about one girl's battle with Tourette's syndrome) surrounded by other girls who liked to read. I was finally finding my niche.

The book club wasn't the only place I started fitting in. I soon joined the ranks of the "theater people." I worked my way up by starting at the very bottom in *Oliver!*, where I was cast as an orphan and had all of one line: "Stop him!" Backstage, I was part of a group that did tongue twisters and chanted "Whether the weather is cold, or whether the weather is hot, we'll be together whatever the weather, whether we like it or not." I always liked being with the group—especially when I met Natalie.

There are some people who can't help but change your life. Natalie was one of them for me. She was everything I wanted to be—thin, smart, pretty, talented, and even though she was home-schooled, universally adored. Much to my surprise, she was also my new best friend. We talked about everything: boys, music, and especially books. Our taste in young adult fiction was pretty much identical. We both loved Meg Cabot, Gordon Korman, and Tamora Pierce. We could (and did) discuss their various works for days. At long last, I had found someone I considered my intellectual equal, if not my superior. This isn't to say I thought the rest of the school was unintelligent or that I was above the other students. In most cases, I was the one who was negligently behind. My math skills were nonexistent and my social skills needed serious work. When it came to books though, I was pretty much in a league of my own. Until Natalie that is.

I did make it to seventh grade. I survived Mrs. P.'s *BUM-MMM-ERs* and a year's worth of indecision as to which boy I had the strongest crush on. Some days I told myself I wasn't interested in any of them. Usually, I imagined dating all of them. Somehow though, I made it past the "Marni likes Tyler" class camping trip (a truth I denied hotly . . . yeah, I was totally clueless) and onto the next level of middle school.

Seventh grade meant big changes. No longer would I be the recipient of the dreaded *BUM-MMM-ER* since I now had a different teacher for every subject. After holding my own as an orphan in *Oliver!* and as a singing tree in *Once on This Island,* I was given real roles in the school plays. Overall, these were major improvements, and I might have stayed in school if it hadn't been for my phys ed (P.E.) class and President John Adams.

P.E. was mandatory, and I had signed up for what I thought

would be the least humiliating form of exercise—dance. I was horribly mistaken. Dance class didn't just embarrass me: it was an embarrassment to itself. The older, well-coordinated students took it upon themselves to teach the rest of us routines that were composed of an "attitude" overdose and hip swishing, none of which I could do, not because I was humiliated (which I was), but because I had no coordination. I tripped my way through routines two-and-a-half beats behind everyone else. I decided the class couldn't get any more mortifying—which is when it did. We were ordered to create our own routine and perform it. In front of *everyone.*

I don't know anyone in their right mind who would look forward to something like that. Maybe if I looked more like Kirsten Dunst in *Bring It On* and less like Velma from *Scooby-Doo,* I wouldn't have dreaded it so much, though I sincerely doubt it. The very thought of doing a simple step ball change had my heart thudding and not in a happy adrenaline way, but in a *Jaws* something-very-bad-is-about-to-happen way. It wasn't just the dancing part that scared me—I had to pick the music as well. I knew that what I listened to wasn't cool. The best mainstream stuff I listened to was Chumbawamba (their song "Tubthumping" was the greatest thing ever). I quickly vetoed doing a number to that particular tune. I couldn't do hip-hop or rap without looking absolutely foolish. Primarily, I listened to pop music on *The Princess Diaries* soundtrack or oldies like Frank Sinatra. The idea of strutting around to "Supergirl" or "Ain't Nuthin' But a She Thing" sent me into a cold sweat.

But hip thrusts weren't enough to send me scurrying from the middle school. Yes, they scared me into looking for alternatives, but I wouldn't actually have left if it hadn't been for John Adams. If you're wondering how a one-term president who died in the 1800s convinced me to become a dropout, you're not alone. I'm not entirely sure how he did it, either. Here's what I do know: I fell in love with John Adams.

Not romantically, of course. He's *dead,* and I am not the type to find that an attractive feature in a guy. I guess what I fell in love with was *learning* about John Adams. He was one seriously cool guy. Not only was he an unbelievably good lawyer (who represented the British after the Boston Massacre because, hey, everyone deserves good representation), he also convinced other countries to help bankroll the United States. Without him, the United States would have remained a backwater British colony. On top of all that, he committed political suicide by keeping the country out of war during his presidency. I guess you could say I became a fan. Weird, I admit.

I sort of stumbled into my John Adams fixation by accident. I was in an American history class that was part joke, part study hall period supervised by the school drama teacher. Anyhow, Mrs. Warner showed us an American Revolution musical called *1776,* so it would look like we were learning. I wasn't exactly impressed. I mean Abigail and John Adams kept singing these long-distance, heart-to-heart songs that were both boring and lame. What I did like, however, was that everyone in the film hated John Adams. They kept singing that he was too disagreeable to write the Declaration of Independence.

I guess there was something about the collective antipathy toward John Adams that stuck with me. I'm not exactly sure what it was since I wasn't really disliked at the middle school. In fact, people didn't seem to form any opinion of me. They labeled me as the smart girl who reads and acts, and basically let me go relatively unscathed. Maybe what drew me to John Adams was that he seemed to speak his mind. If he didn't like you, he wouldn't go around to everyone else whispering that your wig was out of style or whatever. Oh no, he would go right up to you and air his grievances. That's how I pictured him anyway.

I probably wouldn't have bothered to do the research and find out just how cool he was if it hadn't been for my grandparents on my mom's side. They had a tradition of taking each grandchild on a special trip when they turned thirteen. There were only a few rules:

1. The destination had to be in the United States.

2. It had to be somewhere relatively hassle-free.

3. It had to be educational.

Jordan had gone to Washington, D.C. to see the White House, Jonathan went spelunking in Kentucky, and Shayna had chosen Philadelphia. My first impulse was to pick New York City. I was starting to think of myself as an actress and that it was time I experienced the mecca of the theater world: Broadway. I figured we'd see a few plays, check out some museums, and soak in some history at the same time. However, that trip wasn't to be since, in the wake of September 11th, the stress of security would be too much for my grandpa. So it was up to me to find an alternative.

I was in this state of indecision when John Adams came strolling into my life. I began thinking about the hated president, and then I started researching him. I quickly realized that what I wanted to see was his house in Massachusetts. I wanted to see everything: where he ate, where he sat, where he died. I would have been fine devoting the whole trip to John Adams. Instead, though, I decided I wanted to retrace American history around Boston and beyond. My grandparents agreed, and I threw everything I had into my research—which is how John Adams became my favorite president and did something to me that hadn't happened since fifth grade: made me feel like I was learning. I was going through books on his presidency like some people go through M&M's.

Yes, I was a little strange. Not many kids flip out over John Adams, which was part of my problem. Nobody at the middle school wanted to be there. Not that I blamed them, since I didn't either. It's hard to look forward to long drab corridors and English classes where you don't write and you hardly ever read a book. It was even harder to be excited about the place on a social level. Everyone ran around making others feel lousy, all the while searching for their own identity. It was a mess and it sucked all the life and creativity out of me. So when a real mystery man (John Adams) waltzed into my mind and got me interested again, I refused to go back to my old way of life. I didn't want to spend another year and a half in a perpetual state of boredom.

I knew dropping out of middle school would be a tough sell, so I approached my mom as professionally as possible. After securing her undivided attention, we proceeded to discuss my educational needs. I was painfully thorough and pointed out all the failings in my classes. I knew it wasn't enough though—I had to provide a viable alternative to the problem too. Luckily, I had one. I declared I could homeschool just like Natalie. My breathing ceased until she consented to let me switch. I was shocked. I had anticipated her to reply, "Well I know you hate it, honey, but that's life. Only a year and a half left before high school," but she didn't. She gave me a big hug, and said we would find a way to make homeschooling work.

I never regretted making the change. There were a lot of things that needed to be altered and adjusted in my life, and I was finally doing something about it. I was sick and tired of feeling like I had a big sign on me that said "nerd." Like Natalie, I could be anyone I wanted. A fresh start somewhere of my own, somewhere my siblings had never gone, sounded too good to be true. I hadn't been able to figure out who I was in middle school, but I felt like nothing could stop me now. I was ready and eager for a change . . . and I was never to be the same again.

Chapter II

WHEN MY MOM AGREED to let me homeschool, we both knew she wouldn't be my teacher. I don't think we ever really considered it. She despised math, didn't understand science, and had neither the materials nor the time to teach history or English. In the face of all these obstacles, we came up with an excellent solution. I would go to Willow Wind, a homeschooling center not far from my house, for most subjects, and learn American history from my aunt.

It felt like everything I wanted was coming true. I had my chance to start over and completely reinvent myself. No longer regarded as the shy bookish girl with no friends, I became the instigator of excitement. I was outgoing and friendly and instantly had a tight-knit group of friends. Part of me couldn't help being surprised that my new friends liked me. At the middle school, drop-dead beautiful girls like Cecily ("Cee" was willowy, had long, flowing blond hair, and deep blue eyes—your basic Gwyneth Paltrow look-alike) did not occupy the same social circle as me. They also weren't as genuinely sweet as Cee . . . they weren't anywhere close. Suddenly, I was hanging out with kids who were smart, cool, beautiful, talented, and who appreciated my company. Did it get any better than that? Surprisingly, yes.

Natalie and I had stayed best friends, and, since she went to Willow Wind too, we were constantly together. We had the same

classes, went to concerts, shopped, had sleepovers . . . we were inseparable, and I thought I'd never feel lonely again. My life was a
Disney Channel movie, and I wanted it to last forever. Natalie and
I even had our own book club. Since we were both romantics and
nerds, we read *Pride and Prejudice* before throwing a themed party for
two. It began with the five-hour BBC movie version, and continued
with breaks for tea, talk, and croquet. I thought if that was what life
was like in England, the two of us should hop on the nearest plane
to London, since we probably had been born in the wrong country
(and possibly the wrong century).

I thought of Natalie, Cee, and myself as the Unstoppable Trio.
We were careful not to exclude anyone at Willow Wind, but at the
end of the day it was the two of them I was calling on the phone. I
had guy friends at Willow Wind too—a major improvement since
my awkwardness had prevented this in the past. The boys at Willow
Wind were so different that I didn't worry much about what they
thought of me. My friend Eli played the bagpipes, occasionally wore
a kilt, was in my tap dancing class, and always spoke his mind. Dash
was lanky, tall, gentlemanly, and the perfect candidate for a modern-
day knight. To me, they were pretty much perfect.

It wasn't just my social life that changed. I was getting a college-
level education. Dash's mom taught the Great Books class where we
read everything from *The Aeneid* and Dante's *Inferno* to Chinese
poetry. In-class discussions were intense, since everyone did the
readings and criticized even the most acclaimed works of literature.

Eli's mom taught a fantastic Philosophy and Religions class that
was the highlight of everyone's week. I don't know how someone
could not have loved it. For almost two hours a week we became
eccentric mini-philosophers. When we discussed the Sufis, everyone learned how to be a whirling dervish while Rumi's poetry was

read aloud. We wore sheets as togas and answered questions about Greek and Roman deities before chowing down on a platter of Greek food. I was learning, and best of all, no one ever yelled *BUM-MMM-ER!* at me when I was confused. School had become my haven. I never wanted to leave again.

Dating, however, messes everything up. Seriously, the safest way to maintain the status quo is to prohibit people from falling in love (or lust), which, I am aware, is impossible to do. Still, if there was a potion that would prevent crushes, I might have administered a few doses in a backwards *A Midsummer Night's Dream* sort of way.

My friends never saw it coming, and frankly neither did I. When, at my Passover seder, Eli's mom mentioned the possibility of a member of the Unstoppable Trio dating Eli, the three of us paused only to trade incredulous looks before saying, "Yeah, he's great, but that's *never* going to happen." If only that had been true.

Natalie was the first one to change her mind. This came as a surprise to me, since she already had a love interest in the form of a boyfriend. Taylor had been hovering around her in middle school since the first week of *Oliver!* I predicted they'd become the drama club's cutest couple and did my best to assist the inevitable. Mainly, my job was telling Natalie that *of course* Taylor liked her in a girlfriend kind of way. It took longer than I expected for them to start dating, but they were every bit as adorable as I had anticipated, and it had looked like a smooth relationship to me. Soon after, Natalie got to act in another rendition of *Oliver!* with both her boyfriend and Eli. It wasn't a problem that Taylor became Eli's friend too. In fact, it was great. Everything was fine. Until it wasn't.

I guess I can't blame anyone for what happened. It wasn't Natalie's fault she had this I'm-super-smart-yet-delicate thing going for her which boys seemed drawn to. Still, when she broke up with her boyfriend and began dating Eli, I didn't handle it very well. I fully realize it was none of my business who Natalie dated, but I didn't want to see Eli get hurt. I also wanted to avoid what would happen when the inevitable rupture occurred. Battle lines would be drawn, and Team Natalie would be facing off against Team Eli. I knew which side I was supposed to be on. She was my best friend, while I still had to look up Eli's phone number before dialing. My loyalty shouldn't have been in question, which is why it really sucked that I knew I was going to side with Eli, mostly because I didn't think Natalie really cared for him, and to me that was a huge deal. Maybe I was being something of a prude, but I just didn't think it was right to yank a guy around if you weren't really interested. Especially if it might destroy a friendship.

On top of that, I was mad at Natalie and had no idea how to express it. I couldn't find the right words. What had happened between us? We had gone from being best friends to playing the roles of the popular one and her trusty sidekick. It was like we were in our own chick flick, and she had just cast me as the nerdy, pathetic friend who is useful only because she boosts the leading lady's self-esteem. If it were *Pride and Prejudice,* she was now Elizabeth Bennet (witty, skinny, instant guy-magnet) and I was Charlotte Lucas (smart but plain, and willing to settle for the most boring and obnoxious guy ever). And I didn't want to be Charlotte. Even more than that, I didn't want to be treated like Charlotte. I thought that best friends should believe they both had leading lady potential. I could have been mistaken, but Natalie didn't seem to see it that way. So I was mad at her, and the Eli situation just made everything worse.

Suddenly, life at Willow Wind began moving in a downward spiral, although admittedly, Natalie dating Eli wasn't the total disaster I expected. Their eventual breakup seemed fairly amicable, which is more than I can say for the disintegration of our friendship. At some point when I wasn't looking, the two of us had morphed into less-than-friends. Something shifted, and suddenly Natalie and I were locked into a twisted competition to prove our status as protagonists. We went from equals to rivals, and Natalie was definitely the stronger competitor.

When I was at Willow Wind, I thought I was popular; I was pretty universally liked, so I guess I was. A lot of it though, came from being Natalie's friend. And what Natalie giveth, Natalie can taketh away. Our actual disagreement was so small that I figured we could handle it. I told her I was afraid she was just toying with Eli, and that it was important to me she didn't hurt him. She nodded and seemed to understand perfectly. Our underlying issue was still there, but things seemed to be looking up. I didn't think she would call all our friends at Willow Wind to complain about me. Maybe *complain* isn't the right word, but I'm not entirely sure what is. All I know is that suddenly everyone was under the impression I had done something to Natalie along the lines of stabbing her in the back. Nothing could have been further from the truth.

I was suddenly persona non grata. Sure, Cee, Dash, and Eli were still friendly toward me, but it wasn't the same. Natalie was clearly the queen bee, and I was a drone who had stepped out of place, which didn't exactly help with my low self-esteem issues. Maybe I was being paranoid, but it sure felt like we had disintegrated into an episode of *Gossip Girl*. Cee and Dash dated, broke up, and muddled the waters even more. Dash was jealous of Eli: Eli was an object of affection, and the girls who liked him worked hard for attention.

It was a mess that killed my love of theater. With the exception of Dash, everyone involved was an actor with a flair for the dramatic. That's when I learned I wanted my drama to stay on the screen or stage. I didn't want to deal with all of it on a daily basis at my school. What I didn't know was that my life was growing increasingly dramatic—and in a way no one had control over, least of all me.

Chapter 12

HOW I GOT THE NOTION that pulling would make things better is a little complicated. For the record: it wasn't Shayna's fault. She only acted as one of the catalysts for my problem. All the decisions I've made are my own—and I've made plenty of wrong ones. To explain, I need to go back to when I was standing by the rabbit hole, and she pointed out the entrance to me.

Shayna was always critiquing my appearance, probably because it made her feel better about her own. She pointed out my pudgy stomach and recommended exercise and a life sentence of no drumsticks. She was right, but I didn't want to hear it, especially since my family had bugged me about my weight for years. My weight came up in conversation whenever I visited my relatives in California, especially when I saw my Aunt Mirta, a size zero who enjoyed shopping at expensive boutiques. Buying clothes with Mirta was incredibly effective at destroying all my self-confidence in one blow.

So, I had some body image problems, which might explain why I wanted to emulate my skinny friends like Cee and Natalie. I could never really lose weight, mainly because I got too much enjoyment out of food to restrict myself. I'm fortunate that I only obsessed about my weight and didn't sink into anorexia or bulimia. I wonder if it was just sheer luck that I didn't.

When Shayna critiqued my various body parts, especially my stomach, her words always reverberated around my head until some action was taken to drive them out. Shayna was the first person to tell me I needed to shave my legs. It wasn't a suggestion, like "Well, maybe you should consider . . ." According to her, it was a necessity since I resembled a monkey. So, I took a fresh razor from my mom and performed that rite of passage.

Unfortunately, not all of Shayna's beauty demands were that simple. In fact, her next one was that I tweeze my eyebrows. She told me I had a unibrow. I tried to shrug off her comment, but she kept scrunching up her face and repeating it. I didn't know what to think or how to grade eyebrows. In my mind, they were just sort of there to be ignored. I thought mine were okay, but I couldn't get the word out of my head and heard a persistent chant of, "Unibrow, unibrow, unibrow," relentlessly pounding into my brain. I honestly didn't even know what it meant, but I could tell it wasn't good. I began to pull.

It was harmless at first. Nothing could have been more innocent, albeit misguided. I pinched my nails together (or what little there was since I had a nail-biting habit too) and attacked my eyebrows. When I started I hadn't heard of tweezers. Well, I had, but only in terms of removing splinters. I had no idea that anyone would ever use the tool to select what hairs they wanted to remove. Somehow, I had made it to eighth grade without ever considering how people got perfectly shaped eyebrows, which was easily accomplished because I had never looked at eyebrows before. I didn't know that tweezing was supposed to be precise. I just focused my attention on the task ahead of me and pulled. I tugged on my eyebrows wherever my fingers closed around hair. I was sure I was doing a good thing, something to make me prettier. I thought maybe boys might notice me, but it didn't work out the way I'd hoped.

I had no idea what I was doing. I knew that, but I couldn't bring myself to ask anyone for help. I had asked my mom once before about unibrows and she had sort of dismissed the question. I had too little self-confidence to even try to find the answer in an issue of *Seventeen* magazine. They always had skinny, fashionably dressed teenagers on the cover, which only made me feel more uncomfortable with my appearance when I so much as glanced at them. The last thing I wanted to do was discuss my physical flaws with Shayna, so she was out of the running too. That left me with Natalie and Cee. In hindsight, I could have asked them. I'm almost positive that I should have asked them . . . just started the conversation one day with, "Hey, so do you guys know what a unibrow is? Because I have no idea." But they were both so beautiful, I couldn't bring myself to do it.

I decided to get my eyebrows "under control" before mentioning it to anyone. So, when I was alone, I pulled at them. It hurt. No big surprise, right? I was yanking out my eyebrows with my fingers—*of course* it hurt. The thing that struck me as weird wasn't the pain, or even that I kept pulling through the pain, but that after a while there was no pain. That's the part most people don't know because they don't do it long enough to find out. The immediate stab of pain and the muffled "Ouch!" that accompanied my pulling would soon give way to a pleasurable feeling. Pulling made me feel fantastic! Even though the area where I pulled turned a tomato shade of red, the whole thing was both relaxing and exhilarating. It was sort of like a fireworks display: it played with my senses, turned off my brain, and left me longing for the next burst of activity. I didn't realize that until it was way too late. I was hooked before I knew I had begun.

The details of my new habit may seem disturbing. They disturb me, and I'm the one who did it. The truth is, in many ways, pulling is like cracking knuckles or wiggling a loose tooth. It's refreshing in a shot-of-caffeine-to-the-system sort of way. It felt natural. What could be so wrong with pulling when it perked me up and made me feel alive? I sure didn't know the answer to that question, and I wasn't inclined to look into it deeply. The pulling felt so good that I couldn't stop. I really didn't want to quit even if I could.

I think what I loved the most about pulling was that, while I was doing it, I wasn't thinking. I've always been the sort of person who sees a simple situation and begins analyzing it to death. I searched for hidden meanings in everything (and am now left wondering whether that is responsible for the loss of several friendships).

I didn't only overthink my own life, either. I stayed up late at night listening to conversations between characters in the latest book I had read. Not because I wanted to have them in my head, but because I couldn't get them out. To make matters worse, the conversations weren't even in the books. I couldn't just read something and set it aside. The characters would go on past the happily-ever-afters and have adventures in my mind. This might have been fun if it weren't so intrusive. What I wanted was to sleep, not to be the third wheel in my own brain! For a while I listened to the same book on tape every night until I had it memorized, just in the hope that if I knew it well I'd be able to sleep. The only thing that happened was I could soon quote *The Twinkie Squad,* a feat that impressed nobody.

Pulling was far more effective at turning off my brain. It let me zone out. I sort of went into a pulling trance. The real world would slip away, and when I refocused it was to find a pile of hair in front of me, which, while not exactly the nicest way to come back to Earth, wasn't the worst either—or so I thought at the time.

I didn't set out to hurt myself when I started pulling (unless it was on some subconscious level). I honestly thought it was good for me. So good that I began using it as a reward system. When I was bored with my homework but did it anyway, I got to pull. Sometimes I even used pulling as a motivation to keep working. I loved every-thing about it: the way my fingers clenched and tensed, the sound a hair made as it was removed from my eyebrow (so quiet you could hardly hear it), the moist tip of the hair that felt so cool in the palm of my hand. It was satisfying and yet always left me wanting more. I required the sensation, craved it even, and my body had no choice but to give me what I demanded. So, I pulled and listened and played with the hairs. It became a habit. I took solace in my pulling and used it to escape the world around me. That's why I continued doing it long after I should have stopped.

My mom was the first person to notice I had gone too far . . . or at least the first person to comment on it. I realized I had a problem only a few weeks before she did. My eyebrows were becoming per-ilously thin, and I was getting the distinct impression it was not an attractive look. I couldn't seem to stop though. It felt so natural. I couldn't quite believe how the action had become a habit in the space of a few weeks, but that didn't change the facts. Fact: My eyebrows had dwindled to the point of nonexistence. Fact: I loved pulling, and I never wanted to stop. Fact: I had to figure out a way to stop.

All the facts in the world wouldn't have made it easier for me to stop, though. Especially since I wasn't sure I really had a problem. I knew the state of my eyebrows needed to be fixed, but I figured that didn't necessarily mean there was something wrong with me.

When I couldn't figure out a way to help myself, my mom inter-vened. She gently asked me what was going on. Of course, by the time she had worked up the nerve to confront me, my eyebrows were even thinner. I barely had a line of hair over each eye. I knew it looked bad. I knew it, but I still couldn't bring myself to stop. I didn't tell my mom the whole story. I left out the part about how pulling made me feel alive and relaxed and happy and how I didn't really want to stop. I didn't think it would change the situation—and I was probably right. I either had to stop pulling or show up for my first day at Ashland High School without eyebrows. That prospect sounded almost as bad to me as going to school naked. Maybe worse, since in my case there was no waking up from the nightmare.

My mom warned ominously that unless it ended, I would resemble an elderly woman with makeup pencil lines where my eyebrows should have been. The image of a hairless existence has haunted me ever since. That I might have to try one of those hair-growth products they advertise for bald people on late-night television terrified me. I couldn't look at people's faces the same way anymore. I fixated on eyebrows, examining the shape and degree of bushiness, all the while praying they weren't reciprocating. Whenever I spotted what I termed "unnecessary hairs" on other people, I longed to pluck them. I actually fantasized about taking a pair of tweezers to strangers, to friends, to relatives.

I was sure I had gone off the deep end. My urges led me to use tweezers so I could be more precise in my tweezing. That didn't mean I had control over the pulling. My brother Jonathan kept looking at me quizzically and asking what was different. He couldn't put his finger on what had changed, but even he knew something wasn't how it used to be. I just shrugged my shoulders and hoped with all my might that no one would be able to figure it out. Once I was hooked, my time was spent in an anxious, terrified state as I tried to hide my pulling from the world. The more I thought about people finding out, the worse I felt. My stomach wriggled, and my heart sped up. The only thing that calmed me down was to pull, which only made the problem worse.

Somehow, I managed to stifle my urge the summer before high school. I don't know how, and I really wish I did. If I were to guess, it was because the prospect of being considered a freak in high school scared me to the point of immobility. I also think it was because at that time, I didn't know how to hide my condition. The only trick in my arsenal was eyebrow pencil, and I swore to myself that I would never use it ever again. I knew using the pencil made me look better than having nothing there, but the idea of being dependent upon it for the rest of my life almost made me break out into a cold sweat.

For a month and a half, I was able to stay pretty much clean. Much to my relief, my eyebrows grew back, and I began high school with no one aware of my condition. I just wondered how I was going to survive without friends.

Chapter 13

HIGH SCHOOL IS INFINITELY better than middle school. By ninth grade, most kids are done being cruel to others just to make themselves feel better. Another improvement is the fact that high school actually matters. Colleges check high school transcripts, so being smart and working hard actually pays off. Getting out of high school and into a good university was enough to motivate most of my classmates to study. It was more than enough to ensure I kept hitting the books. Frankly, I didn't care about high school, but I knew all along that college was my end game.

College was my version of Neverland, except instead of staying a kid, I would live the life I'd imagined for myself. College was where I would calmly sip coffee while discussing obtuse philosophical theories. College was where I was supposed to become cool and collected and put together. All I had to do was survive four years of public schooling (I was done with Willow Wind), and I would be on my way.

So, I was very careful and deliberate in creating my high school plan, penciling in four years of French, science, math, and other important subjects. With Shayna's help, I planned a schedule that showed I was both well-balanced and studious. What it actually proved, though, was that I was overly ambitious.

Biology was way over my head. As one of two freshmen to land in the class, I sat mutely in a room filled with intimidating sophomores and juniors, and tried to understand why I should care about mitosis. (My answer: I shouldn't.) My complete lack of interest in the subject left me scrambling for a way to pick up my grade. I scurried over to the library and read the extra credit books about disease and destruction just to stay in the B range. I didn't enjoy the books, but the worst part of the extra credit deal was the inquisition style, one-on-one book report with Mr. M. afterwards.

"So, Marni," he slowly drawled after class. "What's *The Hot Zone* about?"

I was fully prepared.

"Well, there is a disease that's spreading, and it makes people *hemorrhage* and die."

Maybe if I had been a science person, I would have known that hemorrhage is pronounced "hem-ridge" not "hem-or-hodge." Instead, I was an English-and-American-history kind of girl with a tendency to mispronounce things.

Mr. M. looked completely mystified, which only made me babble longer. It also led me to misuse the word *hemorrhage* about a hundred times more.

"Um . . . yeah," I dribbled out finally.

"Marni," said Mr. M., "what is a hem-or-hodge?"

In my nervous state I relied on a sudden burst of hand gestures to get my point across.

"You know, when someone is bleeding out. Hemorrhage."

It was like a painful game of charades with me wildly motioning blood spurting from my arteries. That afternoon it became clear we didn't speak the same language, and that when it came to science, I would always be in the wrong.

My luck didn't improve in French class. The endless verb conjugations, the masculine and feminine words, and the snooty accent all evaded me. I would sit in a state of confusion thinking, *"Merde, merde, merde!"* ("Shit, shit, shit!"), while the perky popular girls chatted away Parisian-style. I dreaded the class, especially when we were dealing with numbers.

The French go out of their way to destroy American brains with their number system. For example, instead of just saying ninety-three in a straightforward manner, they have to say four times twenty plus thirteen. As if this isn't confusing at all. *Not.*

It was the number game (also known as the public humiliation game) that really got to me. The teacher would pass out cards with two numbers on them. In English, it would go like this:

ME: I have 45. Who has 78?
OTHER CLASSMATE: I have 78. Who has 27?

Simple, right? The problem was that I couldn't pronounce my numbers in French or even figure them out for that matter. I only knew my card was being called because everyone groaned and searched for the blockhead who wasn't speaking up. Did I mention that the whole thing was timed? The popular girls would roll their eyes in exasperation, and when it was discovered I was the weak link, things only got worse. They'd march up to me after class and demand to know why I couldn't get it right. I thought it was fairly obvious: I sucked at French and was even worse at math.

Math class was straight-up boring. At Willow Wind, I had a free tutor with a sense of humor. Getting used to a classroom setting after that was a hard adjustment. I had no idea what we were doing in class and struggled to keep my eyes open. I ended up copying most of my homework from the back of the book. Yes, technically this is cheating, but since I wasn't learning, I doubted my education was being compromised. That's how I rationalized it anyway.

I doubt I would have passed any of my math classes if it hadn't been for Gwyn. Our reconciliation couldn't have happened at a better time. Since the two of us lived on the same street, we had seen each other from time to time throughout middle school (and in my case Willow Wind). It was always very friendly. We chatted a little if we passed ways, and we said hi in the grocery store. Still, ever since I had my flash that Gwyn didn't really care about me, I had steered clear. As Gwyn later put it (and I agree), I was being an idiot.

During high school, we both walked down our hill to the high school at the same time, and we fell into our old pattern of talking. At first, it felt awkward. I had no idea what to say. "Hey, how has life been treating you since we parted ways at the end of elementary school?" The conversation flowed naturally though, partly because Gwyn hadn't really changed. She was still short, sarcastic, methodical, and absolutely wonderful. It wasn't long before I was back to my old routine of stopping at her house every day after school. Since no one in her family had an aversion to cooking (unlike me and my mom), her refrigerator was always stocked with deliciousness. The two of us would make nachos, listen to music, and hang out, while she explained math to me. With a cheese-laden chip in hand, I learned a billion times more math from Gwyn than I ever did from any teacher.

The best part about reuniting with Gwyn, though, was that I got my best friend back. There was no drama with Gwyn, she never said one thing and did another. She was very up front—what you see is what you get. Life with Gwyn made everything better.

However, even Gwyn couldn't save me from freshman health, which was probably the class where I was the furthest behind. I didn't know the first thing about drugs and had only tasted alcohol once at my bat mitzvah, when unbeknownst to me, the rabbi put wine in my glass instead of grape juice. Everyone else in my class knew about uppers and downers and that *DUI* didn't stand for "Dolphin Under Interrogation." They knew about sex and drugs (and probably rock and roll), while I was clueless. I didn't feel like I could really ask either, especially not about sex. Even though I didn't know the answer, I couldn't imagine inquiring, "Yeah, so is it true that, um . . . a certain part of the male anatomy goes . . . up?" I decided it was time to get some answers from a source I could trust. So, I turned to Chris.

The only reason I knew a boy I could ask for advice was because we had met on a cruise I had gone on with my grandparents. It was a great trip, as I could spend all day seeing various ports in Europe, and spend my nights as far away from Shayna as possible. In order to meet some new people, I went to the teen club and was fortunate enough to find Chris and Josh. They were both thin boys with dark brown hair, but that was where the similarities ended. Chris was prone to swearing and wanted to have a convincing Canadian accent. Josh, on the other hand, was superpolite and only revealed his authentic Canadian accent once he heard Chris butchering it. With my mom's permission, I found myself wandering the ship with them until two in the morning. The knowledge that I'd probably never see them again was incredibly liberating. We shared our pasts, danced, joked around, drank tea at midnight, and ran around the ship until the three of us were officially friends. On the last night of the trip, we all exchanged e-mail addresses and promised to write. I never imagined I would remain in contact with both of them. This came in handy in many ways—not least of all for my health class.

Chris was a high school senior in New York, and I felt cool simply by association. I asked him all my embarrassing questions for some insight into the male psyche. The information he provided me with was more than a little terrifying. My mouth dropped open as I read his e-mails and I would burst out into laughter with my face flushed red with embarrassment. Chris also offered me some horrendous advice. He said that if I really wanted a boyfriend, I should just grab a guy, pull him into a bathroom, and start making out. There were so many problems with this idea, I didn't know where to begin.

For starters, there was no way I could have pulled it off. At the very least, I would have tripped and crashed into a sink or ended up on the floor. Plus, if I had the nerve to grab a guy (which I didn't), they would probably want to know what the hell I was doing. To which I would wittily reply "Um . . ." Somehow, I doubted my bumbling attempts at seduction would result in my having a boyfriend. I also knew I didn't want my first kiss to be in a bathroom with someone flushing a few stalls away. Not exactly romantic.

So instead of taking advice from Chris, I listened to Josh. Josh lived in Canada, played hockey in his free time, and told me to just be myself. Not surprisingly, I decided to go with that and concentrate on surviving high school without the status of a social pariah. It wasn't as hard as I thought. The popular kids ignored me, but once again I found my niche. I was lucky enough to find some genuinely nice kids who were painfully straightlaced and exceptionally largehearted. My friends were band geeks and science nerds who shared my love of classic oldies and puns. None of us were particularly wild, not that we had much of an opportunity since we usually spent our weekends doing homework. We didn't party, drink, or break rules, which doesn't mean we were boring—just tame. Around them, I could do anything, including singing at the top of my lungs in a British accent during lunch and sweet-talking the cafeteria ladies into free muffins. There were perks that came with my "good girl" image and my solitary dimple.

I regained my footing slowly as I created new friends and reconnected with old ones. Still, my freshman year at Ashland High School was rough. The fact that Shayna was there didn't make it any easier. Having an older sister should have come with benefits. It didn't. It just made my status as a pathetic little freshman all the more obvious. Shayna had a reputation as being one of the smartest girls in the school, which added pressure on me to measure up. She was also a princess, literally. She applied for a scholarship, and the next thing we knew she was taking princess lessons and preparing for the Oregon title of Pear Blossom Princess. Despite the fact that this was as lame as it sounds and that she came in third place, she still received money for college and got to wear a tiara. Trust me—it's not easy being the younger sibling of a royal.

It didn't matter how invisible I tried to be: recognition was impossible to avoid. People kept asking if I knew my sister was running for Pear Blossom Princess. I always replied politely that I did and wondered how they thought I could've missed that detail. According to Shayna, a lot of people mentioned me to her and what they had to say wasn't exactly complimentary.

At school, we maintained a sort of truce. It was considered sacred ground and came with its own set of rules for how we would interact. These included:

1. No conversation.
2. Limited eye contact.
3. No participation or membership in any of her clubs/activities.

4. Limited conversations with her friends.

5. No existence allowed except an invisible one.

These rules, of course, were only for my benefit. If I followed them to the letter, she was less likely to scream at me in private. I followed them exactly and walked a respectful fifteen feet behind her on our way to school. I scurried past her in the hallways and scuttled out of my English/global studies class as she entered for AP world history.

We both tried diligently to avoid each other and be associated with our brothers. It didn't matter that Shayna and I used different last names—we were both lumped together. Shayna used her Hebrew middle name, while I signed everything with my mom's maiden name. It didn't stop teachers from comparing us to each other. Since she was so quick-witted and sharp, I was certain any comparison between us did not bode well for me.

That wasn't the only problem lurking in wait.

Chapter 14

IT STARTED OUT MUCH AS it had before—a quick tug at my eyebrows every now and again and everything seemed better. I've heard stories that sometimes in dangerous situations when the adrenaline is flowing and whatnot, people become hyperaware of their surroundings. Hair pulling isn't like that. I didn't become more aware . . . rather, I became more awake. I pulled and felt better, which was always followed by regret. I would look at my face and ask why I was so set on destroying it.

Pulling became my addiction—my personal heroin. Hair-oine. But just because I was hooked didn't mean I was careless. I'd learned several lessons from the first time I had pulled, the most firmly entrenched was the importance of discretion. If no one knew you were pulling, then no one would be able to comment on it. No one would warn against a future that involved tattooed or penciled-on eyebrows. I knew I had to be secretive, or I would be discovered. So I diversified.

Eyelashes have a completely different feel to them. The gesture is the same, but the sensation is even more enjoyable. The perfect tug gets a simultaneous popping sound as the eyelash is removed and the eyelid adheres to the eye. It became the newest branch of my obsession, but it wasn't enough. I needed something else to be effective. So, I began pulling my hair. First it was the back of my head, then above my forehead, and finally behind my ears. As soon as one spot was demolished, I moved on to another. It was sort of like deforestation. I was clear-cutting my hair in one area before abandoning it for untouched locations. I wasn't proud of myself, but I couldn't stop.

Abraham Lincoln once said, "You may fool all the people some of the time; you can even fool some of the people all the time; but you can't fool all of the people all the time." He was dead-on. Not that I didn't have a plan. When I pulled from the top of my head, I knew I had to wear a baseball cap for a month, so no one would think I was balding. When I pulled out my eyebrows, I had to position my bangs so that the eyebrows themselves were barely visible. When I pulled out my bangs, I had to lop off some of my hair to get more bangs to hide what I had done. Hats and scarves helped hide the pulling behind my ears, and I wore them daily.

I was also careful about when I pulled. I couldn't get away with doing it in conversation, but in class I would assess the risk factor, and, if I didn't think anyone was looking, I would tug. Pulling behind the ear was the easiest to hide in the presence of others. It looked like I was just toying with my hair, not that I was yanking it out one piece at a time.

The best time to pull was during tests. Everyone was so focused on the paper in front of them that no one noticed if I was methodically yanking out my bangs. Tests were also the times I felt the need to pull the most; I pulled to relax, and consequently whenever I was stressed or sleep-deprived, my urge became even more pronounced. I remember taking a chemistry exam my senior year, and, even though I had been so proud of the way my bangs were growing back in, in the course of that one test all my hard work was undone. I left the science room a few hours later hoping the janitors wouldn't notice that 2 percent of my hair was on the floor surrounding my desk instead of on my scalp. I tried to prevent anyone from noticing by surreptitiously spreading the hair around a bit and throwing some of it away in the trash. Sometimes I had no choice but to roll my hair up in a ball and stick it in a sweatshirt pocket for later disposal. At the end of the day, I often had huge hairballs that I would stare at in amazement, wondering how all that hair could've been attached to my head that morning and ripped out by late afternoon.

Despite my best efforts to pull discreetly, I wasn't fooling everybody. In fact, I wasn't fooling anybody. Most of my classmates must have known there was *something* going on, but they didn't want to say anything to my face. Part of the reason was probably because they had no idea what was actually wrong with me. If I had been throwing up in the bathroom stall after lunch every day, I'm sure someone would have reported me to the school psychiatrist so I could get help for bulimia. I suspect that since no one knew what to make of my pulling, they just did nothing. I much preferred that to the alternative.

The first person to give me a hard time about my eyebrows (or lack thereof) was Samantha. She was one of those girls you couldn't help taking an instant dislike to, or at least, I couldn't. She had a way of speaking that made it clear to whomever she was addressing that they were infinitely inferior. I never was one to appreciate that. Nor did I like having her repeatedly approach me during our English/global studies class and ask me in her squeaky, high-pitched voice what happened to my eyebrows.

I never knew what to say. "Sorry, I have this compulsion to rip my hair out. And how was your weekend?" I doubted *that* would go over well. I knew how I wanted to reply. I wanted to look her in the eye and answer earnestly, "They got caught in a blender." I tried to picture her expression. Shock? Confusion? Disdain? I wasn't sure what her reaction would be, but I knew I could never say it. If I had mentioned a blender (or any other household appliance) or admitted I had a problem, it would have spread everywhere. I really didn't want to be the girl with a "problem" who had everybody whispering. It would be only a small step from that to meetings with the school counselors. I had left therapy behind me when I entered Willow Wind, and I was in no rush to return. All I wanted was to fly happily under the radar with my friends on the geek squad.

So I didn't mention any blenders. I didn't say anything. Instead, I pasted a blank expression on my face and pretended to be distracted by some inanimate object in the distance. I would do a double take as if just realizing she was speaking to me before excusing myself to talk to the teacher about my latest essay. Samantha never believed my act for a second. She also didn't read it as a clear signal to get lost and never mention my eyebrows again. In fact, she brought it up throughout the year. If Samantha's goal was to mortify me, she succeeded beyond her wildest dreams. I considered myself properly humiliated. After an encounter with her, all I felt capable of doing was disappearing into television and books. A trip to the school library was always in order to lighten my mood. At least it was until a librarian decided to pry.

I remember being happy when I crossed the threshold into the library that day. Samantha hadn't been bothering me recently, and I thought with pride that my eyebrows were growing back in nicely. It was as I perused the books on display that Mr. S. sidled up to me. Mr. S. had never bothered me before. He wasn't my favorite librarian, but it's hard to compete with Judy, who usually worked the checkout desk and gave me energy bars when I missed lunch. Still, I didn't really mind Mr. S. We'd had a few conversations about books, but that was pretty much it. We certainly weren't close enough for me to tell him a secret—particularly not my deepest, darkest one.

So it was unusual, but not surprising, when Mr. S. walked over to me. I figured he would say, "Hi, Marni, how's your day going?" or "Have you seen this new book?" or something equally neutral. Instead, he asked what happened to my eyelashes. Until then, I hadn't realized it was noticeable. I was so focused on my eyebrows, I wasn't aware that my eyelashes were noticeably sparse. I stared at him blankly, said something like "I have to go," and fled. It wasn't just the question that had startled me—mostly it was the questioner. I felt indignant. What right did the Mr. S's and the Samanthas of the world have to interrogate me? I wasn't their friend. They didn't know me at all. To make matters worse, I was being attacked in the library—my happy place, my haven, my sanctuary . . . my sacred ground. Of course, the question would have hurt no matter where I was standing. It hurt in the classroom, and it hurt in the library, and it hurt in my bedroom, where I played it over and over again in my head. I was stuck in a world of hurt, and the only thing that cleared my head was more pulling. And so the hurting continued.

Chapter 15

I HAPPILY TOOK MY GEEKDOM to a whole new level my freshman year. As soon as I joined speech and debate, I was certain I had found my calling. I was destined to become a debate nerd who would inspire mini–debate nerds for years to come. I loved being a member of the Ashland Speech and Debate team. Part of the appeal was that it never made me feel lame—instead, I felt quite the opposite, since I was taught debate by senior boys who intimidated every freshman within a mile radius into silence. They were incredibly smart and could randomly cite all sorts of philosophic theories to support their arguments. I hoped their coolness might rub off by association.

I marked myself down for four years of speech and debate in my high school plan and did everything I could to become a valued member of the team. I even donated my dad's old suits and an enormous bag of ties from my great-uncle, single-handedly outfitting roughly half of the debate boys. I was completely dedicated until Ms. T. shattered my plans.

Ms. T. was the debate coach who made Samantha appear hypersensitive and compassionate in comparison. To be honest, I still haven't come up with an analogy that does her justice—devil incarnate and Cruella de Vil are both missing a certain something. I mean, how do you describe a woman who went out of her way to torture you?

Ms. T.'s animosity toward me was so obvious that everyone on the team knew about it. Nick, a sophomore who, funnily enough, bore an uncanny resemblance to a young Nick Lachey, actually created a game out of her hatred. It was called "Let's Get Marni in Trouble." The object of the game was to see how many times he could get Ms. T. to glare at me. It didn't take much of an effort, since the slightest disturbance in the classroom produced instant death-ray glances. I had to steel myself before entering the class, since I was submitting myself to an hour of intense hatred every time. Things only got worse when she accidentally left me at a Fred Meyer in Forest Grove, Oregon.

The speech and debate team always went to Fred Meyer the night before a tournament. Like Target or Walmart, it was the perfect place to stock up on last-minute debate supplies (like pens and legal pads) before the competition. Anyhow, I was dressed up in my suit and heels looking for something to eat from the deli section, when my teammates boarded the bus without conducting a proper head check, which is how I was abandoned in a hick town in the middle of nowhere. I reached the parking lot just in time to see the orange tail lights fade into the night. So there I was at eleven o'clock at night with almost no money, no cell phone, and five hours away from home. To make matters worse, I had just completed an extra credit project in health class (to compensate for my low grade on a drug quiz) on rape. I thoroughly researched the topic and had stared at terrifying statistics on sexual assaults. One situation in particular I was repeatedly warned against: standing alone in dark parking lots at night. So it shouldn't come as a surprise that I began to freak out.

I started quivering uncontrollably and muttering to myself to get a grip. I needed to formulate a plan, but all I could hear was Shayna's voice reverberating in my head from all those years ago, telling me her greatest fear was that someday I would be raped. That night, it became my biggest fear too. I kept my head, though. I thought about *Pride and Prejudice* and asked myself what the heroine, Elizabeth Bennet, would do in my situation. I didn't have the faintest idea, but the question helped keep the panic at bay. When the bus didn't come rumbling back, I decided that if Elizabeth Bennet had access to modern technology in the form of telephones, she would be calling someone for assistance.

I got lucky. By a stroke of fortune, I remembered the name of the hotel the team was staying at and, with the help of a Fred Meyer employee, was patched through to Ms. T. Our conversation was short and began with me blurting out, "You left me!" and Ms. T. asking for the identity of the caller. It took well over a half an hour for the bus to pull into Fred Meyer to stage my rescue. By that point, my body was shaking feverishly and continued to jerk for hours until the adrenaline began to settle into my system. Ms. T. wasn't on the bus to pick me up, and she hadn't asked how I was doing over the phone. *Nice.* I never knew why she disliked me with every fiber of her bony little body, but after awhile, the feeling was mutual.

I'm not sure why abandoning me at Fred Meyer made her hate me more, but it did. Her glances became increasingly contemptuous as time went on. Still, instead of ditching the team at the end of first semester like any normal person would have, I withstood her hatred my entire freshman year because I loved the team. Although admittedly, I did have some other incentives to stay, one of which was the boys.

I was the only freshman girl on the team. This was both astounding and rather uncomfortable. However, I was not the only freshman, not by a long shot. It also just so happened that all the boys I had a crush on were also debating. Despite my continued inability to flirt, a skill I had not even attempted to master, I could still hang out with them. I knew eating pizza together at tournaments didn't exactly make us friends. It just elevated me to good acquaintance status, which was as high as I ever expected to go, since the guys on the team were attractive and popular, and their female counterparts had practically pasted a RESERVED sign on their foreheads in shiny lip gloss.

I did try to flirt once. Well, sort of. I never really got to the flirting part before screwing it up. After school one day, I spotted Jeremy standing outside a classroom. Jeremy was one of the nicest boys among the freshmen, possibly among the entire high school population. He had wavy, dark hair and big, brown eyes. Most of the girls I knew would have agreed he was crush-worthy. Mainly though, he was just plain nice, and I never worried that, like Nick, he'd try to get Ms. T. to glare at me.

Anyhow, I saw him standing there looking all nice and adorable, and I impulsively decided to take my friend Chris' advice. Not the grabbing and kissing advice, but the flirting advice. As in: *Just try it.* So I casually walked up to him and said, "Hey, Jeremy, what's up with you?"

I just wish I had been able to say it . . . not spray it. One second Jeremy was perfectly dry and cute, and the next, his face was soaked with my saliva. I was horrified. This had *never* happened to me before, and I had no idea what to do. Jeremy was too nice to comment, but he delicately dabbed at himself and mentioned something about waiting for a friend. I just nodded foolishly and flashed back to a quiz in a girly magazine I had read in the dentist's office about embarrassing situations. There was one question that involved accidental sprayage. I desperately tried to remember what options A, B, and C had been, since the asteroid I was praying for wasn't coming fast enough. I decided the way to go was to act lighthearted about it.

"I guess I really got you there," I said sheepishly. "Sorry about that."

Jeremy assured me it was fine, and, after a few more minutes of awkwardness, I made a hasty retreat. I promised myself that if I spotted a really big rock on the way home I would curl up into a little ball under it and die.

That probably helps explain why I remained single throughout high school. I'd like to think the real reason was because dating at school seemed kind of gross. People had known each other for so long they were sort of like siblings. However, this is coming from someone who never had a single date, so what do I know? Maybe I'm just trying to rationalize my boyfriendless existence. The truth? I wanted one. Although it's possible I didn't want a boyfriend so much as I wanted to find Mr. Darcy from *Pride and Prejudice*. Unfortunately, he didn't attend Ashland High School (I double-checked). I didn't actually even want to date the guys I had crushes on, which might explain why my interest didn't last long. In my senior year, Jeremy was telling me how ardently he loved me (technically, it was Lysander telling Helena in Shakespeare's *A Midsummer Night's Dream*, but *still*...), and I was completely immune.

Possibly, my pulling was also a factor in my boyfriendless existence. Not because boys were repulsed by my condition (I worked damn hard at hiding it to avoid just that predicament), but because my pulling made it impossible to picture myself dating anyone. In the movies, the guy raises the girl's face up to gaze into before slowly kissing her. I didn't think it would work too well if some guy looked at my face closely pre-kiss and noticed my eyebrows were missing. I also couldn't exactly let a guy romantically push the bangs out of my eyes. If he tried I would surely stiffen up, hold my breath, and hope he didn't notice that underneath that curtain of bangs was a stubble of growth as my old bangs tried desperately to return to their rightful place. My fear of a boyfriend (or potential boyfriend) running away in disgust stopped me from ever trying to flirt. I kept telling myself that once my pulling was under control, I would try to put myself out there. That never happened.

Despite my failure at flirting, the debate boys were still a pretty big incentive to stay on the team. I also really enjoyed debating. I loved that when I held the floor, I could say anything I wanted to persuade people. I was also slowly getting good. It took me a while to get the knack of debating, since Ms. T. had prevented me from debating at the first tournament, but I started winning awards. I was sure if I went to debate camp over the summer, as a sophomore I'd be able to demolish my opponents.

Ms. T. told everyone that debate camp was essential. I had done my research and was prepared to spend my summer talking about utilitarianism, justice, and equality. I decided to look beyond the nonstop hostility, the snide comments, the underhanded insults, and the glaring from Ms. T. to focus on what really mattered—debating. At least, I did until Ms. T. made me stay after class one day so we could have a "little talk" without any witnesses. That was when I learned the true definition of cruel.

"Marni," Ms. T. began, "I don't think you should go to debate camp."

Since she had been declaring the importance of debate camp for well over a month, I was plenty shocked.

I tried to look calm and serene as I replied, "Oh? And why is that?"

"I don't think you're mature enough for it," she said, coldly.

I sat back, flabbergasted. This coming from a woman who had messed up a head count and left me stranded at Fred Meyer. But she was just getting started. Ms. T. went on to inform me that:

1. No one on the team liked me.
2. I wasn't a "good fit."
3. My English/global studies teacher had described me as "pushy" and said I "did not know when to quit."
4. The senior boys didn't like me sitting near them in the back of the bus.
5. I showed a complete lack of respect for the team, its hierarchy, and its traditions.
6. My footwear was inappropriate.

Okay, she might not have called me out for forgetting to wear heels to the first tournament, but I could tell she was thinking about it. And those were just some of the highlights. By the time she had finished verbally abusing me in every possible manner, the hallways were deserted. I had no idea how long the roast had gone on, but if insults were a way to measure time, I should've been graduating from high school and never looking back.

When I finally left the room and the intense glare of her steely blue eyes, I felt unable to do even the simplest of things, like breathing. I knew walking home wasn't a physical possibility. I'd barely gone a few steps to use the phone before I broke down. I'm still amazed my mom was able to understand what I gargled into the receiver. I was shattered, and my sobbing was uncontrollable.

My mom rushed into action and categorically refused to let me have anything to do with Ms. T. ever again. Leaving the team wasn't enough to make things better though. Telling the school principal the truth—that Ms. T. was an abusive teacher who tortured students and favored the boys—wasn't enough. The sight of wispy blonde curls still scared me. I'd panic at the mere thought of running into her. I even had a nightmare about Ms. T. that summer when I was traveling with my mom and Shayna. Out of nowhere, in the middle of the night, I bolted upright and sobbed in a petrified voice, "Ms. T.!"

My mom patted my shoulders and hugged me and told me it was over. It was all over. One therapist and two years later, I was finally able to start putting speech and debate behind me. Considering it was in speech and debate that I first experienced anti-Semitism (a group of boys from a different team called me "Jew Girl" and told me to "go control the economy"), it's sort of amazing it didn't take even longer. Speech and debate was also where I first told the truth about my eyebrows. There were plenty of reasons I needed therapy to move beyond it.

Chapter 16

I THOUGHT I'D LOST MY MIND. That's what the pulling did to me—it made me question my sanity, which is probably the scariest thing that has ever happened to me. Once I started thinking I had gone insane, I lost the ability to trust myself. After all, everything I was thinking was coming from a madwoman, so why should I listen to anything she had to say? I was splitting myself into first person and third person and wondering if I even was a person and, if so, what kind of a person that was. It certainly wasn't the type of person I wanted to be. My pulling made me despise myself, loathe myself, hold myself in abhorrence . . . the words don't really matter if the sentiment remains the same. Other people's reaction to my missing facial hair stung but didn't come close to the pain and intensity of my self-resentment.

I had no idea what was wrong with me. All I knew was that I wanted to pull, and, according to society, that made me a freak. No one came up to me and said, "If you are ripping your hair out, you should be put into a mental institution," but that's what I thought. No one ever convinced me otherwise. Sure, health class covered anorexia and bulimia, but that was about it. I remember sitting there waiting for someone to mention ripping out hair. I even considered mentioning it casually. I would just ask, "And is hair pulling a common stress disorder too?" But I knew if I did my secret would be revealed. So I kept my mouth shut and extracted meaning from the silence. I thought the absence of conversation on pulling meant it was somehow worse than other disorders. I pictured a whole spectrum of disorders. On one end you had the ones we learned about in class that society could understand, and on the other end you had me. I thought pulling was so wrong it was unspeakable.

I didn't talk about it outside of class, either. No way. If people wanted to know I was mentally unhinged, they could figure it out for themselves. So, I protected my secret and instantly regretted the one time I let my guard down. Instead of confessing to my mom or Gwyn or even Chris or Josh through the privacy of e-mails, I opened up to one of my teammates on the speech and debate team. There were several reasons why I never should have told this particular girl. We weren't friends (I don't even remember her name), she was a high school senior, she had a reputation for being a ditz, and she barely knew me. Considering all that, telling her seems downright stupid. She got the information out of me, though, because I was sick of lying, and she asked point blank about my eyebrows. I considered the blender response or the blank look, but I just couldn't do it. I couldn't keep pretending not to hear the question.

So I told her the truth. I told her I had pulled out all the hair from my eyebrows and that I couldn't stop myself. Being honest was terrifying, but something had to give and I decided it was me. In hindsight, I wish I had told anyone *but* her. The reaction my words received wasn't pretty. She scrunched up her face in revulsion and said what I dreaded most, "Gross!" I doubted it could get any worse. She wasn't finished though.

I shriveled up inside and only felt smaller when I heard her advice: "Well, *stop*." For the record, stopping cold turkey sounded excellent to me. The only problem was that pulling was an addiction I had constant access to indulging. I doubt anyone would put an alcoholic in a room full of bourbon, whiskey, and wine, and casually tell them to just kick the habit.

I decided I didn't want to tell anyone my secret ever again. However, my newfound resolution, like so many of my other intentions, didn't last, and I found myself bottling my secret in until I cracked. Roughly two months after my unfortunate confession, I had a breakdown. Not quite a meltdown of Britney Spears' proportions, but pretty bad nonetheless.

I was out of control with the pulling, miserable on speech and debate, and feeling very alone in the world. I barely had eyebrows, and my eyelashes were equally sparse. My mom nervously asked me what happened to my eyebrows, and the next thing I knew, I was bawling. My tears were uncontrollable, and I was inconsolable. My body quaked with tremors, and I felt like I was back outside Fred Meyer's, terrified I was about to be raped. The world was spinning beyond my control, and all I could do was let the tears move their way past my nonexistent eyelashes and down my face. I didn't want to pull, but I couldn't stop, and the whole thing made me feel inhuman. Instead I felt like some insect, and instead of biting off my mate's head after mating, I was the type of bug that ripped out my own hair. I was the praying mantis of humans. This sentiment gushed out of me with the tears, while my mom listened and stroked my hair. It felt so good to be touched there, but I was terrified she would be repulsed too. I couldn't bear to see my mom revolted like the girl from speech and debate.

I should have realized that it would take a lot more than hair removal to separate my mom from my side. She pulled me onto her lap and hugged me tightly as my story spilled out. It took several hours before I was calm enough to keep my words from getting garbled, which was when my mom decided it was time to know what we were up against with my pulling. She did what I had been too scared to do before—type the words "hair pulling" into the Google search bar. I think I was afraid that articles would appear showing the link between pulling and insanity. That was something I wasn't willing to face. My mom, however, thought it was time we got some answers.

She sat me down next to the computer and clicked on the first official-looking website, which was where I found out the name of the thing that had been torturing me for years: *trichotillomania* (commonly referred to as "trich"). Before that day, I didn't know there *was* an official name for my pulling, let alone so many addicts like me out there. On some level, I knew I wasn't totally alone, but at Ashland High School it sure felt that way.

The website we discovered changed everything for me. I found out there was an estimated one to two million people with trich in America alone. The reason for the broad range was because people like me were really good at hiding it. The website didn't say I was insane. It told me the urge felt irresistible and that all things considered, my case wasn't all that bad. It pointed out that some people continue pulling even when they are asleep. I also knew that not everyone was lucky enough to have a supportive mom and the resources to pay for therapy. That was a lot more than plenty of people could say.

Understanding that what I had was real and not a sign of insanity made a huge difference in my life. I could trust myself again. I stopped talking about "that crazy girl" when I was referring to myself in my head. It took a while, but eventually I stopped picturing myself as a praying mantis too. Knowing that what I had was real, somewhat common, and even had a name helped me come to terms with my addiction. I didn't need to feel ashamed I had a compulsive urge because lots of people have compulsive behaviors. It started to occur to me that maybe I was part of a silent majority— people who suffer from something but are too scared to talk about it with anyone. More importantly, after finding out about trich, I felt like I could talk to Gwyn about my pulling.

I was still scared to confide in her. My mom was obligated to love me no matter what, and Gwyn wasn't. Still, I thought if there was anyone my age I could count on for support, it was Gwyn. I couldn't stop obsessing about her reaction, though, and I planned out the perfect way to tell her everything.

It began with a walk around the Southern Oregon University campus, which was conveniently located near our houses. The evening was beautiful, cold, and crisp, and it felt good to stretch my legs while we walked familiar streets we had crossed together since elementary school. It took me a while to get around to the real reason I had asked her to go on the walk. She knew there was something I had to say, since usually when we were together we stayed in her house and sang (very badly) to whatever her iPod randomly selected. She waited patiently for me to spit it out and continued to listen until the whole story was dangling in the brisk air. Gwyn never so much as flinched. She just nodded her head at appropriate moments and asked me a series of questions. Gwyn asked me about the extent of my pulling, whether I needed any medical treatment for it, and whether I ate my hair. Her questions were important, and she asked them calmly, almost clinically, in the matter-of-fact way that had always been Gwyn's style.

Once she was satisfied my health wasn't in any serious danger and she didn't need her parents (both of whom were doctors) to take me to the hospital, she told me my condition didn't matter to her. I had been her friend when I couldn't tie my own shoes and had traded my Fruit Roll-up for her fruit leathers. We had been friends when I was the geekiest, dorkiest girl at Lincoln Elementary School, couldn't climb the rope ladder, and read books during lunch. My pulling was meaningless compared to all that. We would be friends even if I was completely bald. Gwyn's confident smile reminded me that at the end of the day, friends are there to have your back, even when some of your family fails to support you.

My dad and I had gotten into a pattern where everything was quid pro quo. "I'll take you to a museum, honey—if you fly down to see me exclusively." Great. Trich was no different to him; it was just another thing to haggle over. My mom wanted me in therapy. She thought it was best if I got as much help as possible to beat my addiction. I think it was hard for her to see firsthand what I was doing to myself too. Whenever I was stressed or sleep-deprived, the pulling became worse, and I would lose huge chunks of eyebrow in the space of a few hours. My mom wanted me to see a professional psychologist as soon as possible.

But, therapy meant I had to get my dad to pay half the bill, something he typically resisted. He had only helped pay for therapy before because he thought Carrie the Therapist would pressure me into speaking to him more often. Still, I figured he would find my trich so disturbing that he would cover half of therapy. Of course, it was never that simple with my dad.

It's a rare individual who can use his daughter's disorder to make life even *more* miserable for her, but my dad could do it without qualms or apologies. He refused to supply a dime if there were changes I could make at home to solve my "problem." His first recommendation was to get rid of our dogs. He decided (being such an expert on trich and all . . . *not!*) that there was a link between my pets and my pulling. According to my father, our two dogs were creating stress in my life.

My dad had other suggestions too, most of which involved medication. I was not interested in pursuing this path. I could feel pretty crummy sometimes (just like everyone else), but that didn't stop me from being an upbeat, optimistic person. I got a rush of happiness from Rollerblading, goofing around with my friends, and watching cheesy romantic comedies, among other things. I didn't want to lose any of that because of medications. I was haunted by a Cheryl Wheeler song that questions whether people can really tell the difference between feeling peace and Prozac. I didn't want to feel nothing at all—I'd already experienced living numb in middle school. That had been enough to steer me away from medication, although I have heard for some people it can be helpful. I didn't need Tom Cruise spouting Scientology to know that drugs just weren't the best option for me. In fact, my mom rolled her eyes when I told her my dad's suggestion and replied, "You don't need that." It took awhile for my dad to realize there was no way I would get rid of the pets, put myself on drugs, or trade in my home for some type of rehab facility. After a lot of begging, pleading, and pulling, he agreed to help pay for my therapy. That was where I began working out my pulling issues and a drug-free existence was recommended to me. I just wish everyone in my family had been able to stay clean.

Chapter 17

MY COUSIN ANDY HAD always been one of the most important people in my life. As kids, we were inseparable troublemakers who thrived on stirring up problems with our shenanigans. Andy and I had a lot in common: we were both friendly, extroverted, vaguely mischievous, and intelligent. Growing up, I secretly thought we were the same person. I imagined us as a penny—we were different on just the matter of our genders, but inside we were made of the same metal. Maybe that's why I turned to pulling while he turned to drugs.

I had never understood drugs, which is why I did the extra credit rape project in high school. When I heard the term "uppers" and "downers," I stared in confusion, before asking why anyone would want to get depressed on drugs. As far as I was concerned, drugs were what the "bad" kids did in their free time. None of my friends had expressed an interest in experimenting with altered states of consciousness, so I chose to pretend that drugs just didn't exist. When Andy became an addict, I had to reevaluate everything.

Andy wasn't just some random druggie; he was my on-again, off-again role model. While I was walking the straight and narrow, he was partying and socializing and being "cool." I had accepted my status as Queen of the Nerds with much pleasure, but I still longed for a bit of excitement. I wanted to see the world through Andy's eyes. At least I did, until that involved cocaine and heroin. Hearing reports from my grandma about how Andy was having run-ins with the police, how he was getting into trouble at his wretched private high school, how he was slipping up and getting himself hurt scared me. I just didn't know what I could do stuck in Ashland while he battled his demons in Manhattan Beach, California.

The summer before my senior year of high school, I flew down to Los Angeles to stay at my grandma's just as Andy hit rock bottom. He had been busted for drug possession again and needed to go to rehab or juvenile hall. Grandma was absolutely frantic. She had always felt the need to fix everyone's problems and was working double-time to extract Andy from the mess he'd made of his life. Grandma kept making arrangements and whispering secretively into the cell phone the whole time I was in Los Angeles. I knew I was only underfoot and that the way I could be most helpful was to ensure that I wasn't in the way.

I escaped to the closest Barnes & Noble every day to get my mind off the Andy situation. I still felt tense and worried, but I was able to submerge my fears in books. Morally, I did have a few pangs about my behavior. I knew it was wrong to go into a bookstore, spend all day reading, and leave without making a single purchase. On the other hand, I never could have afforded to buy all those books. So, I did my best to blend into the background and even hid under a desk in order to inconspicuously enjoy everything the YA fiction section had to offer.

My visit with Grandma, however, wasn't the relaxing stay I had originally imagined. Instead, I couldn't wait to fly out to Atlanta and join the group of Jewish teenagers from all over the United States who would be traveling across the country on a bus with me. That was my *real* summer plan.

The program was called Etgar 36, and it promised I would feel an increased sense of connection with my country while I met with people involved in solving important issues (like homelessness, gun control, immigration, and abortion). I was excited about the trip, but mainly I was looking forward to leaving Los Angeles. It was killing me to be in the same state, the same freaking city, as my cousin, and still be unable to help him pull his life together. I thought going away on Etgar would help clear my head.

I was partly right. Etgar was an amazing experience that completely surpassed everything they advertised on the website. We did so many things in the course of a day—meetings, museums, historical landmarks, national monuments—it was insane in the best possible way. It was hard to find the energy to obsess over my cousin when I was always on the move and surrounded by interesting teenagers. Even the quiet time I spent on the bus staring out the window as states rolled by me was spent in peaceful thought. Instead of the mountains I was used to seeing, there were stretches where my view went uninterrupted. I would soak in the sights and wonder what it would be like to walk off into a horizon that seemed to stretch to eternity.

The group of us boarded the bus in Atlanta and made our way back across the country to Los Angeles before splitting into two camps: a group of kids who would fly to Chicago and continue onward (I was in this group) and the kids who would head back home. I had mixed feelings about returning to the city I had just left, even though it was only for a day. All my anxiety over Andy came bubbling up to the surface, especially when I heard we were scheduled to go to a Jewish rehab center for dinner. I didn't know who I could confide in about my fears for Andy. I had made a bunch of friends on the cross-country trip, but I didn't think Andy's drug use was my secret to tell. I wanted to protect him as much as possible, so I kept my mouth shut.

The rehab center sent all my tightly bottled control spattering everywhere. Just walking in the front doors scared me. I knew any minute my fears about Andy were going to smother me. The truth was, I was terrified that Andy, the cousin I had played hide-and-go-seek with, was going to disappear. I would be left looking at an empty shell. I was afraid that even though we had been best friends, distance and time had made it impossible for me to reach him. I'd always felt out of control with my trich, but Andy's problem was absolutely beyond me alone—that was what made panic rise. There was nothing I could do to help him.

The drug addicts sat in a circle with our group and told their stories. They explained how they had gotten hooked on various substances and how their addictions had taken over their lives. They said that what they cared about the most, what they needed the most, was getting their fix. I pictured Andy the whole time, imagined the words coming from his mouth, and the desperation kept swelling. We weren't even eighteen years old. Pulling and rehab weren't supposed to happen to Andy and me. The addicts sharing their life stories weren't supposed to become us.

I had a mini-epiphany while we heard about one man's experience with heroin—addiction isn't just for the "bad" kids. All my life, I had been thinking about addiction like a stupid anti-drug poster. "Just say no." It's not that easy. I had avoided drugs and alcohol, I had taken all the AP classes, I had steered clear from video games, I had immersed myself in books from a young age. And at the end of all that, I was still trapped under the weight of addiction.

Something clicked in my brain at that rehab center, and I realized I'd been right about Andy all along. We were the same person.

We both turned to something that made us feel good, that helped us escape from our minds and the world. The only real difference was that his addiction was illegal and had landed him in rehab, whereas my addiction was misunderstood and socially stigmatizing. The stereotype of the "good kid" I had always tried to fill and the "bad kid" that Andy's private school was trying to make him out to be, appeared to me then as nothing more than a pile of *merde*. He was my cousin, my flip side, and, as far as I was concerned, there was no one better.

I called my mom that night and told her how worried I was about him. I asked her just how badly Andy was doing and choked back tears when I heard her answer. My mom told me to let the family worry about Andy and enjoy myself on the trip. She pointed out what I already knew—it was out of my hands. All of this happened while the group was chowing down on pizza. I spent the dinner with my cell phone to my ear, trying not to bawl. My mom suggested I talk to an addict at the rehab if I thought it would make me feel better. I decided it was better than doing nothing, so I asked our first speaker if there was any way I could make things easier for Andy. The man just shook his head and told me straight up that, "All you can do is be supportive."

I wanted to see Andy, or even just talk to him on the phone, and tell him again that I was sure he could kick the habit. I've always had faith in Andy. Maybe that's a little strange considering the state he was in, but I still believed he could beat the drugs and alcohol. If there was anyone who had the inner strength to chase demons away, it was Andy. But I couldn't talk to him. Andy was at his rehab center, so I had to be content with passing the message through my mom to my grandma to him.

It was time for my group to fly to Chicago, and I didn't want to go. My family was in turmoil and while only a few weeks ago I couldn't wait to leave, now all I wanted was to stay put. Andy, my grandma, and my mom were all on the West Coast. That was where I thought I should be too. I had enjoyed the Etgar experience, and three weeks on a bus had been a wonderful adventure, but I was ready to see it draw to a close.

I had signed up for the full Etgar package, though, which meant waving good-bye to my closest friends in Los Angeles and continuing on to Chicago. I felt strange touching down in the Windy City. I had always wanted to see it, and now my enthusiasm seemed all dried up. Maybe it was the jet lag, but I decided it would be best if I stayed to myself. There were still a bunch of great kids in the group, but things had become a bit cliquish, and my closest friends had exited stage left in California. With only ten more days to go, I was prepared to spend my time with just my thoughts and music for company. Luckily, I never had to take such drastic measures.

There was one late arrival joining us in Chicago. It was a girl who had gone on the first half of the trip the year before and was planning to finish the second half with us. I don't think anyone really cared. We were all too preoccupied with our own lives to think much about the new girl. It's possible that if she hadn't been one of my roommates that first night we wouldn't have bonded. Not that I was excited about having my room of three girls become a room of four. What I really wanted was my king-sized bed I had left behind in Ashland. Still, I knew I was already cohabitating with a confirmed narcissist who hijacked the bathroom every morning. What was one more undesirable roommate?

I didn't make a particularly good first impression on the new girl. I was frustrated with my other roommate and irked with myself for feeling so gloomy. So, I did what any irrational teenage girl would do. I grabbed my iPod and started dancing in the closet. Blasting the soundtrack from *Dirty Dancing: Havana Nights* did have a soothing effect, and I finally emerged ready to meet the roommate. Enter Stephanie.

Stephanie was completely unlike anyone I had ever met before. After introducing herself, she felt the need to say, "I'm horny." This led to a moment of more than a little awkwardness. I quickly learned that Stephanie was virtually incapable of censoring herself. She said what she thought without wasting time trying to be tactful. I actually found it refreshing. Her candor was part of her charm. I also thought she was a little insane. Who makes out with a boy on a summer trip the first night and proceeds to discuss the indiscretion, in detail, with her boyfriend over the phone? Stephanie.

The crazy thing is, we meshed instantly and became really good friends. Stephanie helped me find my misplaced enthusiasm and together we made an unbeatable team. I had a buddy again, someone to keep an eye out for me and vice versa. We swapped music, shared a room, went shopping, and were generally inseparable. She never stopped surprising me. I confided in her about the time I slobbered all over Jeremy and in return she told me about the time she dated an Orthodox Jew whose father hadn't approved. (The fact that they were caught making out in front of the Torah might not have helped.)

Stephanie kept me laughing and made me try new things. She was the one who took me (clueless as ever) to my first sex store. It was a complete accident. I hadn't seen the name of the store—I just noticed some of our friends inside and agreed to check it out. I noticed the door handles shaped in the letters CK, which I thought stood for Calvin Klein or something. They didn't. They actually stood for Condom Kingdom. Inside was the largest display of unmentionables imaginable. I got super embarrassed, but the other girls just seemed curious. Aaron, the only boy in the group, shifted nervously like we might inquire about the size of his anatomy, while Stephanie pointed out various objects in her possession or that her boyfriend was about to get for her. That was a little too much information for me. We left without making a purchase but with a new appreciation for the male physique.

It took me a while to completely open up to Stephanie. We were close enough for me to really care about her opinion of me, and I didn't want to creep her out with my trich. I almost didn't say anything, but much to my surprise the topic came up while riding on the bus from Washington, D.C. to North Carolina. It started with me telling her about my dad's attempt at amends by sending me possums in a nutshell—a hand-painted walnut that opened to reveal a picnic scene of possums. He told me that any woman would want it and certainly any fourteen-year-old girl, because who doesn't love a good possum in a walnut? Stephanie and I were talking about parents and life when I realized she deserved to know about the pulling. We had braved horrible roommates, dingy motels, cockroaches, and mobs of people scrambling to buy the last *Harry Potter* book. I knew her secrets—it was only fair that she knew mine.

I was nervous about telling Stephanie about trich. I had barely gotten to the word "pulling" when she asked me if I had trich. I was shocked. I had no idea how she could have figured it out so quickly. Had she seen any hairless patches and suspected my secret? The answer to that was, surprisingly—no. Stephanie knew I meant trich because she had trich. She didn't need me to explain because she dealt with the same problem every day. For the first time, I had found someone I knew who understood precisely what I was talking about.

There are a lot of fears that go along with trich that you don't really have until you start pulling. That's part of what made me feel so alone—not knowing anyone who had the same anxieties as I did. I didn't know anyone else who was afraid of getting haircuts, not because they might be trimmed too close, but because the people in the shop would stare at your head in horror and ask what had happened. I was terrified of getting lice on Etgar (there was an outbreak, but it was cleared up pretty fast), not because I feared the little buggers but because I didn't want anyone looking closely at my scalp. I had once loved windy days, but with trich those no longer held any enjoyment. Walking to school knowing that a gust of air could expose me to ridicule and censure forced me to constantly hold my bangs down. This made me look odd in itself. There are also the fears of a teacher requiring you to take off a hat, someone wanting to put your hair into a French braid, going into a swimming pool where individual hairs cling together and reveal the pulling even to the untrained eye. All of these things don't usually occur to people who don't suffer from trich.

"Normal" people don't have to contend with the daily fear of discovery. They also don't have to be perpetually on guard and ready for an attack. Yet, that was the reality of my life with trich. One second I could be just another kid on the Mock Trail team and the next Mr. S might be informing me that "Bangs don't look professional enough" and demanding I use barrettes to hold them back. When I would refuse (pinning my bangs back would expose my pulling), he would pressure the others to get me to conform and I would just stand there stuttering, "I can't." Over the years, I'd learned there was no way to predict when that kind of humiliation would occur which created a never-ending atmosphere of fear. That's why it was wonderful to talk to someone who knew exactly what I was up against.

The two of us didn't close our mouths once until we had reached the hotel hours later. There was so much to share. That had been the one secret between us, and with that wall down, we could ask anything without fear. She asked me if there had been any signs growing up that I had trich. Apparently, she had pulled out all the hair from her stuffed animals as a child. Stephanie had also had a rougher time getting support from her parents. They tried to frighten her into a pull-free life and succeeded only in scaring her.

We shared our pasts and I felt less . . . haunted. Trich had always been my solitary burden, up to me alone to feel, and now it was different. I wasn't alone. Trich and life in general might have been working to make me feel helpless and lonely, but it couldn't succeed with Stephanie by my side. I had proof that it wasn't just me. When Stephanie told me she had trich, suddenly those millions of other people with trich weren't just part of a statistic on a website. Stephanie and I had found each other and that gave me a lot of hope. Maybe, I wouldn't feel the need to hide my flaw, my addiction, forever. Surrounded by people like Stephanie, Gwyn, and my mom, maybe I could someday be able to love myself and admit I had trich at the same time. I felt like I could let the world know who Marni really is without fear.

Epilogue

JUST IN CASE YOU'RE WONDERING . . . I did get into college. I'm currently a student at Lewis & Clark College in Oregon where I *still* have had no romantic success with boys. I still embarrass myself on a regular basis, but I take it in stride. At least there is no shortage of amusement, and, quite frankly, I wouldn't want my life any other way.

I still pull. I wish I could say that college has shown me the error of my ways, but that just isn't true. I pull because it feels so good, it is still too hard to quit. Since I've been in college, I have become better at keeping my pulling in check. I think this is because I am happier in college than I ever was in high school. Maybe it isn't the Neverland I originally imagined, but it has its magical moments. As far as the pulling goes, all I can do is try my hardest and take it one day at a time. I remain optimistic that someday I'll be able to kick the habit entirely.

I still talk to Stephanie, and she gives me updates about the craziness in her life. College has done nothing to dilute my amazement at her tenacity. She also continues to pull but flat-out refuses to let it control her life. While Stephanie and I still struggle with trich, Andy has done an amazing job of turning his life around. He got out of rehab, took a long look at himself, and started making changes. Now he is in college, proving everyone who ever doubted him wrong. The two of us have been able to relate because of our addictions in a way I never imagined possible. If there is a silver lining to having trich, it is the way it has brought me closer to Andy.

Shayna is doing great. She is graduating from college this year and is ready to meet the challenges of the so-called real world. We've grown closer over the years, and we can now talk on the phone about the latest episodes of our favorite shows. Hopefully, someday things will be even better, but for now, I'm happy with our relationship.

I still have trouble deciphering my dad. Recently, the two of us saw each other for the first time in five years. He took me shopping, spent an exorbitant amount of money, and left—our relationship just as fuzzy and unclear as before. I pretty much haven't heard from him since. I have no great expectations on this front. Seemingly he contacts me when it serves his purposes.

In hindsight, high school doesn't seem quite so dreadful. I still remember hating it and longing to leave, but it turns out I wasn't as invisible as I thought. In fact, I was nominated for a bunch of Senior "Most Likelys" (and won Forever Sober, which I am still trying to disprove). I keep in touch with my high school friends, including Gwyn, and relish having conversations with them that don't include SAT scores and upcoming AP tests. That's another refreshing thing I found out about college: test scores don't really matter. Once you are in, you're in. After that, all that matters is what you do with yourself.

So what's next? Three years of college and countless essays from now I'll probably be an English major and doing . . . something. What did you expect? I don't know where my life is going. I'm absolutely clueless about my real ending. Hopefully, this book will go on to critical acclaim, change lives, and score me an invitation to talk to Jon Stewart on *The Daily Show* (or Oprah). If not, well, I intend to keep writing and hope I can support myself by doing what I love. I still panic at the thought of joining the working class and intend to take advantage of college while it lasts.

Anyhow, that's me. Or at least me right now. Let's face it—I'm going to change a lot between now and . . . forty. This only encapsulates my first nineteen years of life and hopefully has made you feel a little less alone in the world. That's what writing it has done for me. Sure it was frightening to write about my life and put it out into the world for friends, acquaintances, and strangers to see. In fact, when I first started writing, it felt like I was dragging myself out of the closet. After hiding this huge part of myself all through high school, the idea of revealing it in college terrified me.

I wanted to make a new start at Lewis & Clark, and telling the world about my problems didn't seem like the best way to do that. I instantly began to fear social rejection and outcast status. I couldn't exactly look to any notable figures to explain the disorder to my friends either, since there is no Ellen DeGeneres of trich. It made me nervous at first to be discussing something so private that is never discussed. It scared me so much, I had to see the school therapist for advice.

But then this really amazing thing happened: by being candid and honest, other people started telling me their own stories. It seems that, not only does everyone have their own inner demons—they also know someone else who is battling an addiction. I've met other kids with trich because of this book, and the more I discuss what I've been through, the more comfortable with myself I've become. I've gotten more out of this book than all my therapy sessions because I'm not only helping myself. I'm doing this to help others. And if that works, if you feel like you have more compassion and understanding for people with compulsive behaviors, then this book and my life have been a success. I think that would be the nicest possible outcome.

As a kid, I turned to books for help, and now (hopefully) I've written a book that other kids can turn to. That seems fitting to me. But what do I know? I'm just Marni.

Best of luck,
Marni Bates

Book Club Discussion Questions for MARNI

1. Prior to reading *Marni,* had you heard of trichotillomania? What did you learn about this stress disorder? Its causes? Its symptoms?

2. Despite the fact that the author struggles with a difficult family dynamic and challenging stress disorder, much of her writing has a light and often humorous tone. How does the writing style of *Marni* work for the subject matter she is writing about?

3. Marni writes about the lack of discussion on pulling in her high school health classes. What stress-related and emotional disorders do you see among your peers? How are they different from trich? What are the similarities? Is information on these disorders readily available?

4. Much of *Marni* is devoted to the dysfunctional relationship the author has with her estranged dad. In what ways do you think this relationship may have played a role in the author developing trich?

5. In *Marni* we follow the author's journey from a precocious elementary student to high school senior. What do you think Marni's biggest challenge or issue was at the beginning of the book? Did she resolve this issue by the end of the book? Why or why not?

6. Have you ever felt like you had a personal secret that was too

embarrassing to share with anyone else? Did you end up letting anyone in on what was happening or keep it buried within yourself? How did your choice make you feel? Does it still affect you today?

7. Students with disorders like binging and cutting can often hide their habits from the rest of the world. But Marni was always in fear of being discovered—someone might notice her nonexistent eyebrows or the pile of hair she left behind after a pulling session in class. How would it feel to go through high school living in fear of having your darkest, deepest secret discovered? How might this impact your self-esteem? Your body image? Your social life?

8. Did you relate to the author and her experiences? If so, in what ways?

9. Did Marni have any "a ha" moments where she made an important discovery about herself which allowed her to grow? What were these moments? What did she learn in each one?